Access Your Online Resources

Don't miss out on the Online Resources included with your purchase!

Your purchase of this product unlocks access to our Online Resources page. Elevate your study experience with our **interactive practice test interface**, along with all of the additional resources that we couldn't include in this book.

Flip to the Online Resources section at the end of this book to find the link and a QR code to get started!

AFOQT

Study Guide 2025-2026

AFOQT Prep Book Secrets

2 Full-Length
Practice Tests

100+ Online
Video Tutorials

8th Edition

Written and edited by Matthew Bowling

Printed in the United States of America

This paper meets the requirements of ANSI/NISO Z39.48-1992 (Permanence of Paper).

Paperback
ISBN 13: 978-1-5167-2735-3
ISBN 10: 1-5167-2735-5

DEAR FUTURE EXAM SUCCESS STORY

First of all, **THANK YOU** for purchasing Mometrix study materials!

Second, congratulations! You are one of the few determined test-takers who are committed to doing whatever it takes to excel on your exam. **You have come to the right place.** We developed these study materials with one goal in mind: to deliver you the information you need in a format that's concise and easy to use.

In addition to optimizing your guide for the content of the test, we've outlined our recommended steps for breaking down the preparation process into small, attainable goals so you can make sure you stay on track.

We've also analyzed the entire test-taking process, identifying the most common pitfalls and showing how you can overcome them and be ready for any curveball the test throws you.

Standardized testing is one of the biggest obstacles on your road to success, which only increases the importance of doing well in the high-pressure, high-stakes environment of test day. Your results on this test could have a significant impact on your future, and this guide provides the information and practical advice to help you achieve your full potential on test day.

Your success is our success

We would love to hear from you! If you would like to share the story of your exam success or if you have any questions or comments in regard to our products, please contact us at **800-673-8175** or **support@mometrix.com**.

Thanks again for your business and we wish you continued success!

Sincerely,
The Mometrix Test Preparation Team

TABLE OF CONTENTS

Introduction

Thank you for purchasing this resource! You have made the choice to prepare yourself for a test that could have a huge impact on your future, and this guide is designed to help you be fully ready for test day. Obviously, it's important to have a solid understanding of the test material, but you also need to be prepared for the unique environment and stressors of the test, so that you can perform to the best of your abilities.

For this purpose, the first section that appears in this guide is the **Secret Keys**. We've devoted countless hours to meticulously researching what works and what doesn't, and we've boiled down our findings to the five most impactful steps you can take to improve your performance on the test. We start at the beginning with study planning and move through the preparation process, all the way to the testing strategies that will help you get the most out of what you know when you're finally sitting in front of the test.

We recommend that you start preparing for your test as far in advance as possible. However, if you've bought this guide as a last-minute study resource and only have a few days before your test, we recommend that you skip over the first two Secret Keys since they address a long-term study plan.

If you struggle with **test anxiety**, we strongly encourage you to check out our recommendations for how you can overcome it. Test anxiety is a formidable foe, but it can be beaten, and we want to make sure you have the tools you need to defeat it.

Review Video Directory

As you work your way through this guide, you will see numerous review video links interspersed with the written content. If you would like to access all of these review videos in one place, click on the video directory link found on the online resources page: **mometrix.com/resources719/afoqt-27353**

Secret Key #1 – Plan Big, Study Small

There's a lot riding on your performance. If you want to ace this test, you're going to need to keep your skills sharp and the material fresh in your mind. You need a plan that lets you review everything you need to know while still fitting in your schedule. We'll break this strategy down into three categories.

Information Organization

Start with the information you already have: the official test outline. From this, you can make a complete list of all the concepts you need to cover before the test. Organize these concepts into groups that can be studied together, and create a list of any related vocabulary you need to learn so you can brush up on any difficult terms. You'll want to keep this vocabulary list handy once you actually start studying since you may need to add to it along the way.

Time Management

Once you have your set of study concepts, decide how to spread them out over the time you have left before the test. Break your study plan into small, clear goals so you have a manageable task for each day and know exactly what you're doing. Then just focus on one small step at a time. When you manage your time this way, you don't need to spend hours at a time studying. Studying a small block of content for a short period each day helps you retain information better and avoid stressing over how much you have left to do. You can relax knowing that you have a plan to cover everything in time. In order for this strategy to be effective though, you have to start studying early and stick to your schedule. Avoid the exhaustion and futility that comes from last-minute cramming!

Study Environment

The environment you study in has a big impact on your learning. Studying in a coffee shop, while probably more enjoyable, is not likely to be as fruitful as studying in a quiet room. It's important to keep distractions to a minimum. You're only planning to study for a short block of time, so make the most of it. Don't pause to check your phone or get up to find a snack. It's also important to **avoid multitasking**. Research has consistently shown that multitasking will make your studying dramatically less effective. Your study area should also be comfortable and well-lit so you don't have the distraction of straining your eyes or sitting on an uncomfortable chair.

The time of day you study is also important. You want to be rested and alert. Don't wait until just before bedtime. Study when you'll be most likely to comprehend and remember. Even better, if you know what time of day your test will be, set that time aside for study. That way your brain will be used to working on that subject at that specific time and you'll have a better chance of recalling information.

Finally, it can be helpful to team up with others who are studying for the same test. Your actual studying should be done in as isolated an environment as possible, but the work of organizing the information and setting up the study plan can be divided up. In between study sessions, you can discuss with your teammates the concepts that you're all studying and quiz each other on the details. Just be sure that your teammates are as serious about the test as you are. If you find that your study time is being replaced with social time, you might need to find a new team.

Secret Key #2 – Make Your Studying Count

You're devoting a lot of time and effort to preparing for this test, so you want to be absolutely certain it will pay off. This means doing more than just reading the content and hoping you can remember it on test day. It's important to make every minute of study count. There are two main areas you can focus on to make your studying count.

Retention

It doesn't matter how much time you study if you can't remember the material. You need to make sure you are retaining the concepts. To check your retention of the information you're learning, try recalling it at later times with minimal prompting. Try carrying around flashcards and glance at one or two from time to time or ask a friend who's also studying for the test to quiz you.

To enhance your retention, look for ways to put the information into practice so that you can apply it rather than simply recalling it. If you're using the information in practical ways, it will be much easier to remember. Similarly, it helps to solidify a concept in your mind if you're not only reading it to yourself but also explaining it to someone else. Ask a friend to let you teach them about a concept you're a little shaky on (or speak aloud to an imaginary audience if necessary). As you try to summarize, define, give examples, and answer your friend's questions, you'll understand the concepts better and they will stay with you longer. Finally, step back for a big picture view and ask yourself how each piece of information fits with the whole subject. When you link the different concepts together and see them working together as a whole, it's easier to remember the individual components.

Finally, practice showing your work on any multi-step problems, even if you're just studying. Writing out each step you take to solve a problem will help solidify the process in your mind, and you'll be more likely to remember it during the test.

Modality

Modality simply refers to the means or method by which you study. Choosing a study modality that fits your own individual learning style is crucial. No two people learn best in exactly the same way, so it's important to know your strengths and use them to your advantage.

For example, if you learn best by visualization, focus on visualizing a concept in your mind and draw an image or a diagram. Try color-coding your notes, illustrating them, or creating symbols that will trigger your mind to recall a learned concept. If you learn best by hearing or discussing information, find a study partner who learns the same way or read aloud to yourself. Think about how to put the information in your own words. Imagine that you are giving a lecture on the topic and record yourself so you can listen to it later.

For any learning style, flashcards can be helpful. Organize the information so you can take advantage of spare moments to review. Underline key words or phrases. Use different colors for different categories. Mnemonic devices (such as creating a short list in which every item starts with the same letter) can also help with retention. Find what works best for you and use it to store the information in your mind most effectively and easily.

Secret Key #3 – Practice the Right Way

Your success on test day depends not only on how many hours you put into preparing, but also on whether you prepared the right way. It's good to check along the way to see if your studying is paying off. One of the most effective ways to do this is by taking practice tests to evaluate your progress. Practice tests are useful because they show exactly where you need to improve. Every time you take a practice test, pay special attention to these three groups of questions:

- The questions you got wrong
- The questions you had to guess on, even if you guessed right
- The questions you found difficult or slow to work through

This will show you exactly what your weak areas are, and where you need to devote more study time. Ask yourself why each of these questions gave you trouble. Was it because you didn't understand the material? Was it because you didn't remember the vocabulary? Do you need more repetitions on this type of question to build speed and confidence? Dig into those questions and figure out how you can strengthen your weak areas as you go back to review the material.

Additionally, many practice tests have a section explaining the answer choices. It can be tempting to read the explanation and think that you now have a good understanding of the concept. However, an explanation likely only covers part of the question's broader context. Even if the explanation makes perfect sense, **go back and investigate** every concept related to the question until you're positive you have a thorough understanding.

As you go along, keep in mind that the practice test is just that: practice. Memorizing these questions and answers will not be very helpful on the actual test because it is unlikely to have any of the same exact questions. If you only know the right answers to the sample questions, you won't be prepared for the real thing. **Study the concepts** until you understand them fully, and then you'll be able to answer any question that shows up on the test.

It's important to wait on the practice tests until you're ready. If you take a test on your first day of study, you may be overwhelmed by the amount of material covered and how much you need to learn. Work up to it gradually.

On test day, you'll need to be prepared for answering questions, managing your time, and using the test-taking strategies you've learned. It's a lot to balance, like a mental marathon that will have a big impact on your future. Like training for a marathon, you'll need to start slowly and work your way up. When test day arrives, you'll be ready.

Start with the strategies you've read in the first two Secret Keys—plan your course and study in the way that works best for you. If you have time, consider using multiple study resources to get different approaches to the same concepts. It can be helpful to see difficult concepts from more than one angle. Then find a good source for practice tests. Many times, the test website will suggest potential study resources or provide sample tests.

Practice Test Strategy

If you're able to find at least three practice tests, we recommend this strategy:

Untimed and Open-Book Practice

Take the first test with no time constraints and with your notes and study guide handy. Take your time and focus on applying the strategies you've learned.

Timed and Open-Book Practice

Take the second practice test open-book as well, but set a timer and practice pacing yourself to finish in time.

Timed and Closed-Book Practice

Take any other practice tests as if it were test day. Set a timer and put away your study materials. Sit at a table or desk in a quiet room, imagine yourself at the testing center, and answer questions as quickly and accurately as possible.

Keep repeating timed and closed-book tests on a regular basis until you run out of practice tests or it's time for the actual test. Your mind will be ready for the schedule and stress of test day, and you'll be able to focus on recalling the material you've learned.

Secret Key #4 – Pace Yourself

Once you're fully prepared for the material on the test, your biggest challenge on test day will be managing your time. Just knowing that the clock is ticking can make you panic even if you have plenty of time left. Work on pacing yourself so you can build confidence against the time constraints of the exam. Pacing is a difficult skill to master, especially in a high-pressure environment, so **practice is vital**.

Set time expectations for your pace based on how much time is available. For example, if a section has 60 questions and the time limit is 30 minutes, you know you have to average 30 seconds or less per question in order to answer them all. Although 30 seconds is the hard limit, set 25 seconds per question as your goal, so you reserve extra time to spend on harder questions. When you budget extra time for the harder questions, you no longer have any reason to stress when those questions take longer to answer.

Don't let this time expectation distract you from working through the test at a calm, steady pace, but keep it in mind so you don't spend too much time on any one question. Recognize that taking extra time on one question you don't understand may keep you from answering two that you do understand later in the test. If your time limit for a question is up and you're still not sure of the answer, mark it and move on, and come back to it later if the time and the test format allow. If the testing format doesn't allow you to return to earlier questions, just make an educated guess; then put it out of your mind and move on.

On the easier questions, be careful not to rush. It may seem wise to hurry through them so you have more time for the challenging ones, but it's not worth missing one if you know the concept and just didn't take the time to read the question fully. Work efficiently but make sure you understand the question and have looked at all of the answer choices, since more than one may seem right at first.

Even if you're paying attention to the time, you may find yourself a little behind at some point. You should speed up to get back on track, but do so wisely. Don't panic; just take a few seconds less on each question until you're caught up. Don't guess without thinking, but do look through the answer choices and eliminate any you know are wrong. If you can get down to two choices, it is often worthwhile to guess from those. Once you've chosen an answer, move on and don't dwell on any that you skipped or had to hurry through. If a question was taking too long, chances are it was one of the harder ones, so you weren't as likely to get it right anyway.

On the other hand, if you find yourself getting ahead of schedule, it may be beneficial to slow down a little. The more quickly you work, the more likely you are to make a careless mistake that will affect your score. You've budgeted time for each question, so don't be afraid to spend that time. Practice an efficient but careful pace to get the most out of the time you have.

Secret Key #5 – Have a Plan for Guessing

When you're taking the test, you may find yourself stuck on a question. Some of the answer choices seem better than others, but you don't see the one answer choice that is obviously correct. What do you do?

The scenario described above is very common, yet most test takers have not effectively prepared for it. Developing and practicing a plan for guessing may be one of the single most effective uses of your time as you get ready for the exam.

In developing your plan for guessing, there are three questions to address:

- When should you start the guessing process?
- How should you narrow down the choices?
- Which answer should you choose?

When to Start the Guessing Process

Unless your plan for guessing is to select C every time (which, despite its merits, is not what we recommend), you need to leave yourself enough time to apply your answer elimination strategies. Since you have a limited amount of time for each question, that means that if you're going to give yourself the best shot at guessing correctly, you have to decide quickly whether or not you will guess.

Of course, the best-case scenario is that you don't have to guess at all, so first, see if you can answer the question based on your knowledge of the subject and basic reasoning skills. Focus on the key words in the question and try to jog your memory of related topics. Give yourself a chance to bring the knowledge to mind, but once you realize that you don't have (or you can't access) the knowledge you need to answer the question, it's time to start the guessing process.

It's almost always better to start the guessing process too early than too late. It only takes a few seconds to remember something and answer the question from knowledge. Carefully eliminating wrong answer choices takes longer. Plus, going through the process of eliminating answer choices can actually help jog your memory.

Summary: Start the guessing process as soon as you decide that you can't answer the question based on your knowledge.

How to Narrow Down the Choices

The next chapter in this book (**Test-Taking Strategies**) includes a wide range of strategies for how to approach questions and how to look for answer choices to eliminate. You will definitely want to read those carefully, practice them, and figure out which ones work best for you. Here though, we're going to address a mindset rather than a particular strategy.

Your odds of guessing an answer correctly depend on how many options you are choosing from.

Number of options left	5	4	3	2	1
Odds of guessing correctly	20%	25%	33%	50%	100%

You can see from this chart just how valuable it is to be able to eliminate incorrect answers and make an educated guess, but there are two things that many test takers do that cause them to miss out on the benefits of guessing:

- Accidentally eliminating the correct answer
- Selecting an answer based on an impression

We'll look at the first one here, and the second one in the next section.

To avoid accidentally eliminating the correct answer, we recommend a thought exercise called **the $5 challenge**. In this challenge, you only eliminate an answer choice from contention if you are willing to bet $5 on it being wrong. Why $5? Five dollars is a small but not insignificant amount of money. It's an amount you could afford to lose but wouldn't want to throw away. And while losing $5 once might not hurt too much, doing it twenty times will set you back $100. In the same way, each small decision you make—eliminating a choice here, guessing on a question there—won't by itself impact your score very much, but when you put them all together, they can make a big difference. By holding each answer choice elimination decision to a higher standard, you can reduce the risk of accidentally eliminating the correct answer.

The $5 challenge can also be applied in a positive sense: If you are willing to bet $5 that an answer choice *is* correct, go ahead and mark it as correct.

Summary: Only eliminate an answer choice if you are willing to bet $5 that it is wrong.

Which Answer to Choose

You're taking the test. You've run into a hard question and decided you'll have to guess. You've eliminated all the answer choices you're willing to bet $5 on. Now you have to pick an answer. Why do we even need to talk about this? Why can't you just pick whichever one you feel like when the time comes?

The answer to these questions is that if you don't come into the test with a plan, you'll rely on your impression to select an answer choice, and if you do that, you risk falling into a trap. The test writers know that everyone who takes their test will be guessing on some of the questions, so they intentionally write wrong answer choices to seem plausible. You still have to pick an answer though, and if the wrong answer choices are designed to look right, how can you ever be sure that you're not falling for their trap? The best solution we've found to this dilemma is to take the decision out of your hands entirely. Here is the process we recommend:

Once you've eliminated any choices that you are confident (willing to bet $5) are wrong, select the first remaining choice as your answer.

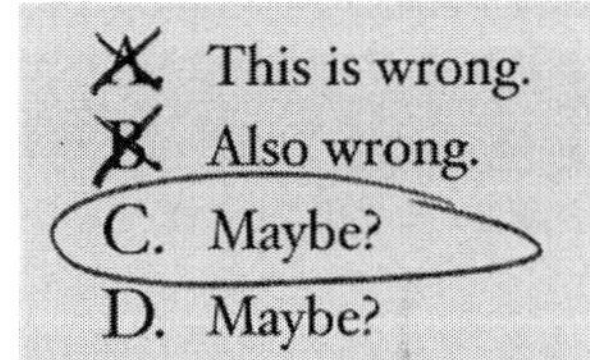

Whether you choose to select the first remaining choice, the second, or the last, the important thing is that you use some preselected standard. Using this approach guarantees that you will not be enticed into selecting an answer choice that looks right, because you are not basing your decision on how the answer choices look.

This is not meant to make you question your knowledge. Instead, it is to help you recognize the difference between your knowledge and your impressions. There's a huge difference between thinking an answer is right because of what you know, and thinking an answer is right because it looks or sounds like it should be right.

Summary: To ensure that your selection is appropriately random, make a predetermined selection from among all answer choices you have not eliminated.

Test-Taking Strategies

This section contains a list of test-taking strategies that you may find helpful as you work through the test. By taking what you know and applying logical thought, you can maximize your chances of answering any question correctly!

It is very important to realize that every question is different and every person is different: no single strategy will work on every question, and no single strategy will work for every person. That's why we've included all of them here, so you can try them out and determine which ones work best for different types of questions and which ones work best for you.

Question Strategies

✓ Read Carefully

Read the question and the answer choices carefully. Don't miss the question because you misread the terms. You have plenty of time to read each question thoroughly and make sure you understand what is being asked. Yet a happy medium must be attained, so don't waste too much time. You must read carefully and efficiently.

✓ Contextual Clues

Look for contextual clues. If the question includes a word you are not familiar with, look at the immediate context for some indication of what the word might mean. Contextual clues can often give you all the information you need to decipher the meaning of an unfamiliar word. Even if you can't determine the meaning, you may be able to narrow down the possibilities enough to make a solid guess at the answer to the question.

✓ Prefixes

If you're having trouble with a word in the question or answer choices, try dissecting it. Take advantage of every clue that the word might include. Prefixes can be a huge help. Usually, they allow you to determine a basic meaning. *Pre-* means before, *post-* means after, *pro-* is positive, *de-* is negative. From prefixes, you can get an idea of the general meaning of the word and try to put it into context.

✓ Hedge Words

Watch out for critical hedge words, such as *likely, may, can, often, almost, mostly, usually, generally, rarely*, and *sometimes*. Question writers insert these hedge phrases to cover every possibility. Often an answer choice will be wrong simply because it leaves no room for exception. Be on guard for answer choices that have definitive words such as *exactly* and *always*.

✓ Switchback Words

Stay alert for *switchbacks*. These are the words and phrases frequently used to alert you to shifts in thought. The most common switchback words are *but, although*, and *however*. Others include *nevertheless, on the other hand, even though, while, in spite of, despite*, and *regardless of*. Switchback words are important to catch because they can change the direction of the question or an answer choice.

⊘ Face Value

When in doubt, use common sense. Accept the situation in the problem at face value. Don't read too much into it. These problems will not require you to make wild assumptions. If you have to go beyond creativity and warp time or space in order to have an answer choice fit the question, then you should move on and consider the other answer choices. These are normal problems rooted in reality. The applicable relationship or explanation may not be readily apparent, but it is there for you to figure out. Use your common sense to interpret anything that isn't clear.

Answer Choice Strategies

⊘ Answer Selection

The most thorough way to pick an answer choice is to identify and eliminate wrong answers until only one is left, then confirm it is the correct answer. Sometimes an answer choice may immediately seem right, but be careful. The test writers will usually put more than one reasonable answer choice on each question, so take a second to read all of them and make sure that the other choices are not equally obvious. As long as you have time left, it is better to read every answer choice than to pick the first one that looks right without checking the others.

⊘ Answer Choice Families

An answer choice family consists of two (in rare cases, three) answer choices that are very similar in construction and cannot all be true at the same time. If you see two answer choices that are direct opposites or parallels, one of them is usually the correct answer. For instance, if one answer choice says that quantity *x* increases and another either says that quantity *x* decreases (opposite) or says that quantity *y* increases (parallel), then those answer choices would fall into the same family. An answer choice that doesn't match the construction of the answer choice family is more likely to be incorrect. Most questions will not have answer choice families, but when they do appear, you should be prepared to recognize them.

⊘ Eliminate Answers

Eliminate answer choices as soon as you realize they are wrong, but make sure you consider all possibilities. If you are eliminating answer choices and realize that the last one you are left with is also wrong, don't panic. Start over and consider each choice again. There may be something you missed the first time that you will realize on the second pass.

⊘ Avoid Fact Traps

Don't be distracted by an answer choice that is factually true but doesn't answer the question. You are looking for the choice that answers the question. Stay focused on what the question is asking for so you don't accidentally pick an answer that is true but incorrect. Always go back to the question and make sure the answer choice you've selected actually answers the question and is not merely a true statement.

⊘ Extreme Statements

In general, you should avoid answers that put forth extreme actions as standard practice or proclaim controversial ideas as established fact. An answer choice that states the "process should be used in certain situations, if..." is much more likely to be correct than one that states the "process should be discontinued completely." The first is a calm rational statement and doesn't even make a definitive, uncompromising stance, using a hedge word *if* to provide wiggle room, whereas the second choice is far more extreme.

☑ Benchmark

As you read through the answer choices and you come across one that seems to answer the question well, mentally select that answer choice. This is not your final answer, but it's the one that will help you evaluate the other answer choices. The one that you selected is your benchmark or standard for judging each of the other answer choices. Every other answer choice must be compared to your benchmark. That choice is correct until proven otherwise by another answer choice beating it. If you find a better answer, then that one becomes your new benchmark. Once you've decided that no other choice answers the question as well as your benchmark, you have your final answer.

☑ Predict the Answer

Before you even start looking at the answer choices, it is often best to try to predict the answer. When you come up with the answer on your own, it is easier to avoid distractions and traps because you will know exactly what to look for. The right answer choice is unlikely to be word-for-word what you came up with, but it should be a close match. Even if you are confident that you have the right answer, you should still take the time to read each option before moving on.

General Strategies

☑ Tough Questions

If you are stumped on a problem or it appears too hard or too difficult, don't waste time. Move on! Remember though, if you can quickly check for obviously incorrect answer choices, your chances of guessing correctly are greatly improved. Before you completely give up, at least try to knock out a couple of possible answers. Eliminate what you can and then guess at the remaining answer choices before moving on.

☑ Check Your Work

Since you will probably not know every term listed and the answer to every question, it is important that you get credit for the ones that you do know. Don't miss any questions through careless mistakes. If at all possible, try to take a second to look back over your answer selection and make sure you've selected the correct answer choice and haven't made a costly careless mistake (such as marking an answer choice that you didn't mean to mark). This quick double check should more than pay for itself in caught mistakes for the time it costs.

☑ Pace Yourself

It's easy to be overwhelmed when you're looking at a page full of questions; your mind is confused and full of random thoughts, and the clock is ticking down faster than you would like. Calm down and maintain the pace that you have set for yourself. Especially as you get down to the last few minutes of the test, don't let the small numbers on the clock make you panic. As long as you are on track by monitoring your pace, you are guaranteed to have time for each question.

☑ Don't Rush

It is very easy to make errors when you are in a hurry. Maintaining a fast pace in answering questions is pointless if it makes you miss questions that you would have gotten right otherwise. Test writers like to include distracting information and wrong answers that seem right. Taking a little extra time to avoid careless mistakes can make all the difference in your test score. Find a pace that allows you to be confident in the answers that you select.

☑ KEEP MOVING

Panicking will not help you pass the test, so do your best to stay calm and keep moving. Taking deep breaths and going through the answer elimination steps you practiced can help to break through a stress barrier and keep your pace.

Final Notes

The combination of a solid foundation of content knowledge and the confidence that comes from practicing your plan for applying that knowledge is the key to maximizing your performance on test day. As your foundation of content knowledge is built up and strengthened, you'll find that the strategies included in this chapter become more and more effective in helping you quickly sift through the distractions and traps of the test to isolate the correct answer.

Now that you're preparing to move forward into the test content chapters of this book, be sure to keep your goal in mind. As you read, think about how you will be able to apply this information on the test. If you've already seen sample questions for the test and you have an idea of the question format and style, try to come up with questions of your own that you can answer based on what you're reading. This will give you valuable practice applying your knowledge in the same ways you can expect to on test day.

Good luck and good studying!

Verbal Analogies

What Are Analogy Questions?

Analogies are pairs of terms that have a common relationship. Analogy questions are presented in the format, "A is to B as C is to D," meaning that terms A and B are related to one another in the same or similar way that terms C and D are related to each other. Terms A and B do not have to be related to terms C and D at all, though they usually will be.

Usually in the question, you will be given terms A, B, and C, and will have to supply term D from the choices given. Occasionally, you may be given only terms A and B, and you will have to select a pair of terms for C and D.

What Sort of Relationships Will There Be?

Below are some examples of the types of analogies that may appear on the exam. Most of the questions you encounter will be relatively simple relationships, but here is an extensive list of the types of analogies that might show up.

Characteristic

Some characteristic analogies will focus on a characteristic of something else.

- *Dog* is to *paw*—The foot of a dog is its paw.
- *Lady* is to *lovely*—A lady has a lovely personality.
- *Outrageous* is to *lies*—Lies can be described as being outrageous.

Some characteristic analogies will focus on something that is NOT a characteristic of something else.

- *Desert* is to *humidity*—A desert does not have humidity.
- *Job* is to *unemployed*—A person without a job is unemployed.
- *Quick* is to *considered*—A quick decision is often not very considered.

Source

- *Casting* is to *metal*—A casting is made from metal.
- *Forest* is to *trees*—A forest is composed of trees.
- *Slogans* is to *banners*—A slogan is printed on banners.

Location

- *Eiffel Tower* is to *Paris*—The Eiffel Tower is a structure in Paris.
- *Welsh* is to *Wales*—The Welsh are the inhabitants of Wales.
- *Pound* is to *England*—The pound is the monetary unit of England.

Sequential

- *One* is to *two*—These are consecutive numbers.
- *Birth* is to *death*—These are the first and last events of a life or project.
- *Spring* is to *summer*—The season of spring immediately precedes summer.

Cause/Effect

- *Storm* is to *hail*—Hail can be caused by a storm.
- *Heat* is to *fire*—Heat results from a fire.
- *Monotony* is to *boredom*—Boredom is a consequence of monotony.

Creator/Creation

- *Carpenter* is to *house*—A carpenter builds a house.
- *Painter* is to *portrait*—A painter makes a portrait.
- *Burroughs* is to *Tarzan*—Edgar Rice Burroughs wrote the novel Tarzan.

Provider/Provision

- *Job* is to *salary*—A job provides a salary.
- *Therapist* is to *treatment*—A therapist treats patients.
- *Army* is to *defense*—An army enables national defense.

Object/Function

- *Pencil* is to *write*—A pencil is used to write.
- *Pressure* is to *barometer*—A barometer measures pressure.
- *Frown* is to *unhappy*—A frown shows unhappiness.

User/Tool

- *Carpenter* is to *hammer*—A carpenter uses a hammer.
- *Teacher* is to *chalk*—A teacher uses chalk.
- *Farmer* is to *tractor*—A farmer drives a tractor.

Whole/Part

- *Door* is to *house*—A door is part of a house.
- *State* is to *country*—A country is made up of states.
- *Day* is to *month*—A month consists of many days.

Grammatical Transformation

- *Ran* is to *run*—These are different tenses of the same verb.
- *Die* is to *dice*—These are singular and plural forms.
- *We* is to *our*—These are pronouns related to groups.

Translation

- *Satan* is to *Lucifer*—These are both names for the devil.
- *Bon voyage* is to *farewell*—These are the French and English words for goodbye.
- *Japan* is to *Nippon*—These are two names for the same country.

Category

- *Door* is to *window*—Both a door and a window are parts of a house.
- *Thigh* is to *shin*—Both a thigh and a shin are parts of a leg.
- *Measles* is to *mumps*—Both measles and mumps are types of diseases.

Synonym or Definition

These are analogies in which both terms have a similar meaning.

- *Chase* is to *pursue*—Both of these terms mean to "go after."
- *Achieve* is to *accomplish*—Both of these terms refer to the successful attainment of a goal.
- *Satiate* is to *satisfy*—Both of these terms mean to gratify a desire.

Antonym or Contrast

These are analogies in which both terms have an opposite meaning.

- *Disguise* is to *reveal*—To disguise something is not to reveal it, but to conceal it.
- *Peace* is to *war*—Peace is a state in which there is no war.
- *Forget* is to *remember*—The word "remember" means not to forget something.

Intensity

These are analogies in which either one term expresses a higher degree of something than the other term.

- *Exum* is to *happy*—To be exuberant is to be extremely happy.
- *Break* is to *shatter*—To shatter is to break violently into many pieces.
- *Deluge* is to *rain*—A deluge is a heavy rain.

What Strategies Can I Use?

A huge vocabulary is not necessary to succeed on analogy questions (though it certainly doesn't hurt). In most cases though, you can determine the answer even if you don't recognize all the words. The strategies listed here will help you develop the ability to recognize basic relationships and apply simple steps and methods to solving them.

Determine the Relationship

Don't focus on the meanings, but rather the relationship between the two words.

To understand the relationship, first create a sentence that links the two words and puts them into perspective. The sentence that you use to connect the words can be simple at first.

- Example:
  - *Wood* is to *fire*
  - *Wood* feeds a *fire*.

Then go through each answer choice and replace the words with the answer choices. If the question is easy, then that may be all that is necessary. If the question is hard, you might have to fine-tune your sentence.

- Example:
  - *Fire* is to *wood* as *cow* is to (*a. grass, b. farmer*)

Using the initial sentence, you would state "Grass feeds a cow." This is correct, but then so is the next answer choice "Farmer feeds a cow." So which is right? Modify the sentence to be more specific.

- Example: "Wood feeds a fire and is consumed."

This modified sentence makes answer choice B incorrect and answer choice A clearly correct, because while "grass feeds a cow and is consumed" is correct, "farmer feeds a cow and is consumed" is definitely wrong.

If your initial sentence seems correct with more than one answer choice, then keep modifying it until only one answer choice makes sense.

Similar Choices

If you don't know the word, don't worry. Start by looking at the answer choices and trying them out. Remember that three of the answer choices will always be wrong. If you can find a common relationship between any three answer choices, then you know they are all wrong. Find the answer choice that does not have a common relationship to the other answer choices and it will be the correct answer.

- Example:
    - *Tough* is to *rugged* as *hard* is to (*a. soft, b. easy, c. delicate, d. rigid*)

In this example the first three choices are all opposites of the term "hard". Even if you don't know that rigid means the same as hard, you know it must be correct, because the other three all had the same relationship. They were all opposites, so they must all be wrong. The one that has a different relationship from the other three must be correct. So don't worry if you don't know a word. Focus on the answer choices that you do understand and see if you can identify common relationships. Even identifying two word pairs with the same relationship (for example, two word pairs that are both opposites) will allow you to eliminate those two answer choices, for they are both wrong.

A simple way to remember this is that if you have two or more answer choices with the exact same relationship, then they are both or all wrong.

- Example: (*a. neat, b. orderly*)

Since the two answer choices above are synonyms and therefore have the same relationship with the matching term, then you know that they both must be wrong, because they both can't be correct, and for all intents and purposes they are the same word.

Be sure to read all of the choices. You may find an answer choice that seems right at first, but you may find a better choice if you continue reading.

Difficult words are usually synonyms or antonyms (opposites). Whenever you have extremely difficult words that you don't understand, look at the answer choices. Try to identify whether two or more of the answer choices are either synonyms or antonyms. Remember that if you can find two word pairs that have the same relationship (for example, they are both synonyms) then you can eliminate them both.

Eliminate Answers

Eliminate choices as soon as you realize they are wrong, but be careful! Make sure you consider all of the possible answer choices. Don't worry if you are stuck between two that seem right. By eliminating the other two possible choices, your odds are now 50/50. Rather than wasting too much time, play the odds. You are guessing, but guessing wisely, because you've been able to knock out some of the answer choices that you know are wrong. If you are eliminating choices and realize that the answer choice you are left with is also obviously wrong, don't panic. Start over and consider each choice again. There may easily be something you missed the first time and will realize on the second pass.

Word Types

The correct answer choice will contain words that are the same type of word as those in the word pair.

- Example:
    - *Artist* is to *paintbrush*

In this example, an artist is a person, while a paintbrush is an object. The correct answer will have one word that describes a person and another word that describes an object.

- Example:
    - *Hedge* is to *gardener* as *rock* is to (*a. wind, b. sculptor*)

In this example, you could create the sentence, "The gardener cuts away at hedges." Both answer choices seem correct with this sentence. "Wind cuts away at rocks" through the process of erosion, and "a sculptor cuts away at rocks" using a hammer and chisel. The difference is that a gardener is a person, as is a sculptor, while the wind is a thing, which makes answer choice B correct.

Nearly and Perfect Opposites

When you have determined which pair of terms you should work with, and know that the provided pair is an opposite, then you must find the opposite of the remaining unmatched term. Nearly opposite may often be more correct, because the goal is to test your understanding of the nuances, or little differences, between words. A perfect opposite may not exist, so don't be concerned if your answer choice is not a complete opposite. Focus upon edging closer to the word. Eliminate the words that you know aren't correct first. Then narrow your search. Cross out the words that are the most similar to the main word until you are left with the one that is the least similar.

Prefixes

Take advantage of every clue that the word might include. Prefixes and suffixes can be a huge help. Usually, they allow you to determine a basic meaning. *Pre-* means before, *post-* means after, *pro-* is positive, and *de-* is negative. From prefixes and suffixes, you can get an idea of the general meaning of the word and look for its opposite. Beware though of any traps. Just because con is the opposite of pro, doesn't necessarily mean *congress* is the opposite of *progress*!

Review Video: Affixes
Visit mometrix.com/academy and enter code: 782422

Positive vs. Negative

Many words can be easily determined to be positive or negative. Words such as *despicable*, *gruesome*, and *bleak* are all negative. Words such as *ecstatic*, *praiseworthy*, and *magnificent* are all positive. You will be surprised at how many words can be considered as either positive or negative. If you recognize a positive/negative relationship between the given pair of terms, then focus in on the answer choices that would duplicate that positive/negative relationship with the remaining term.

Word Strength

When analyzing a word, determine how **strong** it is. For example, *stupendous* and *good* are both positive words. However, *stupendous* is a much stronger positive adjective than *good*. Also, *towering* or *gigantic* are stronger words than *tall* or *large*. Search for an answer choice with either the same or opposite strength (depending on the relationship of the matched terms) to the remaining term.

Type and Topic

Another key is what type of word is the unmatched term. If the unmatched term is an adjective describing height, then look for the answer choice to be an adjective describing height as well. Match both the type and topic of the main word. The type refers the parts of speech, whether the word is an adjective, adverb, or verb. The topic refers to what the definition of the word includes, such as descriptive sizes (large, small, gigantic, etc).

Form a Sentence

Many words seem more natural in a sentence. *Specious reasoning*, *irresistible force*, and *uncanny resemblance* are just a few of the word combinations that usually go together. When faced with an uncommon word that you barely understand, try to put the word in a sentence that makes sense. It will help you to understand the word's meaning and make it easier to determine its relationship. Once you have a good descriptive sentence that utilizes a main term or answer choice properly, plug in the answer choice or main term and see if a solid relationship can be established.

Use Logic

Ask yourself questions about each answer choice to see if they are logical.

- Example:
  - *Aromas* is to *smelt* as *poundings* is to (*a. seen*, *b. heard*)

Would poundings be *seen*? Or would poundings be *heard*? It can logically be deduced that poundings are heard.

The Trap of Familiarity

Don't just choose a word because you recognize it. On difficult questions, you may only recognize one or two words. There won't be any made up words on the test, so don't think that just because you only recognize one word means that word must be correct. If you don't recognize three words, then focus on the one that you do recognize. Is it correct? Try your best to determine if it fits the sentence you created that shows the relationship between terms. If it does, that is great, but if it doesn't, eliminate it. Each word you eliminate increases your chances of getting the question correct.

Tough Questions

If you are stumped on a problem or it appears too hard or too difficult, don't waste time. Move on! Remember though, if you can quickly check for obviously incorrect answer choices, your chances of guessing correctly are greatly improved. Before you completely give up, at least try to knock out a couple of possible answers. Eliminate what you can and then guess at the remainder before moving on.

Read Carefully

Understand the analogy. Read the terms and answer choices carefully. Don't miss the question because you misread the terms. There are only a few words in each question, so you can spend time reading them carefully. Yet a happy medium must be attained, so don't waste too much time. You must read carefully, but efficiently.

BRAINSTORM

If you get stuck on a difficult analogy, spend a few seconds quickly brainstorming. Run through the complete list of possible relationships. Break down each answer choice into all of the potential combinations with the two possible analogous terms. Since there are four answer choices and each answer choice could form a pair with one of two terms, there are only eight possible relationships to test. Look at each relationship and see if it would make sense. Test with sentences to determine if any relationship can be established. By systematically going through all possibilities, you may find something that you would otherwise overlook.

Practice Questions

1. *Stirrup* is to *ear* as *atrium* is to

a. Blood
b. Ventricle
c. Vestibule
d. Heart
e. Chamber

2. *Dwelling* is to *condominium* as *meal* is to

a. Entree
b. Brunch
c. Appetizer
d. Plate
e. Dessert

3. *Fragrant* is to *smell* as *mellifluous* is to

a. Sound
b. Pleasant
c. Fluid
d. Taste
e. Soothing

4. *Bracelet* is to *jewelry* as *pomegranate* is to

a. Seeds
b. Edible
c. Fruit
d. Acidic
e. Citrus

5. *Loud* is to *deafening* as *happy* is to

a. Ecstatic
b. Glad
c. Morose
d. Content
e. Depressed

6. *Facile* is to *easy* as *loquacious* is to

a. Silent
b. Difficult
c. Friendly
d. Lacking
e. Talkative

7. *Abate* is to *increase* as *abhor*

a. Despise
b. Love
c. Tolerate
d. Abdicate
e. Hate

8. ***Quills*** **is to** ***porcupine*** **as** ***tusks*** **is to**

a. Proboscis
b. Horn
c. Ivory
d. Elephant
e. Nose

9. ***Duplicity*** **is to** ***deception*** **as** ***avarice*** **is to**

a. Greed
b. Money
c. Average
d. Accumulate
e. Benevolent

10. ***Whisper*** **is to** ***yell*** **as** ***tap*** **is to**

a. Water
b. Pat
c. Dance
d. Jab
e. Jump

11. ***Eucalyptus*** **is to** ***tree*** **as** ***iris*** **is to**

a. Tulip
b. Purple
c. Eye
d. Face
e. Flower

12. ***Irksome*** **is to** ***tedious*** **as** ***intriguing*** **is to**

a. Fascinating
b. Silly
c. Unlikely
d. Impossible
e. Irritating

Practice Answers

1. D: This is a "part to whole" analogy. Just as the *stirrup* is a part of the *ear*, so is the *atrium* a part of the *heart.*

2. B: In "type" analogies, one word in the stem names a category that encompasses the other. Just as a *condominium* is a type of *dwelling*, so is *brunch* a type of *meal.*

3. A: This analogy is that of adjective to noun. *Fragrant* is an adjective modifying the noun *smell* in a positive way. *Mellifluous* is an adjective modifying the noun *sound* in a positive way.

4. C: In this "type" analogy, one word in the stem names a category that encompasses the other. A *bracelet* is a type of *jewelry*, just as a *pomegranate* is a type of *fruit.*

5. A: In this analogy of relative degree, the second term in each pair indicates a more intense degree of the first term. *Deafening* is a more intense version of *loud,* just as *ecstatic* is a more intense version of *happy.*

6. E: This analogy is based on synonyms. Just as *facile* and *easy* mean about the same thing, so do *loquacious* and *talkative.*

7. B: This analogy is based on antonyms. Just as *abate* means the opposite of *increase,* so does *abhor* mean the opposite of *love.*

8. D: This analogy names prominent features of each animal. *Quills* are a prominent feature of a *porcupine*, just as *tusks* are a prominent feature of an *elephant.*

9. A: This is another synonym-based analogy. *Duplicity* and *deception* mean about the same thing, just as *avarice* and *greed* do. You might have been tempted to choose D, which suggests something that an avaricious person might do, but *greed* is the better answer since it is a noun, like *avarice* is.

10. D: This is an analogy of relative degree. A *yell* is a much louder version of a *whisper*, just as a *jab* is a much harder version of a *tap.*

11. E: This is an analogy indicating types, since a *eucalyptus* is one type of *tree*, and an *iris* is one type of *flower.*

12. A: In this analogy based on synonyms, *irksome* means about the same as *tedious,* just as *intriguing* means about the same as *fascinating.*

Arithmetic Reasoning and Math Knowledge

What Do the Arithmetic Reasoning Questions Look Like?

Arithmetic questions will generally take the form of a simple word problem. You will be posed an everyday situation that requires arithmetic to solve and asked to select the correct answer from the choices given. You may be asked to calculate rates, percentages, averages, or some other practical math quantity, and you may have to convert between different units. It is usually obvious what the question is asking for.

How Can I Prepare?

Since the math needed for these questions is not complicated, that means that you only need to learn or refresh your memory of a few simple operations. Then it's just a matter of practicing them. One of the biggest mistakes people make when trying to learn math is that they read about a concept, look at a worked-out example problem, and when it makes sense, they assume they understand it well enough and move on. Then when the test comes, they don't remember how to solve the problems. Math skills must be practiced in order to be remembered.

What Do the Math Knowledge Questions Look Like?

Math knowledge questions are much less predictable than arithmetic questions. Math knowledge questions may test your knowledge of anything covered in the arithmetic section, plus square roots, exponents, factors, multiples, equations, geometric properties, and more.

How Can I Prepare?

The questions may be more difficult, but the preparation process should be the same: learn the concepts and facts you need to know, then practice them.

What Math Do I Need to Know?

All of the major concepts you will need to excel on the arithmetic and math knowledge sections are covered in the remainder of this chapter.

Arithmetic

Classifications of Numbers

Numbers are the basic building blocks of mathematics. Specific features of numbers are identified by the following terms:

Integer – any positive or negative whole number, including zero. Integers do not include fractions $\left(\frac{1}{3}\right)$, decimals (0.56), or mixed numbers $\left(7\frac{3}{4}\right)$.

Prime number – any whole number greater than 1 that has only two factors, itself and 1; that is, a number that can be divided evenly only by 1 and itself.

Composite number – any whole number greater than 1 that has more than two different factors; in other words, any whole number that is not a prime number. For example: The composite number 8 has the factors of 1, 2, 4, and 8.

Even number – any integer that can be divided by 2 without leaving a remainder. For example: 2, 4, 6, 8, and so on.

Odd number – any integer that cannot be divided evenly by 2. For example: 3, 5, 7, 9, and so on.

Decimal number – any number that uses a decimal point to show the part of the number that is less than one. Example: 1.234.

Decimal point – a symbol used to separate the ones place from the tenths place in decimals or dollars from cents in currency.

Decimal place – the position of a number to the right of the decimal point. In the decimal 0.123, the 1 is in the first place to the right of the decimal point, indicating tenths; the 2 is in the second place, indicating hundredths; and the 3 is in the third place, indicating thousandths.

The **decimal**, or base 10, system is a number system that uses ten different digits (0, 1, 2, 3, 4, 5, 6, 7, 8, 9). An example of a number system that uses something other than ten digits is the **binary**, or base 2, number system, used by computers, which uses only the numbers 0 and 1. It is thought that the decimal system originated because people had only their 10 fingers for counting.

Rational numbers include all integers, decimals, and fractions. Any terminating or repeating decimal number is a rational number.

Irrational numbers cannot be written as fractions or decimals because the number of decimal places is infinite and there is no recurring pattern of digits within the number. For example, pi (π) begins with 3.141592 and continues without terminating or repeating, so pi is an irrational number.

Real numbers are the set of all rational and irrational numbers.

Review Video: Classification of Numbers
Visit mometrix.com/academy and enter code: 461071

Review Video: Prime and Composite Numbers
Visit mometrix.com/academy and enter code: 565581

Numbers in Word Form and Place Value

When writing numbers out in word form or translating word form to numbers, it is essential to understand how a place value system works. In the decimal or base-10 system, each digit of a number represents how many of the corresponding place value—a specific factor of 10—are contained in the number being represented. To make reading numbers easier, every three digits to the left of the decimal place is preceded by a comma. The following table demonstrates some of the place values:

Power of 10	10^3	10^2	10^1	10^0	10^{-1}	10^{-2}	10^{-3}
Value	1,000	100	10	1	0.1	0.01	0.001
Place	thousands	hundreds	tens	ones	tenths	hundredths	thousandths

For example, consider the number 4,546.09, which can be separated into each place value like this:

4: thousands
5: hundreds
4: tens
6: ones
0: tenths
9: hundredths

This number in word form would be *four thousand five hundred forty-six and nine hundredths.*

Review Video: Place Value
Visit mometrix.com/academy and enter code: 205433

The term **rational** means that the number can be expressed as a ratio or fraction. That is, a number, r, is rational if and only if it can be represented by a fraction $\frac{a}{b}$ where a and b are integers and b does not equal 0. The set of rational numbers includes integers and decimals. If there is no finite way to represent a value with a fraction of integers, then the number is **irrational**. Common examples of irrational numbers include: $\sqrt{5}$, $(1+\sqrt{2})$, and π.

Review Video: Rational and Irrational Numbers
Visit mometrix.com/academy and enter code: 280645

Review Video: Ordering Rational Numbers
Visit mometrix.com/academy and enter code: 419578

A number line is a graph to see the distance between numbers. Basically, this graph shows the relationship between numbers. So a number line may have a point for zero and may show negative numbers on the left side of the line. Any positive numbers are placed on the right side of the line. For example, consider the points labeled on the following number line:

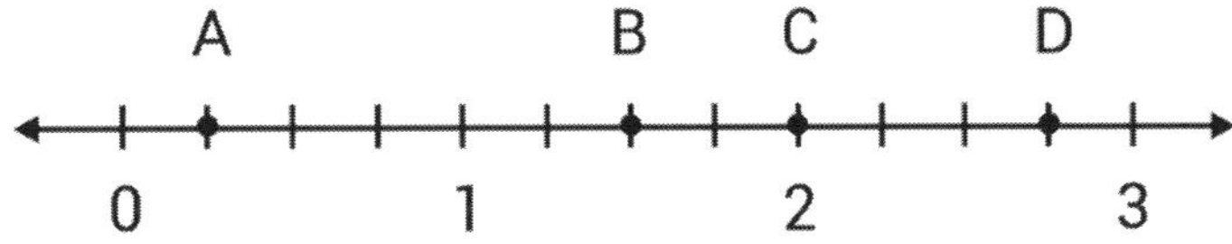

We can use the dashed lines on the number line to identify each point. Each dashed line between two whole numbers is $\frac{1}{4}$. The line halfway between two numbers is $\frac{1}{2}$.

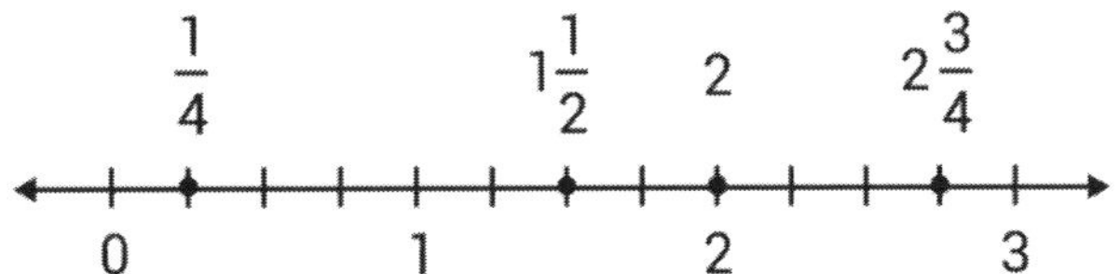

Review Video: The Number Line
Visit mometrix.com/academy and enter code: 816439

Rounding is reducing the digits in a number while still trying to keep the value similar. The result will be less accurate but in a simpler form and easier to use. Whole numbers can be rounded to the nearest ten, hundred, or thousand.

When you are asked to estimate the solution to a problem, you will need to provide only an approximate figure or **estimation** for your answer. In this situation, you will need to round each number in the calculation to the level indicated (nearest hundred, nearest thousand, etc.) or to a level that makes sense for the numbers involved. When estimating a sum **all numbers must be rounded to the same level**. You cannot round one number to the nearest thousand while rounding another to the nearest hundred.

Review Video: Rounding and Estimation
Visit mometrix.com/academy and enter code: 126243

An **operation** is simply a mathematical process that takes some value(s) as input(s) and produces an output. Elementary operations are often written in the following form: *value operation value*. For instance, in the expression $1 + 2$ the values are 1 and 2 and the operation is addition. Performing the operation gives the output of 3. In this way we can say that $1 + 2$ and 3 are equal, or $1 + 2 = 3$.

ADDITION

Addition increases the value of one quantity by the value of another quantity (both called **addends**). Example: $2 + 4 = 6$ or $8 + 9 = 17$. The result is called the **sum**. With addition, the order does not matter, $4 + 2 = 2 + 4$.

When adding signed numbers, if the signs are the same simply add the absolute values of the addends and apply the original sign to the sum. For example, $(+4) + (+8) = +12$ and $(-4) + (-8) = -12$. When the original signs are different, take the absolute values of the addends and subtract the smaller value from the larger value, then apply the original sign of the larger value to the difference. Example: $(+4) + (-8) = -4$ and $(-4) + (+8) = +4$.

SUBTRACTION

Subtraction is the opposite operation to addition; it decreases the value of one quantity (the **minuend**) by the value of another quantity (the **subtrahend**). For example, $6 - 4 = 2$ or $17 - 8 = 9$. The result is called the **difference**. Note that with subtraction, the order does matter, $6 - 4 \neq 4 - 6$.

For subtracting signed numbers, change the sign of the subtrahend and then follow the same rules used for addition. Example: $(+4) - (+8) = (+4) + (-8) = -4$

MULTIPLICATION

Multiplication can be thought of as repeated addition. One number (the **multiplier**) indicates how many times to add the other number (the **multiplicand**) to itself. Example: $3 \times 2 = 2 + 2 + 2 = 6$. With multiplication, the order does not matter, $2 \times 3 = 3 \times 2$ or $3 + 3 = 2 + 2 + 2$, either way the result (the **product**) is the same.

If the signs are the same, the product is positive when multiplying signed numbers. Example: $(+4) \times (+8) = +32$ and $(-4) \times (-8) = +32$. If the signs are opposite, the product is negative. Example: $(+4) \times (-8) = -32$ and $(-4) \times (+8) = -32$. When more than two factors are multiplied together, the sign of the product is determined by how many negative factors are present. If there are an odd number of negative factors then the product is negative, whereas an even number of negative factors indicates a positive product. Example: $(+4) \times (-8) \times (-2) = +64$ and $(-4) \times (-8) \times (-2) = -64$.

Division

Division is the opposite operation to multiplication; one number (the **divisor**) tells us how many parts to divide the other number (the **dividend**) into. The result of division is called the **quotient**. Example: $20 \div 4 = 5$. If 20 is split into 4 equal parts, each part is 5. With division, the order of the numbers does matter, $20 \div 4 \neq 4 \div 20$.

The rules for dividing signed numbers are similar to multiplying signed numbers. If the dividend and divisor have the same sign, the quotient is positive. If the dividend and divisor have opposite signs, the quotient is negative. Example: $(-4) \div (+8) = -0.5$.

> **Review Video: Mathematical Operations**
> Visit mometrix.com/academy and enter code: 208095

Parentheses

Parentheses are used to designate which operations should be done first when there are multiple operations. Example: $4 - (2 + 1) = 1$; the parentheses tell us that we must add 2 and 1, and then subtract the sum from 4, rather than subtracting 2 from 4 and then adding 1 (this would give us an answer of 3).

> **Review Video: Mathematical Parentheses**
> Visit mometrix.com/academy and enter code: 978600

Exponents

An **exponent** is a superscript number placed next to another number at the top right. It indicates how many times the base number is to be multiplied by itself. Exponents provide a shorthand way to write what would be a longer mathematical expression, Example: $2^4 = 2 \times 2 \times 2 \times 2$. A number with an exponent of 2 is said to be "squared," while a number with an exponent of 3 is said to be "cubed." The value of a number raised to an exponent is called its power. So 8^4 is read as "8 to the 4th power," or "8 raised to the power of 4."

> **Review Video: Exponents**
> Visit mometrix.com/academy and enter code: 600998

Roots

A **root**, such as a square root, is another way of writing a fractional exponent. Instead of using a superscript, roots use the radical symbol ($\sqrt{\ }$) to indicate the operation. A radical will have a number underneath the bar, and may sometimes have a number in the upper left: $\sqrt[n]{a}$, read as "the nth root of a." The relationship between radical notation and exponent notation can be described by this equation:

$$\sqrt[n]{a} = a^{\frac{1}{n}}$$

The two special cases of $n = 2$ and $n = 3$ are called square roots and cube roots. If there is no number to the upper left, the radical is understood to be a square root ($n = 2$). Nearly all of the roots you encounter will be square roots. A square root is the same as a number raised to the one-half power. When we say that a is the square root of b ($a = \sqrt{b}$), we mean that a multiplied by itself equals b: ($a \times a = b$).

A **perfect square** is a number that has an integer for its square root. There are 10 perfect squares from 1 to 100: 1, 4, 9, 16, 25, 36, 49, 64, 81, 100 (the squares of integers 1 through 10).

> **Review Video: Roots**
> Visit mometrix.com/academy and enter code: 795655
>
> **Review Video: Perfect Squares and Square Roots**
> Visit mometrix.com/academy and enter code: 648063

Word Problems and Mathematical Symbols

When working on word problems, you must be able to translate verbal expressions or "math words" into math symbols. This chart contains several "math words" and their appropriate symbols:

Phrase	Symbol
equal, is, was, will be, has, costs, gets to, is the same as, becomes	$=$
times, of, multiplied by, product of, twice, doubles, halves, triples	$\times$
divided by, per, ratio of/to, out of	$\div$
plus, added to, sum, combined, and, more than, totals of	$+$
subtracted from, less than, decreased by, minus, difference between	$-$
what, how much, original value, how many, a number, a variable	x, n, etc.

Examples of Translated Mathematical Phrases

- The phrase four more than twice a number can be written algebraically as $2x + 4$.
- The phrase half a number decreased by six can be written algebraically as $\frac{1}{2}x - 6$.
- The phrase the sum of a number and the product of five and that number can be written algebraically as $x + 5x$.
- You may see a test question that says, "Olivia is constructing a bookcase from seven boards. Two of them are for vertical supports and five are for shelves. The height of the bookcase is twice the width of the bookcase. If the seven boards total 36 feet in length, what will be the height of Olivia's bookcase?" You would need to make a sketch and then create the equation to determine the width of the shelves. The height can be represented as double the width. (If x represents the width of the shelves in feet, then the height of the bookcase is $2x$. Since the seven boards total 36 feet, $2x + 2x + x + x + x + x + x = 36$ or $9x = 36$; $x = 4$. The height is twice the width, or 8 feet.)

A great way to make use of some of the features built into the decimal system would be regrouping when attempting longform subtraction operations. When subtracting within a place value, sometimes the minuend is smaller than the subtrahend, **regrouping** enables you to 'borrow' a unit from a place value to the left in order to get a positive difference. For example, consider subtracting 189 from 525 with regrouping.

First, set up the subtraction problem in vertical form:

$$\begin{array}{r} 525 \\ -\ 189 \\ \hline \end{array}$$

Notice that the numbers in the ones and tens columns of 525 are smaller than the numbers in the ones and tens columns of 189. This means you will need to use regrouping to perform subtraction:

	5	2	5
–	1	8	9

To subtract 9 from 5 in the ones column you will need to borrow from the 2 in the tens columns:

	5	1	15
–	1	8	9
			6

Next, to subtract 8 from 1 in the tens column you will need to borrow from the 5 in the hundreds column:

	4	11	15
–	1	8	9
		3	6

Last, subtract the 1 from the 4 in the hundreds column:

	4	11	15
–	1	8	9
	3	3	6

Review Video: Subtracting Large Numbers
Visit mometrix.com/academy and enter code: 603350

The **order of operations** is a set of rules that dictates the order in which we must perform each operation in an expression so that we will evaluate it accurately. If we have an expression that includes multiple different operations, the order of operations tells us which operations to do first. The most common mnemonic for the order of operations is **PEMDAS**, or "Please Excuse My Dear Aunt Sally." PEMDAS stands for parentheses, exponents, multiplication, division, addition, and subtraction. It is important to understand that multiplication and division have equal precedence, as do addition and subtraction, so those pairs of operations are simply worked from left to right in order.

For example, evaluating the expression $5 + 20 \div 4 \times (2 + 3)^2 - 6$ using the correct order of operations would be done like this:

- **P:** Perform the operations inside the parentheses: $(2 + 3) = 5$
- **E:** Simplify the exponents: $(5)^2 = 5 \times 5 = 25$
  - The expression now looks like this: $5 + 20 \div 4 \times 25 - 6$
- **MD:** Perform multiplication and division from left to right: $20 \div 4 = 5$; then $5 \times 25 = 125$
  - The expression now looks like this: $5 + 125 - 6$
- **AS:** Perform addition and subtraction from left to right: $5 + 125 = 130$; then $130 - 6 = 124$

Review Video: Order of Operations
Visit mometrix.com/academy and enter code: 259675

Arithmetic Reasoning and Math Knowledge

Factors and Greatest Common Factor

Factors are numbers that are multiplied together to obtain a **product**. For example, in the equation $2 \times 3 = 6$, the numbers 2 and 3 are factors. A **prime number** has only two factors (1 and itself), but other numbers can have many factors.

A **common factor** is a number that divides exactly into two or more other numbers. For example, the factors of 12 are 1, 2, 3, 4, 6, and 12, while the factors of 15 are 1, 3, 5, and 15. The common factors of 12 and 15 are 1 and 3.

A **prime factor** is also a prime number. Therefore, the prime factors of 12 are 2 and 3. For 15, the prime factors are 3 and 5.

The **greatest common factor** (GCF) is the largest number that is a factor of two or more numbers. For example, the factors of 15 are 1, 3, 5, and 15; the factors of 35 are 1, 5, 7, and 35. Therefore, the greatest common factor of 15 and 35 is 5.

> **Review Video: Factors**
> Visit mometrix.com/academy and enter code: 920086
>
> **Review Video: Prime Numbers and Factorization**
> Visit mometrix.com/academy and enter code: 760669
>
> **Review Video: Greatest Common Factor and Least Common Multiple**
> Visit mometrix.com/academy and enter code: 838699

Multiples and Least Common Multiple

Often listed out in multiplication tables, **multiples** are integer increments of a given factor. In other words, dividing a multiple by the factor will result in an integer. For example, the multiples of 7 include: $1 \times 7 = 7, 2 \times 7 = 14, 3 \times 7 = 21, 4 \times 7 = 28, 5 \times 7 = 35$. Dividing 7, 14, 21, 28, or 35 by 7 will result in the integers 1, 2, 3, 4, and 5, respectively.

The least common multiple (**LCM**) is the smallest number that is a multiple of two or more numbers. For example, the multiples of 3 include 3, 6, 9, 12, 15, etc.; the multiples of 5 include 5, 10, 15, 20, etc. Therefore, the least common multiple of 3 and 5 is 15.

> **Review Video: Multiples**
> Visit mometrix.com/academy and enter code: 626738

Fractions

A **fraction** is a number that is expressed as one integer written above another integer, with a dividing line between them $\left(\frac{x}{y}\right)$. It represents the **quotient** of the two numbers "x divided by y." It can also be thought of as x out of y equal parts.

The top number of a fraction is called the **numerator**, and it represents the number of parts under consideration. The 1 in $\frac{1}{4}$ means that 1 part out of the whole is being considered in the calculation. The bottom number of a fraction is called the **denominator**, and it represents the total number of equal parts. The 4 in $\frac{1}{4}$ means that the whole consists of 4 equal parts. A fraction cannot have a denominator of zero; this is referred to as "*undefined*."

Fractions can be manipulated, without changing the value of the fraction, by multiplying or dividing (but not adding or subtracting) both the numerator and denominator by the same number. If you divide both numbers by a common factor, you are **reducing** or simplifying the fraction. Two fractions that have the same value but are expressed differently are known as **equivalent fractions**. For example, $\frac{2}{10}, \frac{3}{15}, \frac{4}{20}$, and $\frac{5}{25}$ are all equivalent fractions. They can also all be reduced or simplified to $\frac{1}{5}$.

When two fractions are manipulated so that they have the same denominator, this is known as finding a **common denominator**. The number chosen to be that common denominator should be the least common multiple of the two original denominators. Example: $\frac{3}{4}$ and $\frac{5}{6}$; the least common multiple of 4 and 6 is 12. Manipulating to achieve the common denominator: $\frac{3}{4} = \frac{9}{12}; \frac{5}{6} = \frac{10}{12}$.

Review Video: Overview of Fractions
Visit mometrix.com/academy and enter code: 262335

PROPER FRACTIONS AND MIXED NUMBERS

A fraction whose denominator is greater than its numerator is known as a **proper fraction**, while a fraction whose numerator is greater than its denominator is known as an **improper fraction**. Proper fractions have values *less than one* and improper fractions have values *greater than one.*

A **mixed number** is a number that contains both an integer and a fraction. Any improper fraction can be rewritten as a mixed number. Example: $\frac{8}{3} = \frac{6}{3} + \frac{2}{3} = 2 + \frac{2}{3} = 2\frac{2}{3}$. Similarly, any mixed number can be rewritten as an improper fraction. Example: $1\frac{3}{5} = 1 + \frac{3}{5} = \frac{5}{5} + \frac{3}{5} = \frac{8}{5}$.

Review Video: Proper and Improper Fractions and Mixed Numbers
Visit mometrix.com/academy and enter code: 211077

ADDING AND SUBTRACTING FRACTIONS

If two fractions have a common denominator, they can be added or subtracted simply by adding or subtracting the two numerators and retaining the same denominator. If the two fractions do not already have the same denominator, one or both of them must be manipulated to achieve a common denominator before they can be added or subtracted. Example: $\frac{1}{2} + \frac{1}{4} = \frac{2}{4} + \frac{1}{4} = \frac{3}{4}$.

Review Video: Adding and Subtracting Fractions
Visit mometrix.com/academy and enter code: 378080

Multiplying Fractions

Two fractions can be multiplied by multiplying the two numerators to find the new numerator and the two denominators to find the new denominator. Example: $\frac{1}{3} \times \frac{2}{3} = \frac{1 \times 2}{3 \times 3} = \frac{2}{9}$.

Dividing Fractions

Two fractions can be divided by flipping the numerator and denominator of the second fraction and then proceeding as though it were a multiplication problem. Example: $\frac{2}{3} \div \frac{3}{4} = \frac{2}{3} \times \frac{4}{3} = \frac{8}{9}$.

Review Video: Multiplying and Dividing Fractions
Visit mometrix.com/academy and enter code: 473632

Multiplying a Mixed Number by a Whole Number or a Decimal

When multiplying a mixed number by something, it is usually best to convert it to an improper fraction first. Additionally, if the multiplicand is a decimal, it is most often simplest to convert it to a fraction. For instance, to multiply $4\frac{3}{8}$ by 3.5, begin by rewriting each quantity as a whole number plus a proper fraction. Remember, a mixed number is a fraction added to a whole number and a decimal is a representation of the sum of fractions, specifically tenths, hundredths, thousandths, and so on:

$$4\frac{3}{8} \times 3.5 = \left(4 + \frac{3}{8}\right) \times \left(3 + \frac{1}{2}\right)$$

Next, the quantities being added need to be expressed with the same denominator. This is achieved by multiplying and dividing the whole number by the denominator of the fraction. Recall that a whole number is equivalent to that number divided by 1:

$$= \left(\frac{4}{1} \times \frac{8}{8} + \frac{3}{8}\right) \times \left(\frac{3}{1} \times \frac{2}{2} + \frac{1}{2}\right)$$

When multiplying fractions, remember to multiply the numerators and denominators separately:

$$= \left(\frac{4 \times 8}{1 \times 8} + \frac{3}{8}\right) \times \left(\frac{3 \times 2}{1 \times 2} + \frac{1}{2}\right)$$

$$= \left(\frac{32}{8} + \frac{3}{8}\right) \times \left(\frac{6}{2} + \frac{1}{2}\right)$$

Now that the fractions have the same denominators, they can be added:

$$= \frac{35}{8} \times \frac{7}{2}$$

Finally, perform the last multiplication and then simplify:

$$= \frac{35 \times 7}{8 \times 2} = \frac{245}{16} = \frac{240}{16} + \frac{5}{16} = 15\frac{5}{16}$$

Comparing Fractions

It is important to master the ability to compare and order fractions. This skill is relevant to many real-world scenarios. For example, carpenters often compare fractional construction nail lengths when preparing for a project, and bakers often compare fractional measurements to have the correct ratio of ingredients. There are three commonly used strategies when comparing fractions. These strategies are referred to as the common denominator approach, the decimal approach, and the cross-multiplication approach.

Using a Common Denominator to Compare Fractions

The fractions $\frac{2}{3}$ and $\frac{4}{7}$ have different denominators. $\frac{2}{3}$ has a denominator of 3, and $\frac{4}{7}$ has a denominator of 7. In order to precisely compare these two fractions, it is necessary to use a common denominator. A common denominator is a common multiple that is shared by both denominators. In this case, the denominators 3 and 7 share a multiple of 21. In general, it is most efficient to select the least common multiple for the two denominators.

Rewrite each fraction with the common denominator of 21. Then, calculate the new numerators as illustrated below.

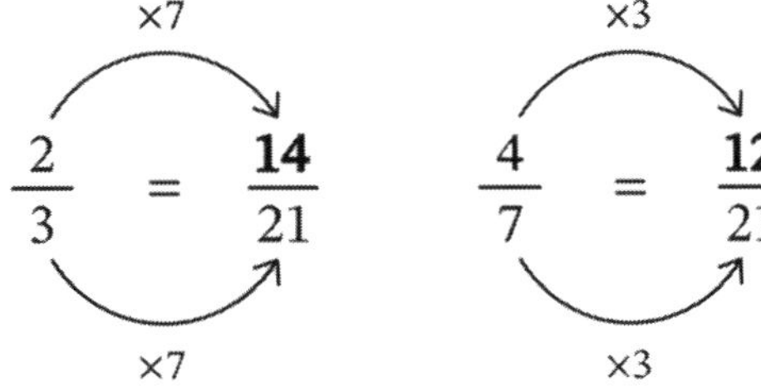

For $\frac{2}{3}$, multiply the numerator and denominator by 7. The result is $\frac{14}{21}$.

For $\frac{4}{7}$, multiply the numerator and denominator by 3. The result is $\frac{12}{21}$.

Now that both fractions have a denominator of 21, the fractions can accurately be compared by comparing the numerators. Since 14 is greater than 12, the fraction $\frac{14}{21}$ is greater than $\frac{12}{21}$. This means that $\frac{2}{3}$ is greater than $\frac{4}{7}$.

Using Decimals to Compare Fractions

Sometimes decimal values are easier to compare than fraction values. For example, $\frac{5}{8}$ is equivalent to 0.625 and $\frac{3}{5}$ is equivalent to 0.6. This means that the comparison of $\frac{5}{8}$ and $\frac{3}{5}$ can be determined by comparing the decimals 0.625 and 0.6. When both decimal values are extended to the thousandths place, they become 0.625 and 0.600, respectively. It becomes clear that 0.625 is greater than 0.600 because 625 thousandths is greater than 600 thousandths. In other words, $\frac{5}{8}$ is greater than $\frac{3}{5}$ because 0.625 is greater than 0.6.

Using Cross-Multiplication to Compare Fractions

Cross-multiplication is an efficient strategy for comparing fractions. This is a shortcut for the common denominator strategy. Start by writing each fraction next to one another. Multiply the numerator of the fraction on the left by the denominator of the fraction on the right. Write down the result next to the fraction on the left. Now multiply the numerator of the fraction on the right by the denominator of the fraction on the left. Write down the result next to the fraction on the right. Compare both products. The fraction with the larger result is the larger fraction.

Consider the fractions $\frac{4}{7}$ and $\frac{5}{9}$.

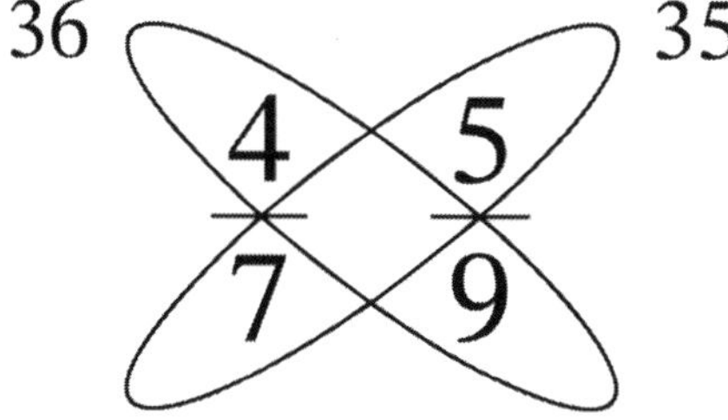

36 is greater than 35. Therefore, $\frac{4}{7}$ is greater than $\frac{5}{9}$.

DECIMALS

Decimals are one way to represent parts of a whole. Using the place value system, each digit to the right of a decimal point denotes the number of units of a corresponding *negative* power of ten. For example, consider the decimal 0.24. We can use a model to represent the decimal. Since a dime is worth one-tenth of a dollar and a penny is worth one-hundredth of a dollar, one possible model to represent this fraction is to have 2 dimes representing the 2 in the tenths place and 4 pennies representing the 4 in the hundredths place:

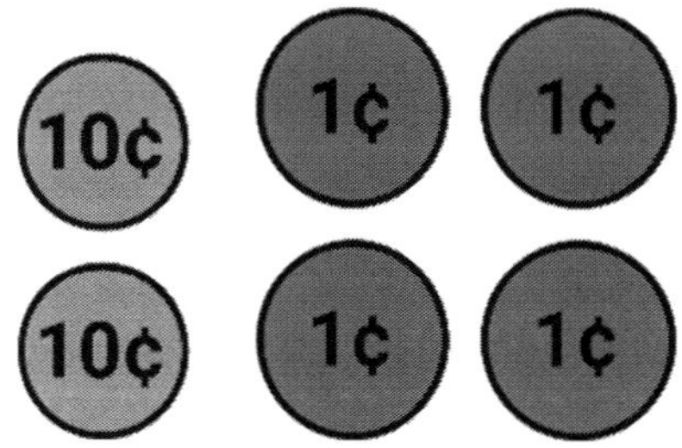

To write the decimal as a fraction, put the decimal in the numerator with 1 in the denominator. Multiply the numerator and denominator by tens until there are no more decimal places. Then simplify the fraction to lowest terms. For example, converting 0.24 to a fraction:

$$0.24 = \frac{0.24}{1} = \frac{0.24 \times 100}{1 \times 100} = \frac{24}{100} = \frac{6}{25}$$

Review Video: Decimals
Visit mometrix.com/academy and enter code: 837268

OPERATIONS WITH DECIMALS

ADDING AND SUBTRACTING DECIMALS

When adding and subtracting decimals, the decimal points must always be aligned. Adding decimals is just like adding regular whole numbers. Example: $4.5 + 2.0 = 6.5$.

If the problem-solver does not properly align the decimal points, an incorrect answer of 4.7 may result. An easy way to add decimals is to align all of the decimal points in a vertical column visually. This will allow you to see exactly where the decimal should be placed in the final answer. Begin adding from right to left. Add each column in turn, making sure to carry the number to the left if a column adds up to more than 9. The same rules apply to the subtraction of decimals.

Review Video: Adding and Subtracting Decimals
Visit mometrix.com/academy and enter code: 381101

MULTIPLYING DECIMALS

A simple multiplication problem has two components: a **multiplicand** and a **multiplier**. When multiplying decimals, work as though the numbers were whole rather than decimals. Once the final product is calculated, count the number of places to the right of the decimal in both the multiplicand and the multiplier. Then, count that number of places from the right of the product and place the decimal in that position.

For example, 12.3×2.56 has a total of three places to the right of the respective decimals. Multiply 123×256 to get 31,488. Now, beginning on the right, count three places to the left and insert the decimal. The final product will be 31.488.

Review Video: How to Multiply Decimals
Visit mometrix.com/academy and enter code: 731574

DIVIDING DECIMALS

Every division problem has a **divisor** and a **dividend**. The dividend is the number that is being divided. In the problem $14 \div 7$, 14 is the dividend and 7 is the divisor. In a division problem with decimals, the divisor must be converted into a whole number. Begin by moving the decimal in the divisor to the right until a whole number is created. Next, move the decimal in the dividend the same number of spaces to the right. For example, 4.9 into 24.5 would become 49 into 245. The decimal was moved one space to the right to create a whole number in the divisor, and then the same was done for the dividend. Once the whole numbers are created, the problem is carried out normally: $245 \div 49 = 5$.

Review Video: Dividing Decimals
Visit mometrix.com/academy and enter code: 560690

Review Video: Dividing Decimals by Whole Numbers
Visit mometrix.com/academy and enter code: 535669

PERCENTAGES

Percentages can be thought of as fractions that are based on a whole of 100; that is, one whole is equal to 100%. The word **percent** means "per hundred." Percentage problems are often presented in three main ways:

- Find what percentage of some number another number is.
    - Example: What percentage of 40 is 8?
- Find what number is some percentage of a given number.
    - Example: What number is 20% of 40?
- Find what number another number is a given percentage of.
    - Example: What number is 8 20% of?

There are three components in each of these cases: a **whole** (W), a **part** (P), and a **percentage** (%). These are related by the equation: $P = W \times \%$. This can easily be rearranged into other forms that may suit different questions better: $\% = \frac{P}{W}$ and $W = \frac{P}{\%}$. Percentage problems are often also word problems. As such, a large part of solving them is figuring out which quantities are what. For example, consider the following word problem:

In a school cafeteria, 7 students choose pizza, 9 choose hamburgers, and 4 choose tacos. What percentage of student choose tacos?

To find the whole, you must first add all of the parts: $7 + 9 + 4 = 20$. The percentage can then be found by dividing the part by the whole $\left(\% = \frac{P}{W}\right)$: $\frac{4}{20} = \frac{20}{100} = 20\%$.

Review Video: Computation with Percentages
Visit mometrix.com/academy and enter code: 693099

Converting Between Percentages, Fractions, and Decimals

Converting decimals to percentages and percentages to decimals is as simple as moving the decimal point. To *convert from a decimal to a percentage*, move the decimal point **two places to the right**. To *convert from a percentage to a decimal*, move it **two places to the left**. It may be helpful to remember that the percentage number will always be larger than the equivalent decimal number. Example:

$$0.23 = 23\% \quad 5.34 = 534\% \quad 0.007 = 0.7\%$$
$$700\% = 7.00 \quad 86\% = 0.86 \quad 0.15\% = 0.0015$$

To convert a fraction to a decimal, simply divide the numerator by the denominator in the fraction. To convert a decimal to a fraction, put the decimal in the numerator with 1 in the denominator. Multiply the numerator and denominator by tens until there are no more decimal places. Then simplify the fraction to lowest terms. For example, converting 0.24 to a fraction:

$$0.24 = \frac{0.24}{1} = \frac{0.24 \times 100}{1 \times 100} = \frac{24}{100} = \frac{6}{25}$$

Fractions can be converted to a percentage by finding equivalent fractions with a denominator of 100. Example:

$$\frac{7}{10} = \frac{70}{100} = 70\% \quad \frac{1}{4} = \frac{25}{100} = 25\%$$

To convert a percentage to a fraction, divide the percentage number by 100 and reduce the fraction to its simplest possible terms. Example:

$$60\% = \frac{60}{100} = \frac{3}{5} \quad 96\% = \frac{96}{100} = \frac{24}{25}$$

Review Video: Converting Fractions to Percentages and Decimals
Visit mometrix.com/academy and enter code: 306233

Review Video: Converting Percentages to Decimals and Fractions
Visit mometrix.com/academy and enter code: 287297

Review Video: Converting Decimals to Fractions and Percentages
Visit mometrix.com/academy and enter code: 986765

Review Video: Converting Decimals, Improper Fractions, and Mixed Numbers
Visit mometrix.com/academy and enter code: 696924

PROPORTIONS

A proportion is a relationship between two quantities that dictates how one changes when the other changes. A **direct proportion** describes a relationship in which a quantity increases by a set amount for every increase in the other quantity, or decreases by that same amount for every decrease in the other quantity. Example: Assuming a constant driving speed, the time required for a car trip increases as the distance of the trip increases. The distance to be traveled and the time required to travel are directly proportional.

An **inverse proportion** is a relationship in which an increase in one quantity is accompanied by a decrease in the other, or vice versa. Example: the time required for a car trip decreases as the speed increases and increases as the speed decreases, so the time required is inversely proportional to the speed of the car.

Review Video: Proportions
Visit mometrix.com/academy and enter code: 505355

RATIOS

A **ratio** is a comparison of two quantities in a particular order. Example: If there are 14 computers in a lab, and the class has 20 students, there is a student to computer ratio of 20 to 14, commonly written as $20:14$. Ratios are normally reduced to their smallest whole number representation, so $20:14$ would be reduced to $10:7$ by dividing both sides by 2.

Review Video: Ratios
Visit mometrix.com/academy and enter code: 996914

CONSTANT OF PROPORTIONALITY

When two quantities have a proportional relationship, there exists a **constant of proportionality** between the quantities. The product of this constant and one of the quantities is equal to the other quantity. For example, if one lemon costs \$0.25, two lemons cost \$0.50, and three lemons cost

$0.75, there is a proportional relationship between the total cost of lemons and the number of lemons purchased. The constant of proportionality is the **unit price**, namely $0.25/lemon. Notice that the total price of lemons, t, can be found by multiplying the unit price of lemons, p, and the number of lemons, n: $t = pn$.

WORK/UNIT RATE

Unit rate expresses a quantity of one thing in terms of one unit of another. For example, if you travel 30 miles every two hours, a unit rate expresses this comparison in terms of one hour: in one hour you travel 15 miles, so your unit rate is 15 miles per hour. Other examples are how much one ounce of food costs (price per ounce) or figuring out how much one egg costs out of the dozen (price per 1 egg, instead of price per 12 eggs). The denominator of a unit rate is always 1. Unit rates are used to compare different situations to solve problems. For example, to make sure you get the best deal when deciding which kind of soda to buy, you can find the unit rate of each. If soda #1 costs $1.50 for a 1-liter bottle, and soda #2 costs $2.75 for a 2-liter bottle, it would be a better deal to buy soda #2, because its unit rate is only $1.375 per 1-liter, which is cheaper than soda #1. Unit rates can also help determine the length of time a given event will take. For example, if you can paint 2 rooms in 4.5 hours, you can determine how long it will take you to paint 5 rooms by solving for the unit rate per room and then multiplying that by 5.

Review Video: Rates and Unit Rates
Visit mometrix.com/academy and enter code: 185363

Algebra

A precursor to working with negative numbers is understanding what **absolute values** are. A number's absolute value is simply the distance away from zero a number is on the number line. The absolute value of a number is always positive and is written $|x|$. For example, the absolute value of 3, written as $|3|$, is 3 because the distance between 0 and 3 on a number line is three units. Likewise, the absolute value of –3, written as $|-3|$, is 3 because the distance between 0 and –3 on a number line is three units. So $|3| = |-3|$.

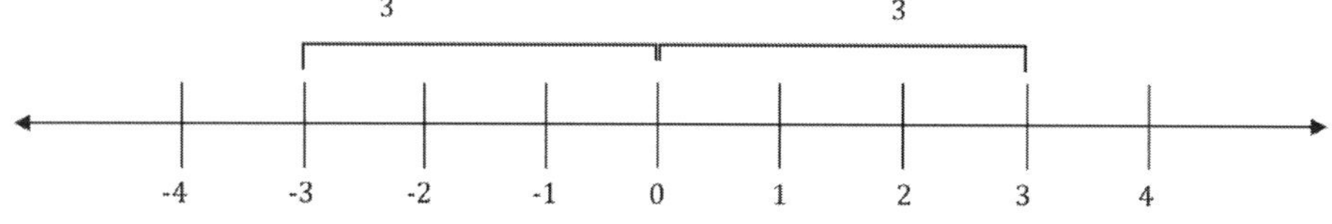

Review Video: Absolute Value
Visit mometrix.com/academy and enter code: 314669

The properties of exponents are as follows:

Property	Description
$a^1 = a$	Any number to the power of 1 is equal to itself
$1^n = 1$	The number 1 raised to any power is equal to 1
$a^0 = 1$	Any number raised to the power of 0 is equal to 1
$a^n \times a^m = a^{n+m}$	Add exponents to multiply powers of the same base number
$a^n \div a^m = a^{n-m}$	Subtract exponents to divide powers of the same base number
$(a^n)^m = a^{n \times m}$	When a power is raised to a power, the exponents are multiplied

Property	Description
$(a \times b)^n = a^n \times b^n$ $(a \div b)^n = a^n \div b^n$	Multiplication and division operations inside parentheses can be raised to a power. This is the same as each term being raised to that power.
$a^{-n} = \frac{1}{a^n}$	A negative exponent is the same as the reciprocal of a positive exponent

Note that exponents do not have to be integers. Fractional or decimal exponents follow all the rules above as well. Example: $5^{\frac{1}{4}} \times 5^{\frac{3}{4}} = 5^{\frac{1}{4}+\frac{3}{4}} = 5^1 = 5$.

> **Review Video: Properties of Exponents**
> Visit mometrix.com/academy and enter code: 532558

Scientific notation is a way of writing large numbers in a shorter form. The form $a \times 10^n$ is used in scientific notation, where a is greater than or equal to 1 but less than 10, and n is the number of places the decimal must move to get from the original number to a. Example: The number 230,400,000 is cumbersome to write. To write the value in scientific notation, place a decimal point between the first and second numbers, and include all digits through the last non-zero digit ($a = 2.304$). To find the appropriate power of 10, count the number of places the decimal point had to move ($n = 8$). The number is positive if the decimal moved to the left, and negative if it moved to the right. We can then write 230,400,000 as 2.304×10^8. If we look instead at the number 0.00002304, we have the same value for a, but this time the decimal moved 5 places to the right ($n = -5$). Thus, 0.00002304 can be written as 2.304×10^{-5}. Using this notation makes it simple to compare very large or very small numbers. By comparing exponents, it is easy to see that 3.28×10^4 is smaller than 1.51×10^5, because 4 is less than 5.

> **Review Video: Scientific Notation**
> Visit mometrix.com/academy and enter code: 976454

Terms and Coefficients

Mathematical expressions consist of a combination of one or more values arranged in terms that are added together. As such, an expression could be just a single number, including zero. A **variable term** is the product of a real number, also called a **coefficient**, and one or more variables, each of which may be raised to an exponent. Expressions may also include numbers without a variable, called **constants** or **constant terms**. The expression $6s^2$, for example, is a single term where the coefficient is the real number 6 and the variable term is s^2. Note that if a term is written as simply a variable to some exponent, like t^2, then the coefficient is 1, because $t^2 = 1t^2$.

Linear Expressions

A **single variable linear expression** is the sum of a single variable term, where the variable has no exponent, and a constant, which may be zero. For instance, the expression $2w + 7$ has $2w$ as the variable term and 7 as the constant term. It is important to realize that terms are separated by addition or subtraction. Since an expression is a sum of terms, expressions such as $5x - 3$ can be written as $5x + (-3)$ to emphasize that the constant term is negative. A real-world example of a single variable linear expression is the perimeter of a square, four times the side length, often expressed: $4s$.

In general, a **linear expression** is the sum of any number of variable terms so long as none of the variables have an exponent. For example, $3m + 8n - \frac{1}{4}p + 5.5q - 1$ is a linear expression, but $3y^3$ is not. In the same way, the expression for the perimeter of a general triangle, the sum of the side lengths $(a + b + c)$ is considered to be linear, but the expression for the area of a square, the side length squared (s^2) is not.

On a graph with two points, (x_1, y_1) and (x_2, y_2), the **slope** is found with the formula $m = \frac{y_2 - y_1}{x_2 - x_1}$; where $x_1 \neq x_2$ and m stands for slope. If the value of the slope is **positive**, the line has an *upward direction* from left to right. If the value of the slope is **negative**, the line has a *downward direction* from left to right. Consider the following example:

A new book goes on sale in bookstores and online stores. In the first month, 5,000 copies of the book are sold. Over time, the book continues to grow in popularity. The data for the number of copies sold is in the table below.

# of Months on Sale	1	2	3	4	5
# of Copies Sold (In Thousands)	5	10	15	20	25

So, the number of copies that are sold and the time that the book is on sale is a proportional relationship. In this example, an equation can be used to show the data: $y = 5x$, where x is the number of months that the book is on sale. Also, y is the number of copies sold. So, the slope of the corresponding line is $\frac{\text{rise}}{\text{run}} = \frac{5}{1} = 5$.

Review Video: Finding the Slope of a Line
Visit mometrix.com/academy and enter code: 766664

Equations that can be written as $ax + b = 0$, where $a \neq 0$, are referred to as **one variable linear equations**. A solution to such an equation is called a **root**. In the case where we have the equation $5x + 10 = 0$, if we solve for x we get a solution of $x = -2$. In other words, the root of the equation is –2. This is found by first subtracting 10 from both sides, which gives $5x = -10$. Next, simply divide both sides by the coefficient of the variable, in this case 5, to get $x = -2$. This can be checked by plugging –2 back into the original equation $(5)(-2) + 10 = -10 + 10 = 0$.

The **solution set** is the set of all solutions of an equation. In our example, the solution set would simply be –2. If there were more solutions (there usually are in multivariable equations) then they would also be included in the solution set. When an equation has no true solutions, it is referred to as an **empty set**. Equations with identical solution sets are **equivalent equations**. An **identity** is a term whose value or determinant is equal to 1.

Linear equations can be written many ways. Below is a list of some forms linear equations can take:

- **Standard Form**: $Ax + By = C$; the slope is $\frac{-A}{B}$ and the y-intercept is $\frac{C}{B}$
- **Slope Intercept Form**: $y = mx + b$, where m is the slope and b is the y-intercept
- **Point-Slope Form**: $y - y_1 = m(x - x_1)$, where m is the slope and (x_1, y_1) is a point on the line
- **Two-Point Form**: $\frac{y - y_1}{x - x_1} = \frac{y_2 - y_1}{x_2 - x_1}$, where (x_1, y_1) and (x_2, y_2) are two points on the given line

- **Intercept Form**: $\frac{x}{x_1} + \frac{y}{y_1} = 1$, where $(x_1, 0)$ is the point at which a line intersects the x-axis, and $(0, y_1)$ is the point at which the same line intersects the y-axis

> **Review Video: Slope-Intercept and Point-Slope Forms**
> Visit mometrix.com/academy and enter code: 113216
>
> **Review Video: Linear Equations Basics**
> Visit mometrix.com/academy and enter code: 793005

SOLVING ONE-VARIABLE LINEAR EQUATIONS

Multiply all terms by the lowest common denominator to eliminate any fractions. Look for addition or subtraction to undo so you can isolate the variable on one side of the equal sign. Divide both sides by the coefficient of the variable. When you have a value for the variable, substitute this value into the original equation to make sure you have a true equation. Consider the following example:

Kim's savings are represented by the table below. Represent her savings, using an equation.

X (Months)	Y (Total Savings)
2	\$1,300
5	\$2,050
9	\$3,050
11	\$3,550
16	\$4,800

The table shows a function with a constant rate of change, or slope, of 250. Given the points on the table, the slopes can be calculated as $\frac{(2{,}050-1300)}{(5-2)}$, $\frac{(3{,}050-2{,}050)}{(9-5)}$, $\frac{(3{,}550-3{,}050)}{(11-9)}$, and $\frac{(4{,}800-3{,}550)}{(16-11)}$, each of which equals 250. Thus, the table shows a constant rate of change, indicating a linear function. The slope-intercept form of a linear equation is written as $y = mx + b$, where m represents the slope and b represents the y-intercept. Substituting the slope into this form gives $y = 250x + b$. Substituting corresponding x- and y-values from any point into this equation will give the y-intercept, or b. Using the point, $(2, 1{,}300)$, gives $1{,}300 = 250(2) + b$, which simplifies as $b = 800$. Thus, her savings may be represented by the equation, $y = 250x + 800$.

RULES FOR MANIPULATING EQUATIONS

LIKE TERMS

Like terms are terms in an equation that have the same variable, regardless of whether or not they also have the same coefficient. This includes terms that *lack* a variable; all constants (i.e., numbers without variables) are considered like terms. If the equation involves terms with a variable raised to different powers, the like terms are those that have the variable raised to the same power.

For example, consider the equation $x^2 + 3x + 2 = 2x^2 + x - 7 + 2x$. In this equation, 2 and −7 are like terms; they are both constants. $3x$, x, and $2x$ are like terms, they all include the variable x raised to the first power. x^2 and $2x^2$ are like terms, they both include the variable x, raised to the second power. $2x$ and $2x^2$ are not like terms; although they both involve the variable x, the variable is not raised to the same power in both terms. The fact that they have the same coefficient, 2, is not relevant.

Review Video: Rules for Manipulating Equations
Visit mometrix.com/academy and enter code: 838871

Carrying Out the Same Operation on Both Sides of an Equation

When solving an equation, the general procedure is to carry out a series of operations on both sides of an equation, choosing operations that will tend to simplify the equation when doing so. The reason why the same operation must be carried out on both sides of the equation is because that leaves the meaning of the equation unchanged, and yields a result that is equivalent to the original equation. This would not be the case if we carried out an operation on one side of an equation and not the other. Consider what an equation means: it is a statement that two values or expressions are equal. If we carry out the same operation on both sides of the equation—add 3 to both sides, for example—then the two sides of the equation are changed in the same way, and so remain equal. If we do that to only one side of the equation—add 3 to one side but not the other—then that wouldn't be true; if we change one side of the equation but not the other then the two sides are no longer equal.

Advantage of Combining Like Terms

Combining like terms refers to adding or subtracting like terms—terms with the same variable—and therefore reducing sets of like terms to a single term. The main advantage of doing this is that it simplifies the equation. Often, combining like terms can be done as the first step in solving an equation, though it can also be done later, such as after distributing terms in a product.

For example, consider the equation $2(x + 3) + 3(2 + x + 3) = -4$. The 2 and the 3 in the second set of parentheses are like terms, and we can combine them, yielding $2(x + 3) + 3(x + 5) = -4$. Now we can carry out the multiplications implied by the parentheses, distributing the outer 2 and 3 accordingly: $2x + 6 + 3x + 15 = -4$. The $2x$ and the $3x$ are like terms, and we can add them together: $5x + 6 + 15 = -4$. Now, the constants 6, 15, and –4 are also like terms, and we can combine them as well: subtracting 6 and 15 from both sides of the equation, we get $5x = -4 - 6 - 15$, or $5x = -25$, which simplifies further to $x = -5$.

Review Video: Solving Equations by Combining Like Terms
Visit mometrix.com/academy and enter code: 668506

Canceling Terms on Opposite Sides of an Equation

Two terms on opposite sides of an equation can be canceled if and only if they *exactly* match each other. They must have the same variable raised to the same power and the same coefficient. For example, in the equation $3x + 2x^2 + 6 = 2x^2 - 6$, $2x^2$ appears on both sides of the equation and can be canceled, leaving $3x + 6 = -6$. The 6 on each side of the equation *cannot* be canceled, because it is added on one side of the equation and subtracted on the other. While they cannot be canceled, however, the 6 and –6 are like terms and can be combined, yielding $3x = -12$, which simplifies further to $x = -4$.

It's also important to note that the terms to be canceled must be independent terms and cannot be part of a larger term. For example, consider the equation $2(x + 6) = 3(x + 4) + 1$. We cannot cancel the x's, because even though they match each other they are part of the larger terms $2(x + 6)$ and $3(x + 4)$. We must first distribute the 2 and 3, yielding $2x + 12 = 3x + 12 + 1$. Now we see that the terms with the x's do not match, but the 12s do, and can be canceled, leaving $2x = 3x + 1$, which simplifies to $x = -1$.

Process for Manipulating Equations

Isolating Variables

To **isolate a variable** means to manipulate the equation so that the variable appears by itself on one side of the equation, and does not appear at all on the other side. Generally, an equation or inequality is considered to be solved once the variable is isolated and the other side of the equation or inequality is simplified as much as possible. In the case of a two-variable equation or inequality, only one variable needs to be isolated; it will not usually be possible to simultaneously isolate both variables.

For a linear equation—an equation in which the variable only appears raised to the first power—isolating a variable can be done by first moving all the terms with the variable to one side of the equation and all other terms to the other side. (*Moving* a term really means adding the inverse of the term to both sides; when a term is *moved* to the other side of the equation its sign is flipped.) Then combine like terms on each side. Finally, divide both sides by the coefficient of the variable, if applicable. The steps need not necessarily be done in this order, but this order will always work.

Review Video: Solving One-Step Equations
Visit mometrix.com/academy and enter code: 777004

Equations with More Than One Solution

Some types of non-linear equations, such as equations involving squares of variables, may have more than one solution. For example, the equation $x^2 = 4$ has two solutions: 2 and –2. Equations with absolute values can also have multiple solutions: $|x| = 1$ has the solutions $x = 1$ and $x = -1$.

It is also possible for a linear equation to have more than one solution, but only if the equation is true regardless of the value of the variable. In this case, the equation is considered to have infinitely many solutions, because any possible value of the variable is a solution. We know a linear equation has infinitely many solutions if when we combine like terms the variables cancel, leaving a true statement. For example, consider the equation $2(3x + 5) = x + 5(x + 2)$. Distributing, we get $6x + 10 = x + 5x + 10$; combining like terms gives $6x + 10 = 6x + 10$, and the $6x$-terms cancel to leave $10 = 10$. This is clearly true, so the original equation is true for any value of x. We could also have canceled the 10s leaving $0 = 0$, but again this is clearly true—in general if both sides of the equation match exactly, it has infinitely many solutions.

Equations with No Solution

Some types of non-linear equations, such as equations involving squares of variables, may have no solution. For example, the equation $x^2 = -2$ has no solutions in the real numbers, because the square of any real number must be positive. Similarly, $|x| = -1$ has no solution, because the absolute value of a number is always positive.

It is also possible for an equation to have no solution even if does not involve any powers greater than one, absolute values, or other special functions. For example, the equation $2(x + 3) + x = 3x$ has no solution. We can see that if we try to solve it: first we distribute, leaving $2x + 6 + x = 3x$. But now if we try to combine all the terms with the variable, we find that they cancel: we have $3x$ on the left and $3x$ on the right, canceling to leave us with $6 = 0$. This is clearly false. In general, whenever the variable terms in an equation cancel leaving different constants on both sides, it means that the equation has no solution. (If we are left with the *same* constant on both sides, the equation has infinitely many solutions instead.)

Features of Equations That Require Special Treatment

Linear Equations

A linear equation is an equation in which variables only appear by themselves: not multiplied together, not with exponents other than one, and not inside absolute value signs or any other functions. For example, the equation $x + 1 - 3x = 5 - x$ is a linear equation; while x appears multiple times, it never appears with an exponent other than one, or inside any function. The two-variable equation $2x - 3y = 5 + 2x$ is also a linear equation. In contrast, the equation $x^2 - 5 = 3x$ is *not* a linear equation, because it involves the term x^2. $\sqrt{x} = 5$ is not a linear equation, because it involves a square root. $(x - 1)^2 = 4$ is not a linear equation because even though there's no exponent on the x directly, it appears as part of an expression that is squared. The two-variable equation $x + xy - y = 5$ is not a linear equation because it includes the term xy, where two variables are multiplied together.

Linear equations can always be solved (or shown to have no solution) by combining like terms and performing simple operations on both sides of the equation. Some non-linear equations can be solved by similar methods, but others may require more advanced methods of solution, if they can be solved analytically at all.

Solving Equations Involving Roots

In an equation involving roots, the first step is to isolate the term with the root, if possible, and then raise both sides of the equation to the appropriate power to eliminate it. Consider an example equation, $2\sqrt{x + 1} - 1 = 3$. In this case, begin by adding 1 to both sides, yielding $2\sqrt{x + 1} = 4$, and then dividing both sides by 2, yielding $\sqrt{x + 1} = 2$. Now square both sides, yielding $x + 1 = 4$. Finally, subtracting 1 from both sides yields $x = 3$.

Squaring both sides of an equation may, however, yield a spurious solution—a solution to the squared equation that is *not* a solution of the original equation. It's therefore necessary to plug the solution back into the original equation to make sure it works. In this case, it does: $2\sqrt{3 + 1} - 1 = 2\sqrt{4} - 1 = 2(2) - 1 = 4 - 1 = 3$.

The same procedure applies for other roots as well. For example, given the equation $3 + \sqrt[3]{2x} = 5$, we can first subtract 3 from both sides, yielding $\sqrt[3]{2x} = 2$ and isolating the root. Raising both sides to the third power yields $2x = 2^3$; i.e., $2x = 8$. We can now divide both sides by 2 to get $x = 4$.

Review Video: Solving Equations Involving Roots
Visit mometrix.com/academy and enter code: 297670

Solving Equations with Exponents

To solve an equation involving an exponent, the first step is to isolate the variable with the exponent. We can then take the appropriate root of both sides to eliminate the exponent. For instance, for the equation $2x^3 + 17 = 5x^3 - 7$, we can subtract $5x^3$ from both sides to get $-3x^3 + 17 = -7$, and then subtract 17 from both sides to get $-3x^3 = -24$. Finally, we can divide both sides by –3 to get $x^3 = 8$. Finally, we can take the cube root of both sides to get $x = \sqrt[3]{8} = 2$.

One important but often overlooked point is that equations with an exponent greater than 1 may have more than one answer. The solution to $x^2 = 9$ isn't simply $x = 3$; it's $x = \pm 3$ (that is, $x = 3$ or

$x = -3$). For a slightly more complicated example, consider the equation $(x - 1)^2 - 1 = 3$. Adding 1 to both sides yields $(x - 1)^2 = 4$; taking the square root of both sides yields $x - 1 = 2$. We can then add 1 to both sides to get $x = 3$. However, there's a second solution. We also have the possibility that $x - 1 = -2$, in which case $x = -1$. Both $x = 3$ and $x = -1$ are valid solutions, as can be verified by substituting them both into the original equation.

Review Video: Solving Equations with Exponents
Visit mometrix.com/academy and enter code: 514557

Solving Equations with Absolute Values

When solving an equation with an absolute value, the first step is to isolate the absolute value term. We then consider two possibilities: when the expression inside the absolute value is positive or when it is negative. In the former case, the expression in the absolute value equals the expression on the other side of the equation; in the latter, it equals the additive inverse of that expression—the expression times negative one. We consider each case separately and finally check for spurious solutions.

For instance, consider solving $|2x - 1| + x = 5$ for x. We can first isolate the absolute value by moving the x to the other side: $|2x - 1| = -x + 5$. Now, we have two possibilities. First, that $2x - 1$ is positive, and hence $2x - 1 = -x + 5$. Rearranging and combining like terms yields $3x = 6$, and hence $x = 2$. The other possibility is that $2x - 1$ is negative, and hence $2x - 1 = -(-x + 5) = x - 5$. In this case, rearranging and combining like terms yields $x = -4$. Substituting $x = 2$ and $x = -4$ back into the original equation, we see that they are both valid solutions.

Note that the absolute value of a sum or difference applies to the sum or difference as a whole, not to the individual terms; in general, $|2x - 1|$ is not equal to $|2x + 1|$ or to $|2x| - 1$.

Review Video: Solving Absolute Value Equations
Visit mometrix.com/academy and enter code: 501208

Spurious Solutions

A **spurious solution** may arise when we square both sides of an equation as a step in solving it or under certain other operations on the equation. It is a solution to the squared or otherwise modified equation that is *not* a solution of the original equation. To identify a spurious solution, it's useful when you solve an equation involving roots or absolute values to plug the solution back into the original equation to make sure it's valid.

Choosing Which Variable to Isolate in Two-Variable Equations

Similar to methods for a one-variable equation, solving a two-variable equation involves isolating a variable: manipulating the equation so that a variable appears by itself on one side of the equation, and not at all on the other side. However, in a two-variable equation, you will usually only be able to isolate one of the variables; the other variable may appear on the other side along with constant terms, or with exponents or other functions.

Often one variable will be much more easily isolated than the other, and therefore that's the variable you should choose. If one variable appears with various exponents, and the other is only raised to the first power, the latter variable is the one to isolate: given the equation $a^2 + 2b = a^3 + b + 3$, the b only appears to the first power, whereas a appears squared and cubed, so b is the variable that can be solved for: combining like terms and isolating the b on the left side of the equation, we get $b = a^3 - a^2 + 3$. If both variables are equally easy to isolate, then it's best to isolate the dependent variable, if one is defined; if the two variables are x and y, the convention is that y is the dependent variable.

Review Video: Solving Equations with Variables on Both Sides
Visit mometrix.com/academy and enter code: 402497

Finding an Unknown in Equivalent Expressions

It is often necessary to apply information given about a rate or proportion to a new scenario. For example, if you know that Jedha can run a marathon (26.2 miles) in 3 hours, how long would it take her to run 10 miles at the same pace? Start by setting up equivalent expressions:

$$\frac{26.2\text{ mi}}{3\text{ hr}} = \frac{10\text{ mi}}{x\text{ hr}}$$

Now, cross multiply and solve for x:

$$\begin{aligned} 26.2x &= 30 \\ x &= \frac{30}{26.2} = \frac{15}{13.1} \\ x &\approx 1.15\text{ hrs } or \text{ 1 hr 9 min} \end{aligned}$$

So, at this pace, Jedha could run 10 miles in about 1.15 hours or about 1 hour and 9 minutes.

Review Video: Cross Multiplying Fractions
Visit mometrix.com/academy and enter code: 893904

Graphical Solutions to Equations

When equations are shown graphically, they are usually shown on a **Cartesian coordinate plane**. The Cartesian coordinate plane consists of two number lines placed perpendicular to each other and intersecting at the zero point, also known as the origin. The horizontal number line is known as the x-axis, with positive values to the right of the origin, and negative values to the left of the origin. The vertical number line is known as the y-axis, with positive values above the origin, and negative values below the origin. Any point on the plane can be identified by an ordered pair in the form (x, y), called coordinates. The x-value of the coordinate is called the abscissa, and the y-value of the coordinate is called the ordinate. The two number lines divide the plane into **four quadrants**: I, II, III, and IV.

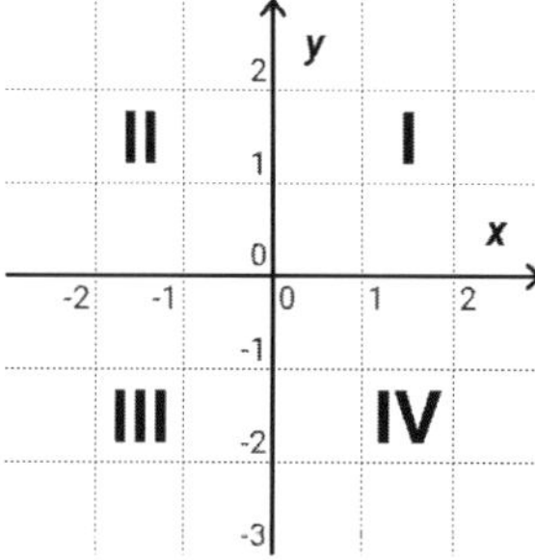

Note that in quadrant I $x > 0$ and $y > 0$, in quadrant II $x < 0$ and $y > 0$, in quadrant III $x < 0$ and $y < 0$, and in quadrant IV $x > 0$ and $y < 0$.

Recall that if the value of the slope of a line is positive, the line slopes upward from left to right. If the value of the slope is negative, the line slopes downward from left to right. If the y-coordinates are the same for two points on a line, the slope is 0 and the line is a **horizontal line**. If the x-coordinates are the same for two points on a line, there is no slope and the line is a **vertical line**. Two or more lines that have equivalent slopes are **parallel lines**. **Perpendicular lines** have slopes that are negative reciprocals of each other, such as $\frac{a}{b}$ and $\frac{-b}{a}$.

Review Video: Cartesian Coordinate Plane and Graphing
Visit mometrix.com/academy and enter code: 115173

Graphing Equations in Two Variables

One way of graphing an equation in two variables is to plot enough points to get an idea for its shape and then draw the appropriate curve through those points. A point can be plotted by substituting in a value for one variable and solving for the other. If the equation is linear, we only need two points and can then draw a straight line between them.

For example, consider the equation $y = 2x - 1$. This is a linear equation—both variables only appear raised to the first power—so we only need two points. When $x = 0, y = 2(0) - 1 = -1$. When $x = 2, y = 2(2) - 1 = 3$. We can therefore choose the points $(0, -1)$ and $(2, 3)$, and draw a line between them:

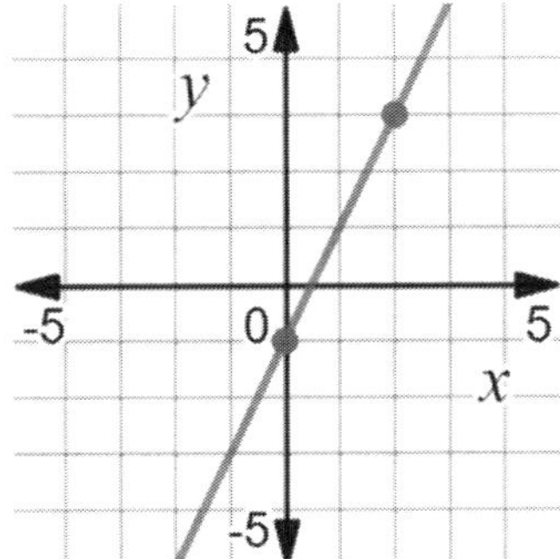

Working with Inequalities

Commonly in algebra and other upper-level fields of math you find yourself working with mathematical expressions that do not equal each other. The statement comparing such expressions with symbols such as $<$ (less than) or $>$ (greater than) is called an *inequality*. An example of an inequality is $7x > 5$. To solve for x, simply divide both sides by 7 and the solution is shown to be $x > \frac{5}{7}$. Graphs of the solution set of inequalities are represented on a number line. Open circles are used to show that an expression approaches a number but is never quite equal to that number.

Review Video: Solving Multi-Step Inequalities
Visit mometrix.com/academy and enter code: 347842

Review Video: Solving Inequalities Using All 4 Basic Operations
Visit mometrix.com/academy and enter code: 401111

Conditional inequalities are those with certain values for the variable that will make the condition true and other values for the variable where the condition will be false. **Absolute inequalities** can have any real number as the value for the variable to make the condition true, while there is no real number value for the variable that will make the condition false. Solving inequalities is done by following the same rules for solving equations with the exception that when multiplying or dividing by a negative number the direction of the inequality sign must be flipped or reversed. **Double inequalities** are situations where two inequality statements apply to the same variable expression. Example: $-c < ax + b < c$.

Review Video: Conditional and Absolute Inequalities
Visit mometrix.com/academy and enter code: 980164

Determining Solutions to Inequalities

To determine whether a coordinate is a solution of an inequality, you can substitute the values of the coordinate into the inequality, simplify, and check whether the resulting statement holds true. For instance, to determine whether $(-2,4)$ is a solution of the inequality $y \geq -2x + 3$, substitute the values into the inequality, $4 \geq -2(-2) + 3$. Simplify the right side of the inequality and the result is $4 \geq 7$, which is a false statement. Therefore, the coordinate is not a solution of the inequality. You can also use this method to determine which part of the graph of an inequality is shaded. The graph of $y \geq -2x + 3$ includes the solid line $y = -2x + 3$ and, since it excludes the point $(-2,4)$ to the left of the line, it is shaded to the right of the line.

Review Video: Graphing Linear Inequalities
Visit mometrix.com/academy and enter code: 439421

Flipping Inequality Signs

When given an inequality, we can always turn the entire inequality around, swapping the two sides of the inequality and changing the inequality sign. For instance, $x + 2 > 2x - 3$ is equivalent to $2x - 3 < x + 2$. Aside from that, normally the inequality does not change if we carry out the same operation on both sides of the inequality. There is, however, one principal exception: if we *multiply* or *divide* both sides of the inequality by a *negative number*, the inequality is flipped. For example, if we take the inequality $-2x < 6$ and divide both sides by –2, the inequality flips and we are left with $x > -3$. This *only* applies to multiplication and division, and only with negative numbers. Multiplying or dividing both sides by a positive number, or adding or subtracting any number regardless of sign, does not flip the inequality. Another special case that flips the inequality sign is when reciprocals are used. For instance, $3 > 2$ but the relation of the reciprocals is $\frac{1}{3} < \frac{1}{2}$.

Compound Inequalities

A **compound inequality** is an equality that consists of two inequalities combined with *and* or *or*. The two components of a proper compound inequality must be of opposite type: that is, one must be greater than (or greater than or equal to), the other less than (or less than or equal to). For instance, "$x + 1 < 2$ or $x + 1 > 3$" is a compound inequality, as is "$2x \geq 4$ and $2x \leq 6$." An *and* inequality can be written more compactly by having one inequality on each side of the common part: "$2x \geq 1$ and $2x \leq 6$," can also be written as $1 \leq 2x \leq 6$.

In order for the compound inequality to be meaningful, the two parts of an *and* inequality must overlap; otherwise, no numbers satisfy the inequality. On the other hand, if the two parts of an *or* inequality overlap, then *all* numbers satisfy the inequality and as such the inequality is usually not meaningful.

Solving a compound inequality requires solving each part separately. For example, given the compound inequality "$x + 1 < 2$ or $x + 1 > 3$," the first inequality, $x + 1 < 2$, reduces to $x < 1$, and the second part, $x + 1 > 3$, reduces to $x > 2$, so the whole compound inequality can be written as "$x < 1$ or $x > 2$." Similarly, $1 \leq 2x \leq 6$ can be solved by dividing each term by 2, yielding $\frac{1}{2} \leq x \leq 3$.

> **Review Video: Compound Inequalities**
> Visit mometrix.com/academy and enter code: 786318

Solving Inequalities Involving Absolute Values

To solve an inequality involving an absolute value, first isolate the term with the absolute value. Then proceed to treat the two cases separately as with an absolute value equation, but flipping the inequality in the case where the expression in the absolute value is negative (since that essentially involves multiplying both sides by −1.) The two cases are then combined into a compound inequality; if the absolute value is on the greater side of the inequality, then it is an *or* compound inequality, if on the lesser side, then it's an *and*.

Consider the inequality $2 + |x - 1| \geq 3$. We can isolate the absolute value term by subtracting 2 from both sides: $|x - 1| \geq 1$. Now, we're left with the two cases $x - 1 \geq 1$ or $x - 1 \leq -1$: note that in the latter, negative case, the inequality is flipped. $x - 1 \geq 1$ reduces to $x \geq 2$, and $x - 1 \leq -1$ reduces to $x \leq 0$. Since in the inequality $|x - 1| \geq 1$ the absolute value is on the greater side, the two cases combine into an *or* compound inequality, so the final, solved inequality is "$x \leq 0$ or $x \geq 2$."

> **Review Video: Solving Absolute Value Inequalities**
> Visit mometrix.com/academy and enter code: 997008

Solving Inequalities Involving Square Roots

Solving an inequality with a square root involves two parts. First, we solve the inequality as if it were an equation, isolating the square root and then squaring both sides of the equation. Second, we restrict the solution to the set of values of x for which the value inside the square root sign is non-negative.

For example, in the inequality, $\sqrt{x - 2} + 1 < 5$, we can isolate the square root by subtracting 1 from both sides, yielding $\sqrt{x - 2} < 4$. Squaring both sides of the inequality yields $x - 2 < 16$, so $x < 18$. Since we can't take the square root of a negative number, we also require the part inside the square root to be non-negative. In this case, that means $x - 2 \geq 0$. Adding 2 to both sides of the inequality yields $x \geq 2$. Our final answer is a compound inequality combining the two simple inequalities: $x \geq 2$ and $x < 18$, or $2 \leq x < 18$.

Note that we only get a compound inequality if the two simple inequalities are in opposite directions; otherwise, we take the one that is more restrictive.

The same technique can be used for other even roots, such as fourth roots. It is *not*, however, used for cube roots or other odd roots—negative numbers *do* have cube roots, so the condition that the quantity inside the root sign cannot be negative does not apply.

> **Review Video: Solving Inequalities Involving Square Roots**
> Visit mometrix.com/academy and enter code: 800288

Special Circumstances

Sometimes an inequality involving an absolute value or an even exponent is true for all values of x, and we don't need to do any further work to solve it. This is true if the inequality, once the absolute value or exponent term is isolated, says that term is greater than a negative number (or greater than or equal to zero). Since an absolute value or a number raised to an even exponent is *always* non-negative, this inequality is always true.

Graphical Solutions to Inequalities

Graphing Simple Inequalities

To graph a simple inequality, we first mark on the number line the value that signifies the end point of the inequality. If the inequality is strict (involves a less than or greater than), we use a hollow circle; if it is not strict (less than or equal to or greater than or equal to), we use a solid circle. We then fill in the part of the number line that satisfies the inequality: to the left of the marked point for less than (or less than or equal to), to the right for greater than (or greater than or equal to).

For example, we would graph the inequality $x < 5$ by putting a hollow circle at 5 and filling in the part of the line to the left:

Graphing Compound Inequalities

To graph a compound inequality, we fill in both parts of the inequality for an *or* inequality, or the overlap between them for an *and* inequality. More specifically, we start by plotting the endpoints of each inequality on the number line. For an *or* inequality, we then fill in the appropriate side of the line for each inequality. Typically, the two component inequalities do not overlap, which means the shaded part is *outside* the two points. For an *and* inequality, we instead fill in the part of the line that meets both inequalities.

For the inequality "$x \leq -3$ or $x > 4$," we first put a solid circle at –3 and a hollow circle at 4. We then fill the parts of the line *outside* these circles:

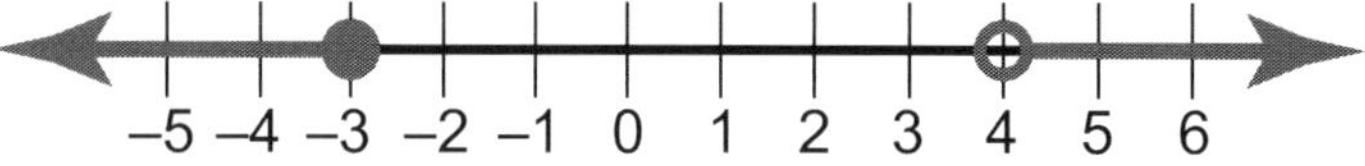

Graphing Inequalities Including Absolute Values

An inequality with an absolute value can be converted to a compound inequality. To graph the inequality, first convert it to a compound inequality, and then graph that normally. If the absolute value is on the greater side of the inequality, we end up with an *or* inequality; we plot the endpoints of the inequality on the number line and fill in the part of the line *outside* those points. If the absolute value is on the smaller side of the inequality, we end up with an *and* inequality; we plot the endpoints of the inequality on the number line and fill in the part of the line *between* those points.

For example, the inequality $|x + 1| \geq 4$ can be rewritten as $x \geq 3$ or $x \leq -5$. We place solid circles at the points 3 and –5 and fill in the part of the line *outside* them:

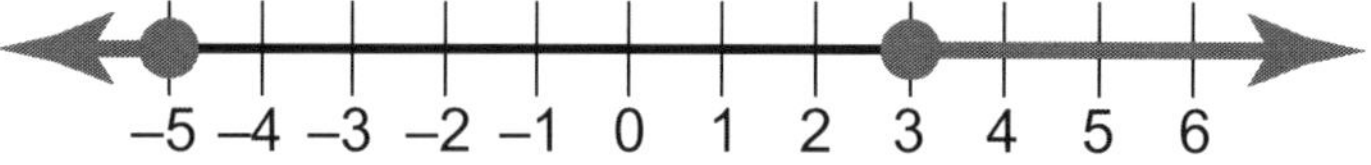

Graphing Inequalities in Two Variables

To graph an inequality in two variables, we first graph the border of the inequality. This means graphing the equation that we get if we replace the inequality sign with an equals sign. If the inequality is strict ($>$ or $<$), we graph the border with a dashed or dotted line; if it is not strict ($\geq$ or $\leq$), we use a solid line. We can then test any point not on the border to see if it satisfies the inequality. If it does, we shade in that side of the border; if not, we shade in the other side. As an example, consider $y > 2x + 2$. To graph this inequality, we first graph the border, $y = 2x + 2$. Since it is a strict inequality, we use a dashed line. Then, we choose a test point. This can be any point not on the border; in this case, we will choose the origin, (0,0). (This makes the calculation easy and is generally a good choice unless the border passes through the origin.) Putting this into the original inequality, we get $0 > 2(0) + 2$, i.e., $0 > 2$. This is *not* true, so we shade in the side of the border that does *not* include the point (0,0):

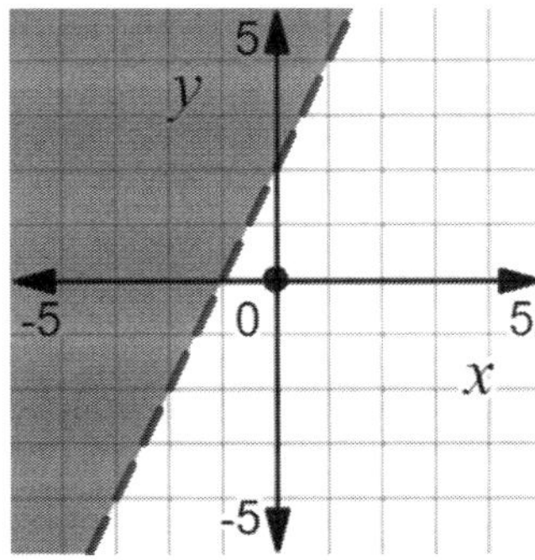

Graphing Compound Inequalities in Two Variables

One way to graph a compound inequality in two variables is to first graph each of the component inequalities. For an *and* inequality, we then shade in only the parts where the two graphs overlap; for an *or* inequality, we shade in any region that pertains to either of the individual inequalities.

Consider the graph of "$y \geq x - 1$ and $y \leq -x$":

We first shade in the individual inequalities:

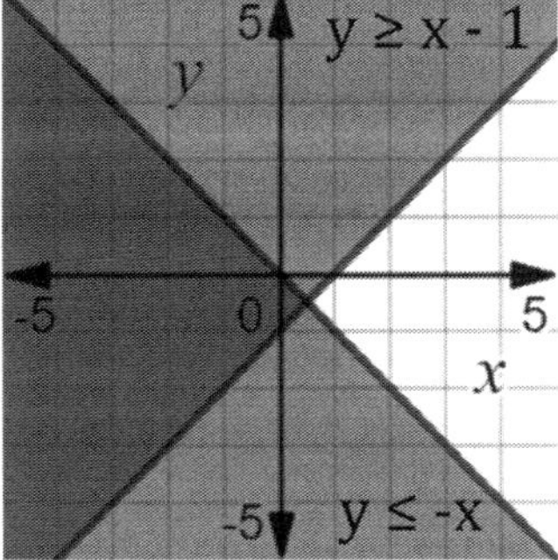

Now, since the compound inequality has an *and*, we only leave shaded the overlap—the part that pertains to *both* inequalities:

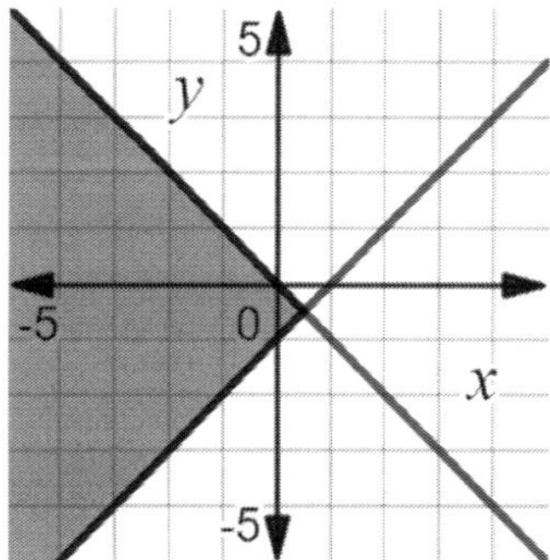

If instead the inequality had been "$y \geq x - 1$ or $y \leq -x$," our final graph would involve the *total* shaded area:

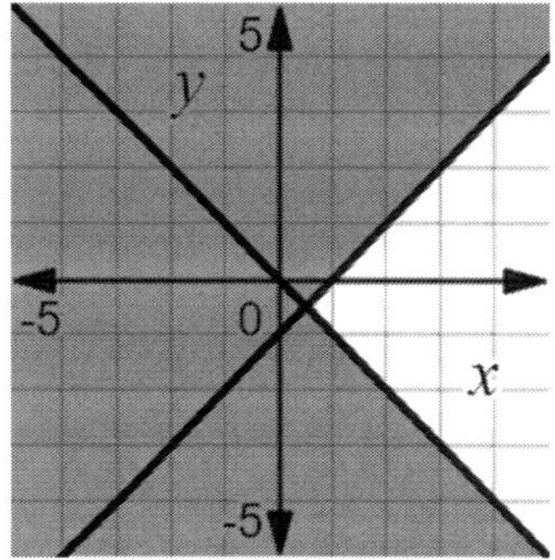

Review Video: Graphing Solutions to Inequalities
Visit mometrix.com/academy and enter code: 391281

SOLVING SYSTEMS OF EQUATIONS

A **system of equations** is a set of simultaneous equations that all use the same variables. A solution to a system of equations must be true for each equation in the system. **Consistent systems** are those with at least one solution. **Inconsistent systems** are systems of equations that have no solution.

Review Video: Solving Systems of Linear Equations
Visit mometrix.com/academy and enter code: 746745

SUBSTITUTION

To solve a system of linear equations by **substitution**, start with the easier equation and solve for one of the variables. Express this variable in terms of the other variable. Substitute this expression in the other equation and solve for the other variable. The solution should be expressed in the form (x, y). Substitute the values into both of the original equations to check your answer. Consider the following system of equations:

$$x + 6y = 15$$
$$3x - 12y = 18$$

Solving the first equation for x: $x = 15 - 6y$

Substitute this value in place of x in the second equation, and solve for y:

$$\begin{aligned} 3(15 - 6y) - 12y &= 18 \\ 45 - 18y - 12y &= 18 \\ 30y &= 27 \\ y &= \frac{27}{30} = \frac{9}{10} = 0.9 \end{aligned}$$

Plug this value for y back into the first equation to solve for x:

$$x = 15 - 6(0.9) = 15 - 5.4 = 9.6$$

Check both equations if you have time:

$$\begin{aligned} 9.6 + 6(0.9) &= 15 \\ 9.6 + 5.4 &= 15 \\ 15 &= 15 \end{aligned} \qquad \begin{aligned} 3(9.6) - 12(0.9) &= 18 \\ 28.8 - 10.8 &= 18 \\ 18 &= 18 \end{aligned}$$

Therefore, the solution is (9.6,0.9).

Review Video: The Substitution Method
Visit mometrix.com/academy and enter code: 565151

Review Video: Substitution and Elimination
Visit mometrix.com/academy and enter code: 958611

Arithmetic Reasoning and Math Knowledge

ELIMINATION

To solve a system of equations using **elimination**, begin by rewriting both equations in standard form $Ax + By = C$. Check to see if the coefficients of one pair of like variables add to zero. If not, multiply one or both of the equations by a non-zero number to make one set of like variables add to zero. Add the two equations to solve for one of the variables. Substitute this value into one of the original equations to solve for the other variable. Check your work by substituting into the other equation. Now, let's look at solving the following system using the elimination method:

$$\begin{aligned} 5x + 6y &= 4 \\ x + 2y &= 4 \end{aligned}$$

If we multiply the second equation by -3, we can eliminate the y-terms:

$$\begin{aligned} 5x + 6y &= 4 \\ -3x - 6y &= -12 \end{aligned}$$

Add the equations together and solve for x:

$$\begin{aligned} 2x &= -8 \\ x &= \frac{-8}{2} = -4 \end{aligned}$$

Plug the value for x back in to either of the original equations and solve for y:

$$-4 + 2y = 4$$
$$y = \frac{4+4}{2} = 4$$

Check both equations if you have time:

$$\begin{aligned} 5(-4) + 6(4) &= 4 \\ -20 + 24 &= 4 \\ 4 &= 4 \end{aligned} \qquad \begin{aligned} -4 + 2(4) &= 4 \\ -4 + 8 &= 4 \\ 4 &= 4 \end{aligned}$$

Therefore, the solution is $(-4,4)$.

Review Video: The Elimination Method
Visit mometrix.com/academy and enter code: 449121

Graphically

To solve a system of linear equations **graphically**, plot both equations on the same graph. The solution of the equations is the point where both lines cross. If the lines do not cross (are parallel), then there is **no solution**.

For example, consider the following system of equations:

$$y = 2x + 7$$
$$y = -x + 1$$

Since these equations are given in slope-intercept form, they are easy to graph; the y-intercepts of the lines are (0,7) and (0,1). The respective slopes are 2 and –1, thus the graphs look like this:

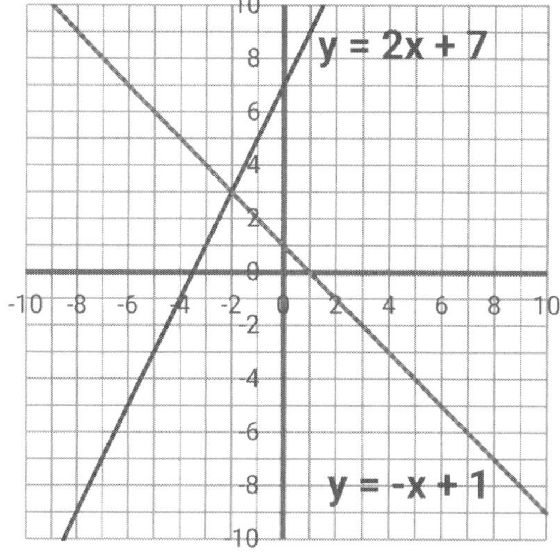

The two lines intersect at the point $(-2,3)$, thus this is the solution to the system of equations.

Solving a system graphically is generally only practical if both coordinates of the solution are integers; otherwise the intersection will lie between gridlines on the graph and the coordinates will be difficult or impossible to determine exactly. It also helps if, as in this example, the equations are in slope-intercept form or some other form that makes them easy to graph. Otherwise, another method of solution (by substitution or elimination) is likely to be more useful.

Review Video: Solving Systems by Graphing
Visit mometrix.com/academy and enter code: 634812

SOLVING SYSTEMS OF EQUATIONS USING THE TRACE FEATURE

Using the trace feature on a calculator requires that you rewrite each equation, isolating the y-variable on one side of the equal sign. Enter both equations in the graphing calculator and plot the graphs simultaneously. Use the trace cursor to find where the two lines cross. Use the zoom feature if necessary to obtain more accurate results. Always check your answer by substituting into the original equations. The trace method is likely to be less accurate than other methods due to the resolution of graphing calculators but is a useful tool to provide an approximate answer.

MONOMIALS AND POLYNOMIALS

A **monomial** is a single constant, variable, or product of constants and variables, such as 7, x, $2x$, or x^3y. There will never be addition or subtraction symbols in a monomial. Like monomials have like variables, but they may have different coefficients. **Polynomials** are algebraic expressions that use addition and subtraction to combine two or more monomials. Two terms make a **binomial**, three terms make a **trinomial**, etc. The **degree of a monomial** is the sum of the exponents of the variables. The **degree of a polynomial** is the highest degree of any individual term.

Review Video: Polynomials
Visit mometrix.com/academy and enter code: 305005

SIMPLIFYING POLYNOMIALS

Simplifying polynomials requires combining like terms. The like terms in a polynomial expression are those that have the same variable raised to the same power. It is often helpful to connect the like terms with arrows or lines in order to separate them from the other monomials. Once you have determined the like terms, you can rearrange the polynomial by placing them together. Remember to include the sign that is in front of each term. Once the like terms are placed together, you can apply each operation and simplify. When adding and subtracting polynomials, only add and subtract the **coefficient**, or the number part; the variable and exponent stay the same.

Review Video: Adding and Subtracting Polynomials
Visit mometrix.com/academy and enter code: 124088

THE FOIL METHOD

In general, multiplying polynomials is done by multiplying each term in one polynomial by each term in the other and adding the results. In the specific case for multiplying binomials, there is a useful acronym, FOIL, that can help you make sure to cover each combination of terms. The **FOIL method** for $(Ax + By)(Cx + Dy)$ would be:

F	Multiply the *first* terms of each binomial	$(\overbrace{Ax}^{first} + By)(\overbrace{Cx}^{first} + Dy)$	ACx^2
O	Multiply the *outer* terms	$(\overbrace{Ax}^{outer} + By)(Cx + \overbrace{Dy}^{outer})$	$ADxy$
I	Multiply the *inner* terms	$(Ax + \overbrace{By}^{inner})(\overbrace{Cx}^{inner} + Dy)$	$BCxy$
L	Multiply the *last* terms of each binomial	$(Ax + \overbrace{By}^{last})(Cx + \overbrace{Dy}^{last})$	BDy^2

Then, add up the result of each and combine like terms: $ACx^2 + (AD + BC)xy + BDy^2$.

For example, using the FOIL method on binomials $(x + 2)$ and $(x - 3)$:

$$\begin{aligned}
&\text{First:} && (\boxed{x} + 2)(\boxed{x} + (-3)) && \rightarrow && (x)(x) && = x^2 \\
&\text{Outer:} && (\boxed{x} + 2)(x + \boxed{(-3)}) && \rightarrow && (x)(-3) && = -3x \\
&\text{Inner:} && (x + \boxed{2})(\boxed{x} + (-3)) && \rightarrow && (2)(x) && = 2x \\
&\text{Last:} && (x + \boxed{2})(x + \boxed{(-3)}) && \rightarrow && (2)(-3) && = -6
\end{aligned}$$

This results in: $(x^2) + (-3x) + (2x) + (-6)$

Combine like terms: $x^2 + (-3 + 2)x + (-6) = x^2 - x - 6$

> **Review Video: Multiplying Terms Using the FOIL Method**
> Visit mometrix.com/academy and enter code: 854792

Dividing Polynomials

Use long division to divide a polynomial by either a monomial or another polynomial of equal or lesser degree.

When **dividing by a monomial**, divide each term of the polynomial by the monomial.

When **dividing by a polynomial**, begin by arranging the terms of each polynomial in order of one variable. You may arrange in ascending or descending order, but be consistent with both polynomials. To get the first term of the quotient, divide the first term of the dividend by the first term of the divisor. Multiply the first term of the quotient by the entire divisor and subtract that product from the dividend. Repeat for the second and successive terms until you either get a remainder of zero or a remainder whose degree is less than the degree of the divisor. If the quotient has a remainder, write the answer as a mixed expression in the form:

$$\text{quotient} + \frac{\text{remainder}}{\text{divisor}}$$

For example, we can evaluate the following expression in the same way as long division:

$$\frac{x^3 - 3x^2 - 2x + 5}{x - 5}$$

$$\begin{array}{r l}
 & x^2 \quad + 2x \quad + 8 \\
x - 5 \,\big) & x^3 - 3x^2 \quad - 2x \quad + 5 \\
 & \underline{-(x^3 - 5x^2)} \\
 & \qquad 2x^2 - 2x \\
 & \qquad \underline{-(2x^2 - 10x)} \\
 & \qquad\qquad 8x + 5 \\
 & \qquad\qquad \underline{-(8x - 40)} \\
 & \qquad\qquad\quad 45
\end{array}$$

$$\frac{x^3 - 3x^2 - 2x + 5}{x - 5} = x^2 + 2x + 8 + \frac{45}{x - 5}$$

When **factoring** a polynomial, first check for a common monomial factor, that is, look to see if each coefficient has a common factor or if each term has an x in it. If the factor is a trinomial but not a perfect trinomial square, look for a factorable form, such as one of these:

$$x^2 + (a + b)x + ab = (x + a)(x + b)$$
$$(ac)x^2 + (ad + bc)x + bd = (ax + b)(cx + d)$$

For factors with four terms, look for groups to factor. Once you have found the factors, write the original polynomial as the product of all the factors. Make sure all of the polynomial factors are prime. Monomial factors may be *prime* or *composite*. Check your work by multiplying the factors to make sure you get the original polynomial.

Below are patterns of some special products to remember to help make factoring easier:

- Perfect trinomial squares: $x^2 + 2xy + y^2 = (x + y)^2$ or $x^2 - 2xy + y^2 = (x - y)^2$
- Difference between two squares: $x^2 - y^2 = (x + y)(x - y)$
- Sum of two cubes: $x^3 + y^3 = (x + y)(x^2 - xy + y^2)$
  - Note: the second factor is *not* the same as a perfect trinomial square, so do not try to factor it further.
- Difference between two cubes: $x^3 - y^3 = (x - y)(x^2 + xy + y^2)$
  - Again, the second factor is *not* the same as a perfect trinomial square.
- Perfect cubes: $x^3 + 3x^2y + 3xy^2 + y^3 = (x + y)^3$ and $x^3 - 3x^2y + 3xy^2 - y^3 = (x - y)^3$

Rational expressions are fractions with polynomials in both the numerator and the denominator; the value of the polynomial in the denominator cannot be equal to zero. Be sure to keep track of values that make the denominator of the original expression zero as the final result inherits the same restrictions. For example, a denominator of $x - 3$ indicates that the expression is not defined when $x = 3$ and, as such, regardless of any operations done to the expression, it remains undefined there.

To **add or subtract** rational expressions, first find the common denominator, then rewrite each fraction as an equivalent fraction with the common denominator. Finally, add or subtract the numerators to get the numerator of the answer, and keep the common denominator as the denominator of the answer.

When **multiplying** rational expressions, factor each polynomial and cancel like factors (a factor which appears in both the numerator and the denominator). Then, multiply all remaining factors in the numerator to get the numerator of the product, and multiply the remaining factors in the denominator to get the denominator of the product. Remember: cancel entire factors, not individual terms.

To **divide** rational expressions, take the reciprocal of the divisor (the rational expression you are dividing by) and multiply by the dividend.

Review Video: Rational Expressions
Visit mometrix.com/academy and enter code: 415183

Simplifying Rational Expressions

To simplify a rational expression, factor the numerator and denominator completely. Factors that are the same and appear in the numerator and denominator have a ratio of 1. For example, look at the following expression:

$$\frac{x-1}{1-x^2}$$

The denominator, $(1-x^2)$, is a difference of squares. It can be factored as $(1-x)(1+x)$. The factor $1-x$ and the numerator $x-1$ are opposites and have a ratio of –1. Rewrite the numerator as $-1(1-x)$. So, the rational expression can be simplified as follows:

$$\frac{x-1}{1-x^2}=\frac{-1(1-x)}{(1-x)(1+x)}=\frac{-1}{1+x}$$

Note that since the original expression is only defined for $x \neq \{-1, 1\}$, the simplified expression has the same restrictions.

Review Video: Reducing Rational Expressions
Visit mometrix.com/academy and enter code: 788868

Solving Quadratic Equations

Quadratic equations are a special set of trinomials of the form $y = ax^2 + bx + c$ that occur commonly in math and real-world applications. The **roots** of a quadratic equation are the solutions that satisfy the equation when $y = 0$; in other words, where the graph touches the x-axis. There are several ways to determine these solutions including using the quadratic formula, factoring, completing the square, and graphing the function.

Review Video: Quadratic Equations Overview
Visit mometrix.com/academy and enter code: 476276

Review Video: Solutions of a Quadratic Equation on a Graph
Visit mometrix.com/academy and enter code: 328231

Quadratic Formula

The **quadratic formula** is used to solve quadratic equations when other methods are more difficult. To use the quadratic formula to solve a quadratic equation, begin by rewriting the equation in standard form $ax^2 + bx + c = 0$, where a, b, and c are coefficients. Once you have identified the values of the coefficients, substitute those values into the quadratic formula

$$x = \frac{-b \pm \sqrt{b^2 - 4ac}}{2a}$$

Evaluate the equation and simplify the expression. Again, check each root by substituting into the original equation. In the quadratic formula, the portion of the formula under the radical $(b^2 - 4ac)$ is called the **discriminant**. If the discriminant is zero, there is only one root: $-\frac{b}{2a}$. If the discriminant is positive, there are two different real roots. If the discriminant is negative, there are no real roots; you will instead find complex roots. Often these solutions don't make sense in context and are ignored.

Review Video: Using the Quadratic Formula
Visit mometrix.com/academy and enter code: 163102

Factoring

To solve a quadratic equation by factoring, begin by rewriting the equation in standard form, $x^2 + bx + c = 0$. Remember that the goal of factoring is to find numbers f and g such that $(x + f)(x + g) = x^2 + (f + g)x + fg$, in other words $(f + g) = b$ and $fg = c$. This can be a really useful method when b and c are integers. Determine the factors of c and look for pairs that could sum to b.

For example, consider finding the roots of $x^2 + 6x - 16 = 0$. The factors of -16 include, -4 and 4, -8 and 2, -2 and 8, -1 and 16, and 1 and -16. The factors that sum to 6 are -2 and 8. Write these factors as the product of two binomials, $0 = (x - 2)(x + 8)$. Finally, since these binomials multiply together to equal zero, set them each equal to zero and solve each for x. This results in $x - 2 = 0$, which simplifies to $x = 2$ and $x + 8 = 0$, which simplifies to $x = -8$. Therefore, the roots of the equation are 2 and -8.

Review Video: Factoring Quadratic Equations
Visit mometrix.com/academy and enter code: 336566

Completing the Square

One way to find the roots of a quadratic equation is to find a way to manipulate it such that it follows the form of a perfect square $(x^2 + 2px + p^2)$ by adding and subtracting a constant. This process is called **completing the square**. In other words, if you are given a quadratic that is not a perfect square, $x^2 + bx + c = 0$, you can find a constant d that could be added in to make it a perfect square:

$$x^2 + bx + c + (d - d) = 0; \ \{\text{Let } b = 2p \text{ and } c + d = p^2\}$$

then:

$$x^2 + 2px + p^2 - d = 0 \text{ and } d = \frac{b^2}{4} - c$$

Once you have completed the square you can find the roots of the resulting equation:

$$\begin{aligned} x^2 + 2px + p^2 - d &= 0 \\ (x + p)^2 &= d \\ x + p &= \pm\sqrt{d} \\ x &= -p \pm \sqrt{d} \end{aligned}$$

It is worth noting that substituting the original expressions into this solution gives the same result as the quadratic formula where $a = 1$:

$$x = -p \pm \sqrt{d} = -\frac{b}{2} \pm \sqrt{\frac{b^2}{4} - c} = -\frac{b}{2} \pm \frac{\sqrt{b^2 - 4c}}{2} = \frac{-b \pm \sqrt{b^2 - 4c}}{2}$$

Completing the square can be seen as arranging block representations of each of the terms to be as close to a square as possible and then filling in the gaps. For example, consider the quadratic expression $x^2 + 6x + 2$:

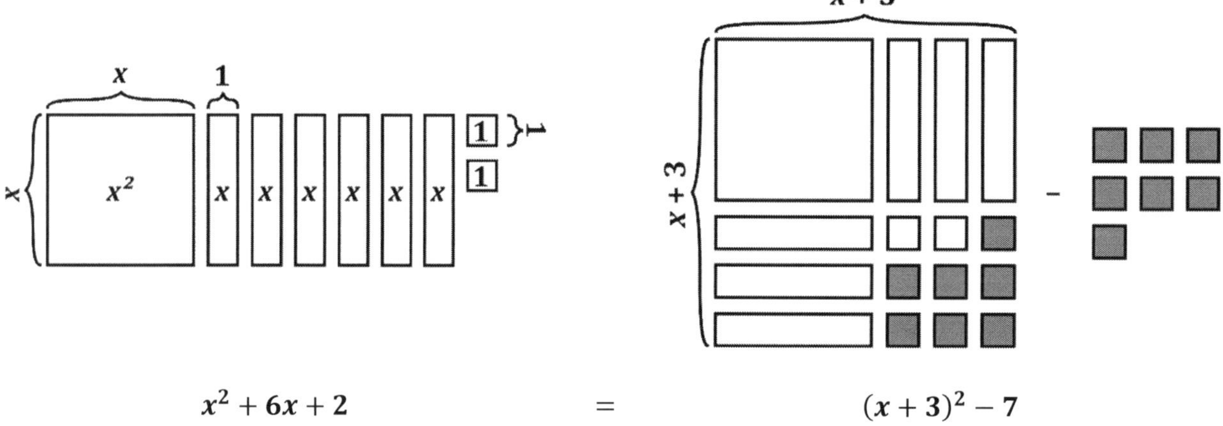

> **Review Video: Completing the Square**
> Visit mometrix.com/academy and enter code: 982479

Using Given Roots to Find Quadratic Equation

One way to find the roots of a quadratic equation is to factor the equation and use the **zero product property**, setting each factor of the equation equal to zero to find the corresponding root. We can use this technique in reverse to find an equation given its roots. Each root corresponds to a linear equation which in turn corresponds to a factor of the quadratic equation.

For example, we can find a quadratic equation whose roots are $x = 2$ and $x = -1$. The root $x = 2$ corresponds to the equation $x - 2 = 0$, and the root $x = -1$ corresponds to the equation $x + 1 = 0$.

These two equations correspond to the factors $(x - 2)$ and $(x + 1)$, from which we can derive the equation $(x - 2)(x + 1) = 0$, or $x^2 - x - 2 = 0$.

Any integer multiple of this entire equation will also yield the same roots, as the integer will simply cancel out when the equation is factored. For example, $2x^2 - 2x - 4 = 0$ factors as $2(x - 2)(x + 1) = 0$.

FUNCTION AND RELATION

When expressing functional relationships, the **variables** x and y are typically used. These values are often written as the **coordinates** (x, y). The x-value is the independent variable and the y-value is the dependent variable. A **relation** is a set of data in which there is not a unique y-value for each x-value in the dataset. This means that there can be two of the same x-values assigned to different y-values. A relation is simply a relationship between the x- and y-values in each coordinate but does not apply to the relationship between the values of x and y in the data set. A **function** is a relation where one quantity depends on the other. For example, the amount of money that you make depends on the number of hours that you work. In a function, each x-value in the data set has one unique y-value because the y-value depends on the x-value.

FUNCTIONS

A function has exactly one value of **output variable** (dependent variable) for each value of the **input variable** (independent variable). The set of all values for the input variable (here assumed to be x) is the domain of the function, and the set of all corresponding values of the output variable (here assumed to be y) is the range of the function. When looking at a graph of an equation, the easiest way to determine if the equation is a function or not is to conduct the vertical line test. If a vertical line drawn through any value of x crosses the graph in more than one place, the equation is not a function.

DETERMINING A FUNCTION

You can determine whether an equation is a **function** by substituting different values into the equation for x. You can display and organize these numbers in a data table. A **data table** contains the values for x and y, which you can also list as coordinates. In order for a function to exist, the table cannot contain any repeating x-values that correspond with different y-values. If each x-coordinate has a unique y-coordinate, the table contains a function. However, there can be repeating y-values that correspond with different x-values. An example of this is when the function contains an exponent. Example: if $x^2 = y$, $2^2 = 4$, and $(-2)^2 = 4$.

Review Video: Definition of a Function
Visit mometrix.com/academy and enter code: 784611

FINDING THE DOMAIN AND RANGE OF A FUNCTION

The **domain** of a function $f(x)$ is the set of all input values for which the function is defined. The **range** of a function $f(x)$ is the set of all possible output values of the function—that is, of every possible value of $f(x)$, for any value of x in the function's domain. For a function expressed in a table, every input-output pair is given explicitly. To find the domain, we just list all the x-values and to find the range, we just list all the values of $f(x)$. Consider the following example:

x	−1	4	2	1	0	3	8	6
$f(x)$	3	0	3	−1	−1	2	4	6

In this case, the domain would be $\{-1, 4, 2, 1, 0, 3, 8, 6\}$ or, putting them in ascending order, $\{-1, 0, 1, 2, 3, 4, 6, 8\}$. (Putting the values in ascending order isn't strictly necessary, but generally makes the set easier to read.) The range would be $\{3, 0, 3, -1, -1, 2, 4, 6\}$. Note that some of these values appear more than once. This is entirely permissible for a function; while each value of x must be matched to a unique value of $f(x)$, the converse is not true. We don't need to list each value more than once, so eliminating duplicates, the range is $\{3, 0, -1, 2, 4, 6\}$, or, putting them in ascending order, $\{-1, 0, 2, 3, 4, 6\}$.

Note that by definition of a function, no input value can be matched to more than one output value. It is good to double-check to make sure that the data given follows this and is therefore actually a function.

Review Video: Domain and Range
Visit mometrix.com/academy and enter code: 778133

Review Video: Domain and Range of Quadratic Functions
Visit mometrix.com/academy and enter code: 331768

Writing a Function Rule Using a Table

If given a set of data, place the corresponding x- and y-values into a table and analyze the relationship between them. Consider what you can do to each x-value to obtain the corresponding y-value. Try adding or subtracting different numbers to and from x and then try multiplying or dividing different numbers to and from x. If none of these **operations** give you the y-value, try combining the operations. Once you find a rule that works for one pair, make sure to try it with each additional set of ordered pairs in the table. If the same operation or combination of operations satisfies each set of coordinates, then the table contains a function. The rule is then used to write the equation of the function in "$y = f(x)$" form.

Direct and Inverse Variations of Variables

Variables that vary directly are those that either both increase at the same rate or both decrease at the same rate. For example, in the functions $y = kx$ or $y = kx^n$, where k and n are positive, the value of y increases as the value of x increases and decreases as the value of x decreases.

Variables that vary inversely are those where one increases while the other decreases. For example, in the functions $y = \frac{k}{x}$ or $y = \frac{k}{x^n}$ where k and n are positive, the value of y increases as the value of x decreases and decreases as the value of x increases.

In both cases, k is the constant of variation.

Properties of Functions

There are many different ways to classify functions based on their structure or behavior. Important features of functions include:

- **End behavior**: the behavior of the function at extreme values ($f(x)$ as $x \to \pm\infty$)
- **y-intercept**: the value of the function at $f(0)$

- **Roots**: the values of x where the function equals zero ($f(x) = 0$)
- **Extrema**: minimum or maximum values of the function or where the function changes direction ($f(x) \geq k$ or $f(x) \leq k$)

Classification of Functions

An **invertible function** is defined as a function, $f(x)$, for which there is another function, $f^{-1}(x)$, such that $f^{-1}(f(x)) = x$. For example, if $f(x) = 3x - 2$ the inverse function, $f^{-1}(x)$, can be found:

$$x = 3(f^{-1}(x)) - 2$$
$$\frac{x+2}{3} = f^{-1}(x)$$

$$f^{-1}(f(x)) = \frac{3x - 2 + 2}{3}$$
$$= \frac{3x}{3}$$
$$= x$$

Note that $f^{-1}(x)$ is a valid function over all values of x.

In a **one-to-one function**, each value of x has exactly one value for y on the coordinate plane (this is the definition of a function) and each value of y has exactly one value for x. While the vertical line test will determine if a graph is that of a function, the horizontal line test will determine if a function is a one-to-one function. If a horizontal line drawn at any value of y intersects the graph in more than one place, the graph is not that of a one-to-one function. Do not make the mistake of using the horizontal line test exclusively in determining if a graph is that of a one-to-one function. A one-to-one function must pass both the vertical line test and the horizontal line test. As such, one-to-one functions are invertible functions.

A **many-to-one function** is a function whereby the relation is a function, but the inverse of the function is not a function. In other words, each element in the domain is mapped to one and only one element in the range. However, one or more elements in the range may be mapped to the same element in the domain. A graph of a many-to-one function would pass the vertical line test, but not the horizontal line test. This is why many-to-one functions are not invertible.

A **monotone function** is a function whose graph either constantly increases or constantly decreases. Examples include the functions $f(x) = x$, $f(x) = -x$, or $f(x) = x^3$.

An **even function** has a graph that is symmetric with respect to the y-axis and satisfies the equation $f(x) = f(-x)$. Examples include the functions $f(x) = x^2$ and $f(x) = ax^n$, where a is any real number and n is a positive even integer.

An **odd function** has a graph that is symmetric with respect to the origin and satisfies the equation $f(x) = -f(-x)$. Examples include the functions $f(x) = x^3$ and $f(x) = ax^n$, where a is any real number and n is a positive odd integer.

Review Video: Even and Odd Functions
Visit mometrix.com/academy and enter code: 278985

Constant functions are given by the equation $f(x) = b$, where b is a real number. There is no independent variable present in the equation, so the function has a constant value for all x. The graph of a constant function is a horizontal line of slope 0 that is positioned b units from the x-axis. If b is positive, the line is above the x-axis; if b is negative, the line is below the x-axis.

Identity functions are identified by the equation $f(x) = x$, where every value of the function is equal to its corresponding value of x. The only zero is the point (0,0). The graph is a line with a slope of 1.

In **linear functions**, the value of the function changes in direct proportion to x. The rate of change, represented by the slope on its graph, is constant throughout. The standard form of a linear equation is $ax + cy = d$, where a, c, and d are real numbers. As a function, this equation is commonly in the form $y = mx + b$ or $f(x) = mx + b$ where $m = -\frac{a}{c}$ and $b = \frac{d}{c}$. This is known as the slope-intercept form, because the coefficients give the slope of the graphed function (m) and its y-intercept (b). Solve the equation $mx + b = 0$ for x to get $x = -\frac{b}{m}$, which is the only zero of the function. The domain and range are both the set of all real numbers.

Review Video: Graphing Linear Functions
Visit mometrix.com/academy and enter code: 699478

Algebraic functions are those that exclusively use polynomials and roots. These would include polynomial functions, rational functions, square root functions, and all combinations of these functions, such as polynomials as the radicand. These combinations may be joined by addition, subtraction, multiplication, or division, but may not include variables as exponents.

Review Video: Common Functions
Visit mometrix.com/academy and enter code: 629798

Absolute Value Functions

An **absolute value function** is in the format $f(x) = |ax + b|$. Like other functions, the domain is the set of all real numbers. However, because absolute value indicates positive numbers, the range is limited to positive real numbers. To find the zero of an absolute value function, set the portion inside the absolute value sign equal to zero and solve for x. An absolute value function is also known as a piecewise function because it must be solved in pieces—one for if the value inside the absolute value sign is positive, and one for if the value is negative. The function can be expressed as:

$$f(x) = \begin{cases} ax + b \text{ if } ax + b \geq 0 \\ -(ax + b) \text{ if } ax + b < 0 \end{cases}$$

This will allow for an accurate statement of the range. The graph of an example absolute value function, $f(x) = |2x - 1|$, is below:

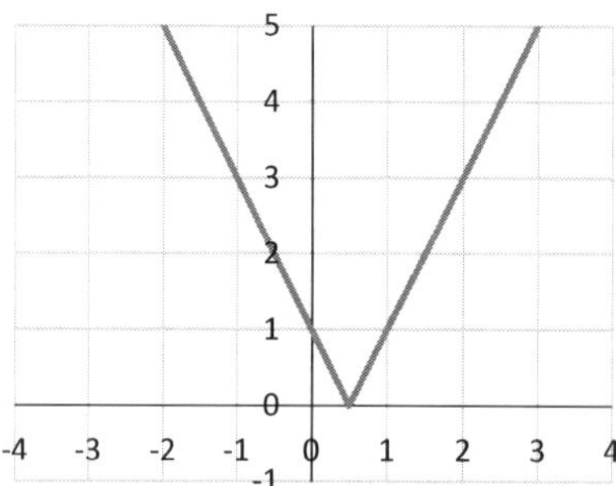

PIECEWISE FUNCTIONS

A **piecewise function** is a function that has different definitions on two or more different intervals. The following, for instance, is one example of a piecewise-defined function:

$$f(x) = \begin{cases} x^2, & x < 0 \\ x, & 0 \leq x \leq 2 \\ (x-2)^2, & x > 2 \end{cases}$$

To graph this function, you would simply graph each part separately in the appropriate domain. The final graph would look like this:

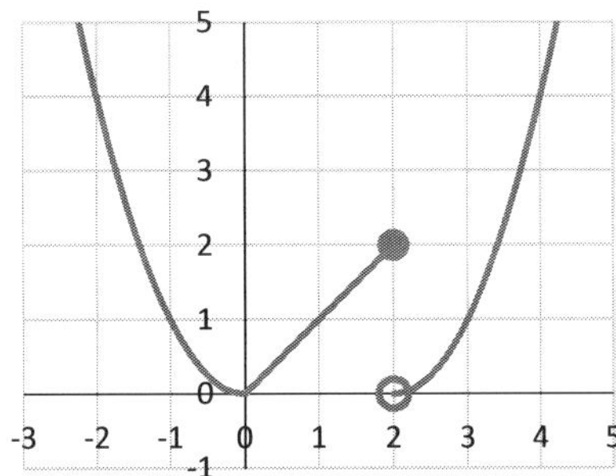

Note the filled and hollow dots at the discontinuity at $x = 2$. This is important to show which side of the graph that point corresponds to. Because $f(x) = x$ on the closed interval $0 \leq x \leq 2$, $f(2) = 2$. The point $(2, 2)$ is therefore marked with a filled circle, and the point (2,0), which is the endpoint of the rightmost $(x - 2)^2$ part of the graph but *not actually part of the function*, is marked with a hollow dot to indicate this.

Review Video: Piecewise Functions
Visit mometrix.com/academy and enter code: 707921

QUADRATIC FUNCTIONS

A **quadratic function** is a function in the form $y = ax^2 + bx + c$, where a does not equal 0. While a linear function forms a line, a quadratic function forms a **parabola**, which is a u-shaped figure that either opens upward or downward. A parabola that opens upward is said to be a **positive quadratic function,** and a parabola that opens downward is said to be a **negative quadratic function**. The shape of a parabola can differ, depending on the values of a, b, and c. All parabolas contain a **vertex**, which is the highest possible point, the **maximum**, or the lowest possible point, the **minimum**. This is the point where the graph begins moving in the opposite direction. A quadratic function can have zero, one, or two solutions, and therefore zero, one, or two x-intercepts. Recall that the x-intercepts are referred to as the zeros, or roots, of a function. A quadratic function will have only one y-intercept. Understanding the basic components of a quadratic function can give you an idea of the shape of its graph.

Example graph of a positive quadratic function, $x^2 + 2x - 3$:

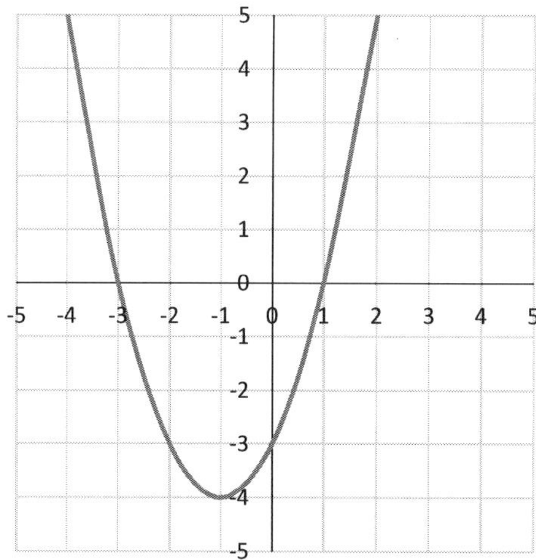

POLYNOMIAL FUNCTIONS

A **polynomial function** is a function with multiple terms and multiple powers of x, such as:

$$f(x) = a_n x^n + a_{n-1} x^{n-1} + a_{n-2} x^{n-2} + \cdots + a_1 x + a_0$$

where n is a non-negative integer that is the highest exponent in the polynomial and $a_n \neq 0$. The domain of a polynomial function is the set of all real numbers. If the greatest exponent in the polynomial is even, the polynomial is said to be of even degree and the range is the set of real numbers that satisfy the function. If the greatest exponent in the polynomial is odd, the polynomial is said to be odd and the range, like the domain, is the set of all real numbers.

RATIONAL FUNCTIONS

A **rational function** is a function that can be constructed as a ratio of two polynomial expressions: $f(x) = \frac{p(x)}{q(x)}$, where $p(x)$ and $q(x)$ are both polynomial expressions and $q(x) \neq 0$. The domain is the set of all real numbers, except any values for which $q(x) = 0$. The range is the set of real numbers that satisfies the function when the domain is applied. When you graph a rational function, you will have vertical asymptotes wherever $q(x) = 0$. If the polynomial in the numerator is of lesser degree than the polynomial in the denominator, the x-axis will also be a horizontal asymptote. If the numerator and denominator have equal degrees, there will be a horizontal asymptote not on the x-axis. If the degree of the numerator is exactly one greater than the degree of the denominator, the graph will have an oblique, or diagonal, asymptote. The asymptote will be along the line $y = \frac{p_n}{q_{n-1}} x + \frac{p_{n-1}}{q_{n-1}}$, where p_n and q_{n-1} are the coefficients of the highest degree terms in their respective polynomials.

> **Review Video: Horizontal Asymptotes**
> Visit mometrix.com/academy and enter code: 747796

SQUARE ROOT FUNCTIONS

A **square root function** is a function that contains a radical and is in the format $f(x) = \sqrt{ax + b}$. The domain is the set of all real numbers that yields a positive radicand or a radicand equal to zero. Because square root values are assumed to be positive unless otherwise identified, the range is all real numbers from zero to infinity. To find the zero of a square root function, set the radicand equal to zero and solve for x. The graph of a square root function is always to the right of the zero and always above the x-axis.

Example graph of a square root function, $f(x) = \sqrt{2x+1}$:

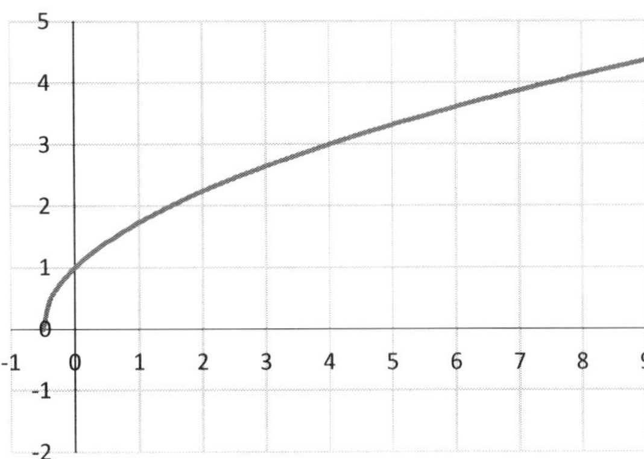

Geometry

Metric Measurement Prefixes

Giga-	One billion	1 *giga*watt is one billion watts
Mega-	One million	1 *mega*hertz is one million hertz
Kilo-	One thousand	1 *kilo*gram is one thousand grams
Deci-	One-tenth	1 *deci*meter is one-tenth of a meter
Centi-	One-hundredth	1 *centi*meter is one-hundredth of a meter
Milli-	One-thousandth	1 *milli*liter is one-thousandth of a liter
Micro-	One-millionth	1 *micro*gram is one-millionth of a gram

Review Video: Metric System Conversion - How the Metric System Works
Visit mometrix.com/academy and enter code: 163709

Measurement Conversion

When converting between units, the goal is to maintain the same meaning but change the way it is displayed. In order to go from a larger unit to a smaller unit, multiply the number of the known amount by the equivalent amount. When going from a smaller unit to a larger unit, divide the number of the known amount by the equivalent amount.

For complicated conversions, it may be helpful to set up conversion fractions. In these fractions, one fraction is the **conversion factor**. The other fraction has the unknown amount in the numerator. So, the known value is placed in the denominator. Sometimes, the second fraction has the known value from the problem in the numerator and the unknown in the denominator. Multiply the two fractions to get the converted measurement. Note that since the numerator and the denominator of the factor are equivalent, the value of the fraction is 1. That is why we can say that the result in the new units is equal to the result in the old units even though they have different numbers.

It can often be necessary to chain known conversion factors together. As an example, consider converting 512 square inches to square meters. We know that there are 2.54 centimeters in an inch and 100 centimeters in a meter, and we know we will need to square each of these factors to achieve the conversion we are looking for.

$$\frac{512 \text{ in}^2}{1} \times \left(\frac{2.54 \text{ cm}}{1 \text{ in}}\right)^2 \times \left(\frac{1 \text{ m}}{100 \text{ cm}}\right)^2 = \frac{512 \cancel{\text{in}^2}}{1} \times \left(\frac{6.4516 \cancel{\text{cm}^2}}{1 \cancel{\text{in}^2}}\right) \times \left(\frac{1 \text{ m}^2}{10{,}000 \cancel{\text{cm}^2}}\right) = 0.330 \text{ m}^2$$

Review Video: Measurement Conversions
Visit mometrix.com/academy and enter code: 316703

Common Units and Equivalents

Metric Equivalents

1000 μg (microgram)	1 mg
1000 mg (milligram)	1 g
1000 g (gram)	1 kg
1000 kg (kilogram)	1 metric ton
1000 mL (milliliter)	1 L
1000 μm (micrometer)	1 mm
1000 mm (millimeter)	1 m
100 cm (centimeter)	1 m
1000 m (meter)	1 km

Distance and Area Measurement

Unit	Abbreviation	US equivalent	Metric equivalent
Inch	in	1 inch	2.54 centimeters
Foot	ft	12 inches	0.305 meters
Yard	yd	3 feet	0.914 meters
Mile	mi	5280 feet	1.609 kilometers
Acre	ac	4840 square yards	0.405 hectares
Square Mile	sq. mi. or mi.^{2}	640 acres	2.590 square kilometers

Capacity Measurements

Unit	Abbreviation	US equivalent	Metric equivalent
Fluid Ounce	fl oz	8 fluid drams	29.573 milliliters
Cup	c	8 fluid ounces	0.237 liter
Pint	pt.	16 fluid ounces	0.473 liter
Quart	qt.	2 pints	0.946 liter
Gallon	gal.	4 quarts	3.785 liters
Teaspoon	t or tsp.	1 fluid dram	5 milliliters
Tablespoon	T or tbsp.	4 fluid drams	15 or 16 milliliters
Cubic Centimeter	cc or cm^3	0.271 drams	1 milliliter

Weight Measurements

Unit	Abbreviation	US equivalent	Metric equivalent
Ounce	oz	16 drams	28.35 grams
Pound	lb	16 ounces	453.6 grams
Ton	tn.	2,000 pounds	907.2 kilograms

Volume and Weight Measurement Clarifications

Always be careful when using ounces and fluid ounces. They are not equivalent.

1 pint = 16 fluid ounces	1 fluid ounce ≠ 1 ounce
1 pound = 16 ounces	1 pint ≠ 1 pound

Having one pint of something does not mean you have one pound of it. In the same way, just because something weighs one pound does not mean that its volume is one pint.

In the United States, the word "ton" by itself refers to a short ton or a net ton. Do not confuse this with a long ton (also called a gross ton) or a metric ton (also spelled *tonne*), which have different measurement equivalents.

1 US ton = 2000 pounds ≠ 1 metric ton = 1000 kilograms

Points and Lines

A **point** is a fixed location in space, has no size or dimensions, and is commonly represented by a dot. A **line** is a set of points that extends infinitely in two opposite directions. It has length, but no width or depth. A line can be defined by any two distinct points that it contains. A **line segment** is a portion of a line that has definite endpoints. A **ray** is a portion of a line that extends from a single point on that line in one direction along the line. It has a definite beginning, but no ending.

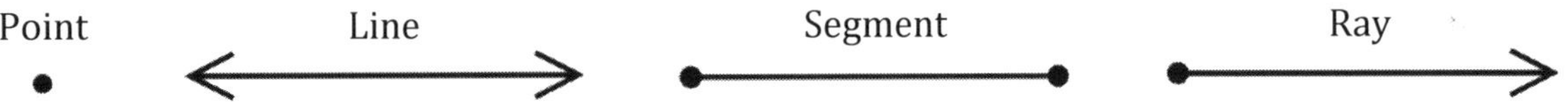

Interactions Between Lines

Intersecting lines are lines that have exactly one point in common. **Concurrent lines** are multiple lines that intersect at a single point. **Perpendicular lines** are lines that intersect at right angles. They are represented by the symbol ⊥. The shortest distance from a line to a point not on the line is a perpendicular segment from the point to the line. **Parallel lines** are lines in the same plane that have no points in common and never meet. It is possible for lines to be in different planes, have no points in common, and never meet, but they are not parallel because they are in different planes.

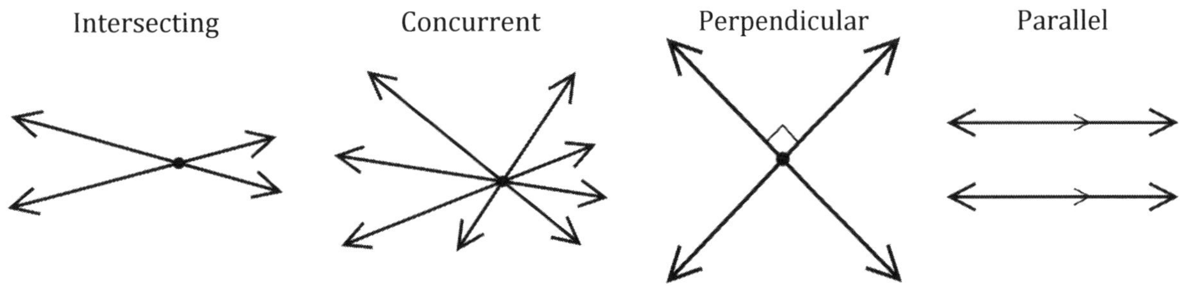

Review Video: Parallel and Perpendicular Lines
Visit mometrix.com/academy and enter code: 815923

A **transversal** is a line that intersects at least two other lines, which may or may not be parallel to one another. A transversal that intersects parallel lines is a common occurrence in geometry. A **bisector** is a line or line segment that divides another line segment into two equal lengths. A

Arithmetic Reasoning and Math Knowledge

perpendicular bisector of a line segment is composed of points that are equidistant from the endpoints of the segment it is dividing.

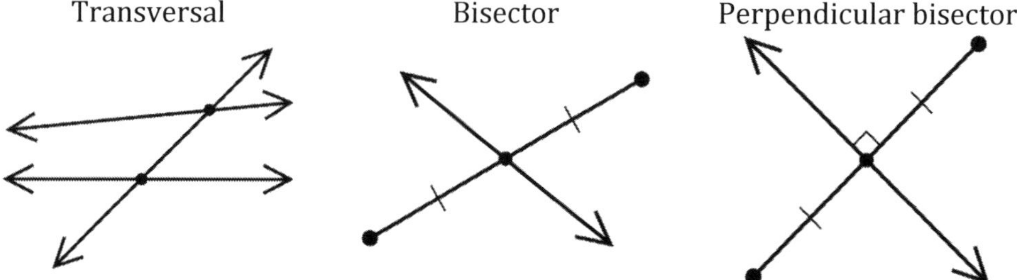

The **projection of a point on a line** is the point at which a perpendicular line drawn from the given point to the given line intersects the line. This is also the shortest distance from the given point to the line. The **projection of a segment on a line** is a segment whose endpoints are the points formed when perpendicular lines are drawn from the endpoints of the given segment to the given line. This is similar to the length a diagonal line appears to be when viewed from above.

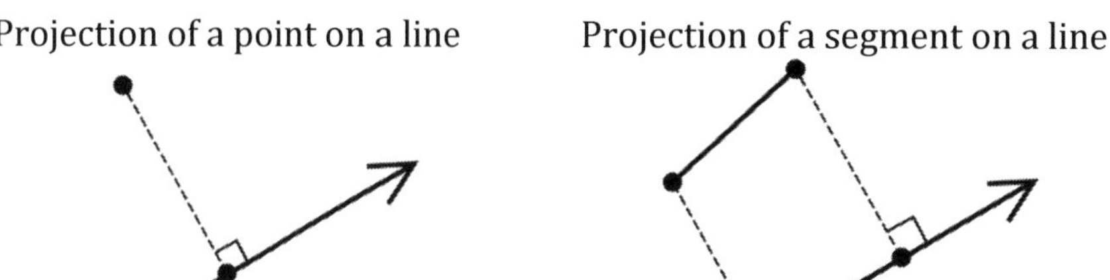

PLANES

A **plane** is a two-dimensional flat surface defined by three non-collinear points. A plane extends an infinite distance in all directions in those two dimensions. It contains an infinite number of points, parallel lines and segments, intersecting lines and segments, as well as parallel or intersecting rays. A plane will never contain a three-dimensional figure or skew lines, which are lines that don't intersect and are not parallel. Two given planes are either parallel or they intersect at a line. A plane may intersect a circular conic surface to form **conic sections**, such as a parabola, hyperbola, circle or ellipse.

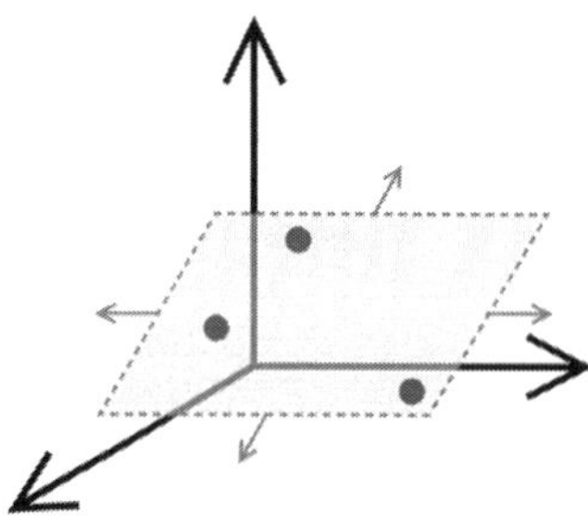

Review Video: Lines and Planes
Visit mometrix.com/academy and enter code: 554267

Angles and Vertices

An **angle** is formed when two lines or line segments meet at a common point. It may be a common starting point for a pair of segments or rays, or it may be the intersection of lines. Angles are represented by the symbol $\angle$.

The **vertex** is the point at which two segments or rays meet to form an angle. If the angle is formed by intersecting rays, lines, and/or line segments, the vertex is the point at which four angles are formed. The pairs of angles opposite one another are called vertical angles, and their measures are equal.

- An **acute** angle is an angle with a degree measure less than 90°.
- A **right** angle is an angle with a degree measure of exactly 90°.
- An **obtuse** angle is an angle with a degree measure greater than 90° but less than 180°.
- A **straight angle** is an angle with a degree measure of exactly 180°. This is also a semicircle.
- A **reflex angle** is an angle with a degree measure greater than 180° but less than 360°.
- A **full angle** is an angle with a degree measure of exactly 360°. This is also a circle.

Review Video: Angles
Visit mometrix.com/academy and enter code: 264624

Relationships Between Angles

Two angles whose sum is exactly 90° are said to be **complementary**. The two angles may or may not be adjacent. In a right triangle, the two acute angles are complementary.

Two angles whose sum is exactly 180° are said to be **supplementary**. The two angles may or may not be adjacent. Two intersecting lines always form two pairs of supplementary angles. Adjacent supplementary angles will always form a straight line.

Two angles that have the same vertex and share a side are said to be **adjacent**. Vertical angles are not adjacent because they share a vertex but no common side.

Review Video: Adjacent Angles
Visit mometrix.com/academy and enter code: 100375

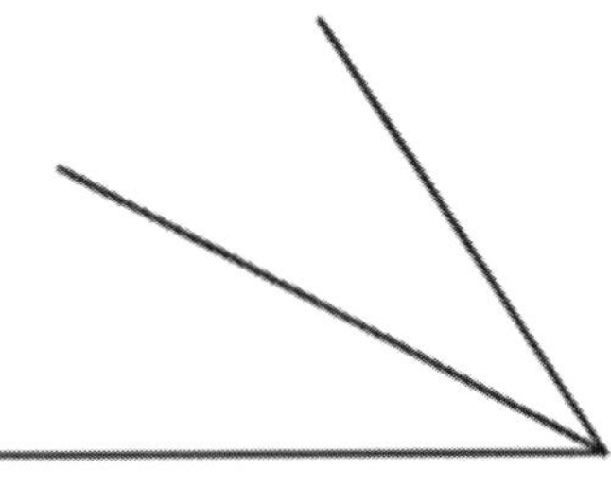

Adjacent
Share vertex and side

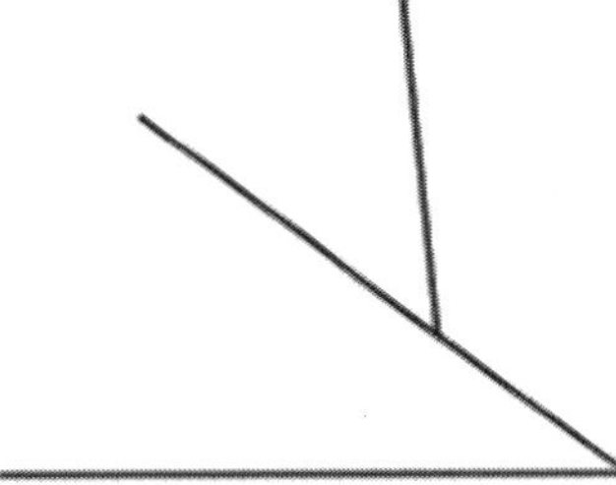

Not adjacent
Share part of a side, but not vertex

When two parallel lines are cut by a transversal, the angles that are between the two parallel lines are **interior angles**. In the diagram below, angles 3, 4, 5, and 6 are interior angles.

When two parallel lines are cut by a transversal, the angles that are outside the parallel lines are **exterior angles**. In the diagram below, angles 1, 2, 7, and 8 are exterior angles.

When two parallel lines are cut by a transversal, the angles that are in the same position relative to the transversal and a parallel line are **corresponding angles**. The diagram below has four pairs of corresponding angles: angles 1 and 5, angles 2 and 6, angles 3 and 7, and angles 4 and 8. Corresponding angles formed by parallel lines are congruent.

When two parallel lines are cut by a transversal, the two interior angles that are on opposite sides of the transversal are called **alternate interior angles**. In the diagram below, there are two pairs of alternate interior angles: angles 3 and 6, and angles 4 and 5. Alternate interior angles formed by parallel lines are congruent.

When two parallel lines are cut by a transversal, the two exterior angles that are on opposite sides of the transversal are called **alternate exterior angles**.

In the diagram below, there are two pairs of alternate exterior angles: angles 1 and 8, and angles 2 and 7. Alternate exterior angles formed by parallel lines are congruent.

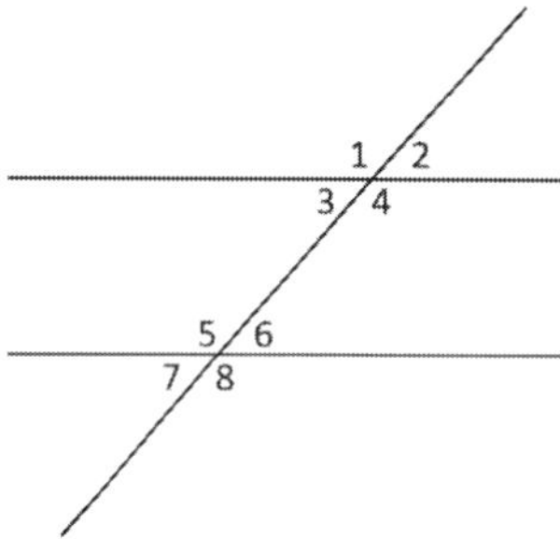

When two lines intersect, four angles are formed. The non-adjacent angles at this vertex are called vertical angles. Vertical angles are congruent. In the diagram, $\angle ABD \cong \angle CBE$ and $\angle ABC \cong \angle DBE$. The other pairs of angles, $(\angle ABC, \angle CBE)$ and $(\angle ABD, \angle DBE)$, are supplementary, meaning the pairs sum to 180°.

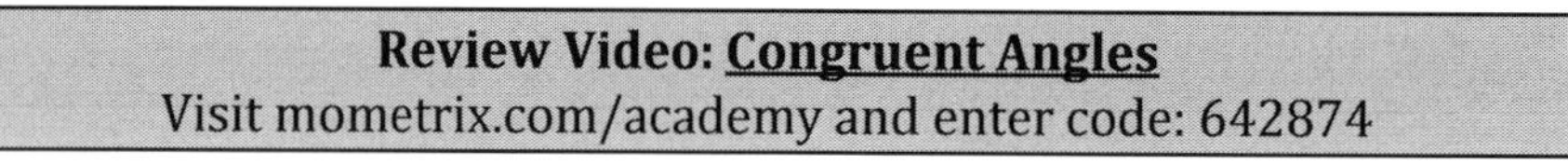
Review Video: Congruent Angles
Visit mometrix.com/academy and enter code: 642874

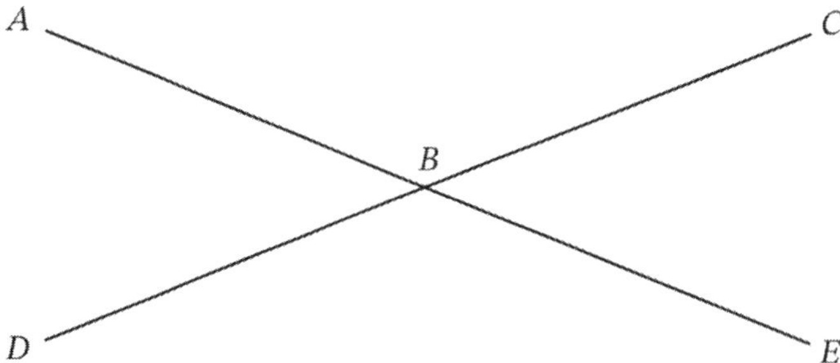

A **polygon** is a closed, two-dimensional figure with three or more straight line segments called **sides**. The point at which two sides of a polygon intersect is called the **vertex**. In a polygon, the number of sides is always equal to the number of vertices. A polygon with all sides congruent and all angles equal is called a **regular polygon**. Common polygons are:

Triangle = 3 sides
Quadrilateral = 4 sides
Pentagon = 5 sides
Hexagon = 6 sides
Heptagon = 7 sides
Octagon = 8 sides
Nonagon = 9 sides
Decagon = 10 sides
Dodecagon = 12 sides

More generally, an n-gon is a polygon that has n angles and n sides.

Review Video: Intro to Polygons
Visit mometrix.com/academy and enter code: 271869

The sum of the interior angles of an n-sided polygon is $(n - 2) \times 180°$. For example, in a triangle $n = 3$. So the sum of the interior angles is $(3 - 2) \times 180° = 180°$. In a quadrilateral, $n = 4$, and the sum of the angles is $(4 - 2) \times 180° = 360°$.

Review Video: Sum of Interior Angles
Visit mometrix.com/academy and enter code: 984991

Convex and Concave Polygons

A **convex polygon** is a polygon whose diagonals all lie within the interior of the polygon. A **concave polygon** is a polygon with a least one diagonal that is outside the polygon. In the diagram below, quadrilateral $ABCD$ is concave because diagonal $\overline{AC}$ lies outside the polygon and quadrilateral $EFGH$ is convex because both diagonals lie inside the polygon.

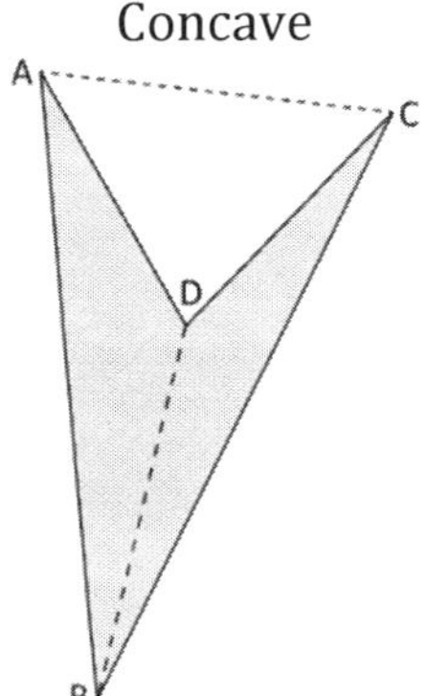

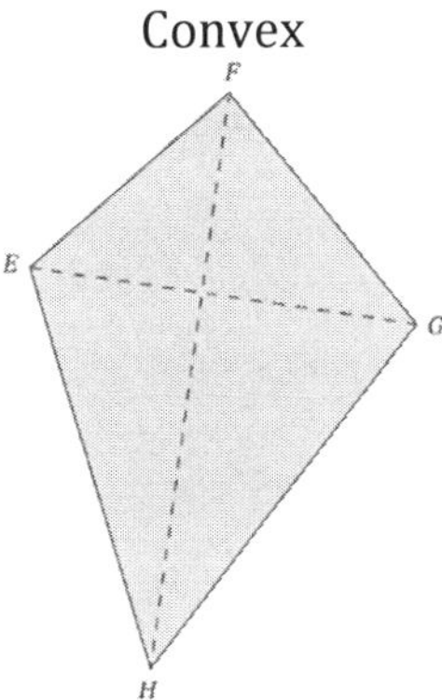

Congruent figures are geometric figures that have the same size and shape. All corresponding angles are equal, and all corresponding sides are equal. Congruence is indicated by the symbol $\cong$.

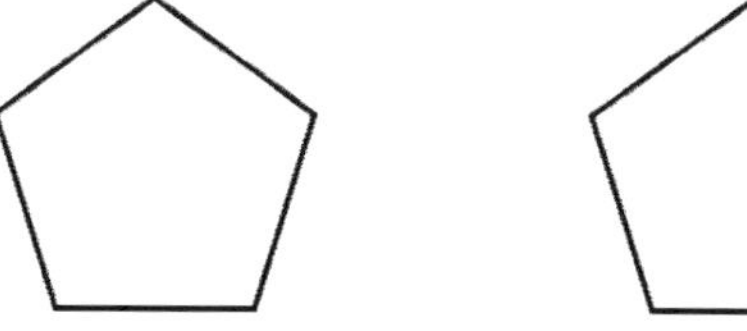

Congruent polygons

Similar figures are geometric figures that have the same shape, but do not necessarily have the same size. All corresponding angles are equal, and all corresponding sides are proportional, but they do not have to be equal. It is indicated by the symbol $\sim$.

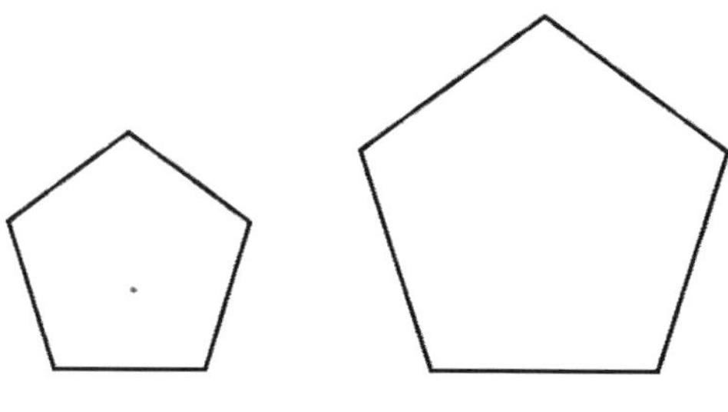

Similar polygons

Note that all congruent figures are also similar, but not all similar figures are congruent.

Review Video: Congruent Shapes
Visit mometrix.com/academy and enter code: 492281

A line that divides a figure or object into congruent parts is called a **line of symmetry**. An object may have no lines of symmetry, one line of symmetry, or multiple (i.e., more than one) lines of symmetry.

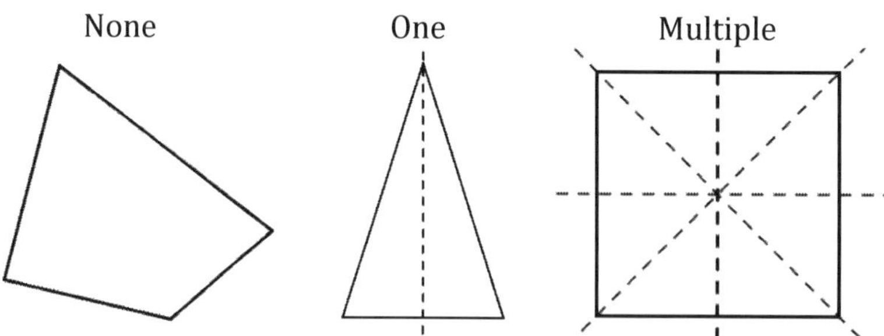

Review Video: Symmetry
Visit mometrix.com/academy and enter code: 528106

A triangle is a three-sided figure with the sum of its interior angles being 180°. The **perimeter of any triangle** is found by summing the three side lengths; $P = a + b + c$. For an equilateral triangle, this is the same as $P = 3a$, where a is any side length, since all three sides are the same length.

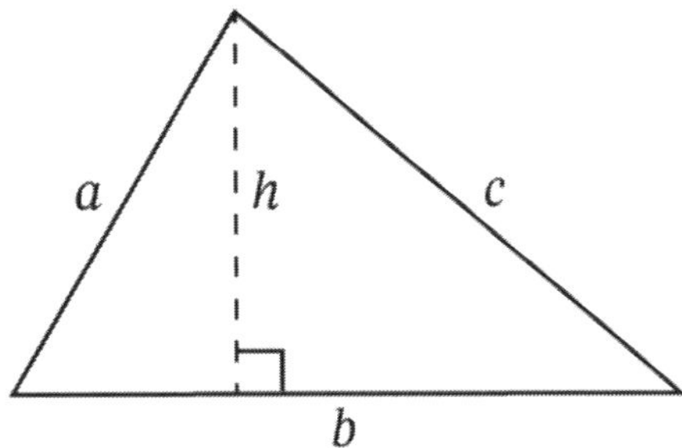

Review Video: Proof that a Triangle is 180 Degrees
Visit mometrix.com/academy and enter code: 687591

Review Video: Area and Perimeter of a Triangle
Visit mometrix.com/academy and enter code: 853779

The **area of any triangle** can be found by taking half the product of one side length referred to as the base, often given the variable b and the perpendicular distance from that side to the opposite vertex called the altitude or height and given the variable h. In equation form that is $A = \frac{1}{2}bh$. Another formula that works for any triangle is $A = \sqrt{s(s-a)(s-b)(s-c)}$, where s is the semiperimeter: $\frac{a+b+c}{2}$, and a, b, and c are the lengths of the three sides. Special cases include isosceles triangles, $A = \frac{1}{2}b\sqrt{a^2 - \frac{b^2}{4}}$, where b is the unique side and a is the length of one of the two congruent sides, and equilateral triangles, $A = \frac{\sqrt{3}}{4}a^2$, where a is the length of a side.

Review Video: Area of Any Triangle
Visit mometrix.com/academy and enter code: 138510

Parts of a Triangle

An **altitude** of a triangle is a line segment drawn from one vertex perpendicular to the opposite side. In the diagram that follows, $\overline{BE}$, $\overline{AD}$, and $\overline{CF}$ are altitudes. The length of an altitude is also called the height of the triangle. The three altitudes in a triangle are always concurrent. The point of concurrency of the altitudes of a triangle, O, is called the **orthocenter**. Note that in an obtuse triangle, the orthocenter will be outside the triangle, and in a right triangle, the orthocenter is the vertex of the right angle.

A **median** of a triangle is a line segment drawn from one vertex to the midpoint of the opposite side. In the diagram that follows, $\overline{BH}$, $\overline{AG}$, and $\overline{CI}$ are medians. This is not the same as the altitude, except the altitude to the base of an isosceles triangle and all three altitudes of an equilateral triangle. The point of concurrency of the medians of a triangle, T, is called the **centroid**. This is the same point as the orthocenter only in an equilateral triangle. Unlike the orthocenter, the centroid is always inside the triangle. The centroid can also be considered the exact center of the triangle. Any shape triangle can be perfectly balanced on a tip placed at the centroid. The centroid is also the point that is two-thirds the distance from the vertex to the opposite side.

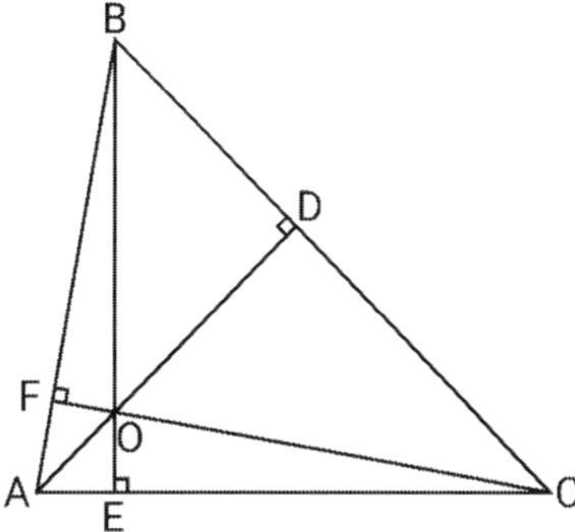

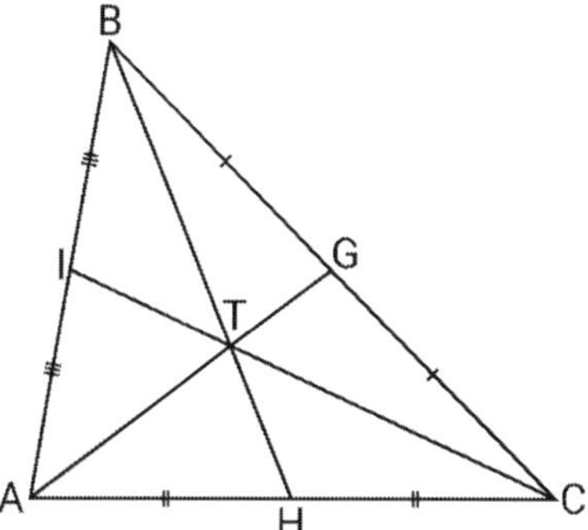

Review Video: Centroid, Incenter, Circumcenter, and Orthocenter
Visit mometrix.com/academy and enter code: 598260

Classifications of Triangles

A **scalene triangle** is a triangle with no congruent sides. A scalene triangle will also have three angles of different measures. The angle with the largest measure is opposite the longest side, and the angle with the smallest measure is opposite the shortest side. An **acute triangle** is a triangle whose three angles are all less than 90°. If two of the angles are equal, the acute triangle is also an **isosceles triangle**. An isosceles triangle will also have two congruent angles opposite the two congruent sides. If the three angles are all equal, the acute triangle is also an **equilateral triangle**. An equilateral triangle will also have three congruent angles, each 60°. All equilateral triangles are also acute triangles. An **obtuse triangle** is a triangle with exactly one angle greater than 90°. The other two angles may or may not be equal. If the two remaining angles are equal, the obtuse triangle is also an isosceles triangle. A **right triangle** is a triangle with exactly one angle equal to 90°. All right triangles follow the Pythagorean theorem. A right triangle can never be acute or obtuse.

The table below illustrates how each descriptor places a different restriction on the triangle:

Angles / Sides	Acute: All angles < 90°	Obtuse: One angle > 90°	Right: One angle = 90°
Scalene: No equal side lengths	$90° > \angle a > \angle b > \angle c$ $x > y > z$	$\angle a > 90° > \angle b > \angle c$ $x > y > z$	$90° = \angle a > \angle b > \angle c$ $x > y > z$
Isosceles: Two equal side lengths	$90° > \angle a, \angle b, or\ \angle c$ $\angle b = \angle c, \quad y = z$	$\angle a > 90° > \angle b = \angle c$ $x > y = z$	$\angle a = 90°$ $\angle b = \angle c = 45°$ $x > y = z$
Equilateral: Three equal side lengths	$60° = \angle a = \angle b = \angle c$ $x = y = z$		

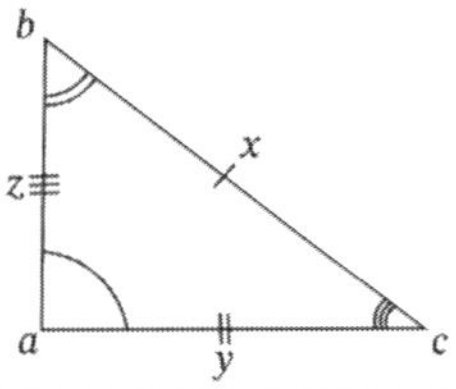

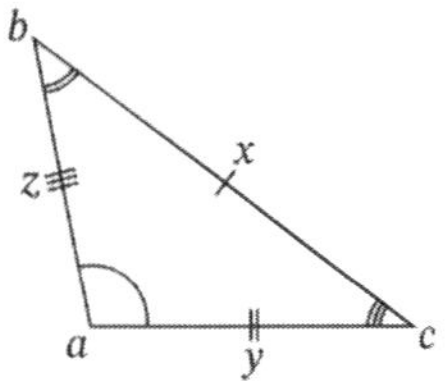

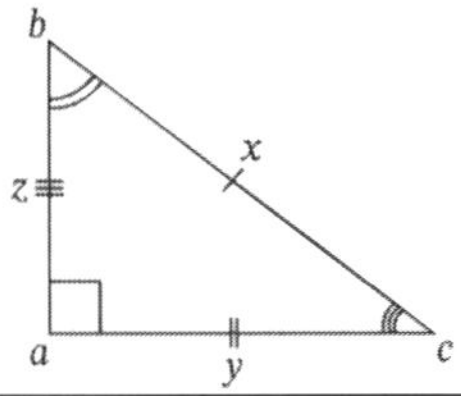

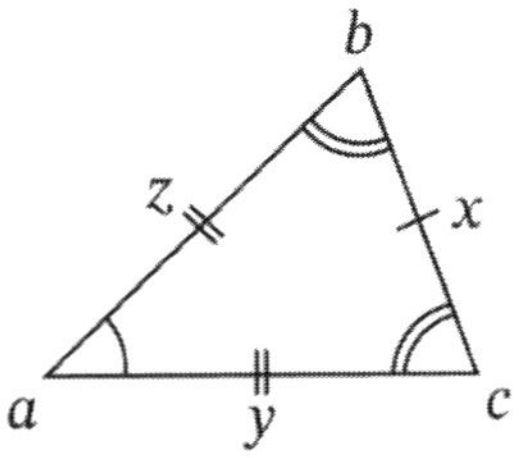

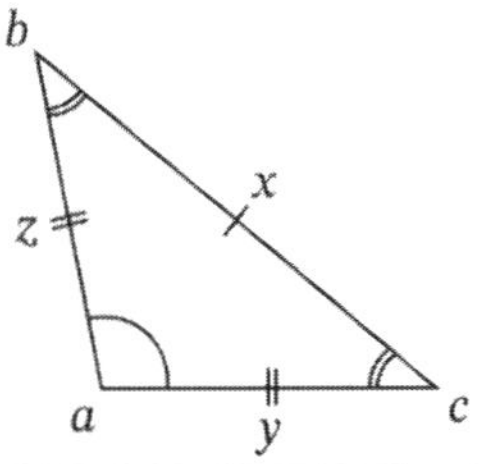

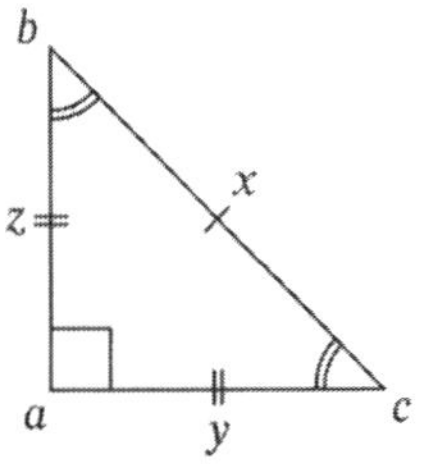

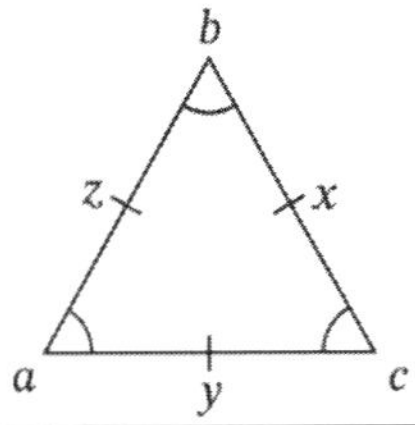

Review Video: Introduction to Types of Triangles
Visit mometrix.com/academy and enter code: 511711

General Rules for Triangles

The **triangle inequality theorem** states that the sum of the measures of any two sides of a triangle is always greater than the measure of the third side. If the sum of the measures of two sides were equal to the third side, a triangle would be impossible because the two sides would lie flat across the third side and there would be no vertex. If the sum of the measures of two of the sides was less than the third side, a closed figure would be impossible because the two shortest sides would never meet. In other words, for a triangle with sides lengths A, B, and C: $A + B > C, B + C > A$, and $A + C > B$.

The sum of the measures of the interior angles of a triangle is always 180°. Therefore, a triangle can never have more than one angle greater than or equal to 90°.

In any triangle, the angles opposite congruent sides are congruent, and the sides opposite congruent angles are congruent. The largest angle is always opposite the longest side, and the smallest angle is always opposite the shortest side.

The line segment that joins the midpoints of any two sides of a triangle is always parallel to the third side and exactly half the length of the third side.

Review Video: General Rules (Triangle Inequality Theorem)
Visit mometrix.com/academy and enter code: 166488

Similarity and Congruence Rules

Similar triangles are triangles whose corresponding angles are equal and whose corresponding sides are proportional. Represented by AAA. Similar triangles whose corresponding sides are congruent are also congruent triangles.

Triangles can be shown to be **congruent** in 5 ways:

- **SSS**: Three sides of one triangle are congruent to the three corresponding sides of the second triangle.
- **SAS**: Two sides and the included angle (the angle formed by those two sides) of one triangle are congruent to the corresponding two sides and included angle of the second triangle.
- **ASA**: Two angles and the included side (the side that joins the two angles) of one triangle are congruent to the corresponding two angles and included side of the second triangle.
- **AAS**: Two angles and a non-included side of one triangle are congruent to the corresponding two angles and non-included side of the second triangle.
- **HL**: The hypotenuse and leg of one right triangle are congruent to the corresponding hypotenuse and leg of the second right triangle.

Review Video: Similar Triangles
Visit mometrix.com/academy and enter code: 398538

Rotation

A **rotation** is a transformation that turns a figure around a point called the **center of rotation**, which can lie anywhere in the plane. If a line is drawn from a point on a figure to the center of rotation, and another line is drawn from the center to the rotated image of that point, the angle between the two lines is the **angle of rotation**. The vertex of the angle of rotation is the center of rotation.

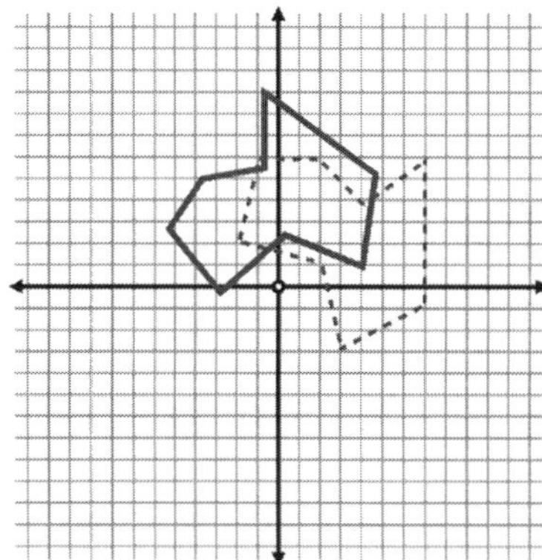

Review Video: Rotation
Visit mometrix.com/academy and enter code: 602600

TRANSLATION AND DILATION

A **translation** is a transformation which slides a figure from one position in the plane to another position in the plane. The original figure and the translated figure have the same size, shape, and orientation. A **dilation** is a transformation which proportionally stretches or shrinks a figure by a **scale factor**. The dilated image is the same shape and orientation as the original image but a different size. A polygon and its dilated image are similar.

Translation

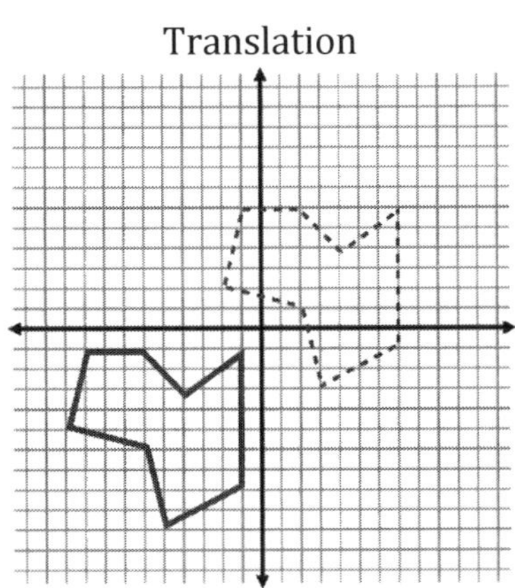

Dilation

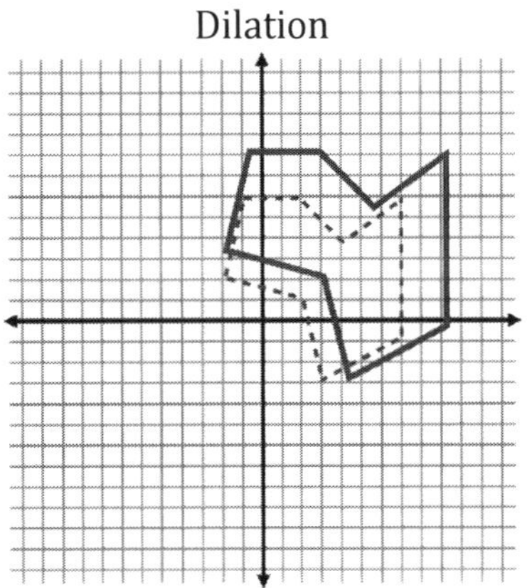

Review Video: Translation
Visit mometrix.com/academy and enter code: 718628

Review Video: Dilation
Visit mometrix.com/academy and enter code: 471630

A **reflection of a figure over a line** (a "flip") creates a congruent image that is the same distance from the line as the original figure but on the opposite side. The **line of reflection** is the perpendicular bisector of any line segment drawn from a point on the original figure to its reflected image (unless the point and its reflected image happen to be the same point, which happens when a figure is reflected over one of its own sides). A **reflection of a figure over a point** (an inversion) in two dimensions is the same as the rotation of the figure 180° about that point. The image of the figure is congruent to the original figure. The **point of reflection** is the midpoint of a line segment which connects a point in the figure to its image (unless the point and its reflected image happen to be the same point, which happens when a figure is reflected in one of its own points).

Reflection of a figure over a line

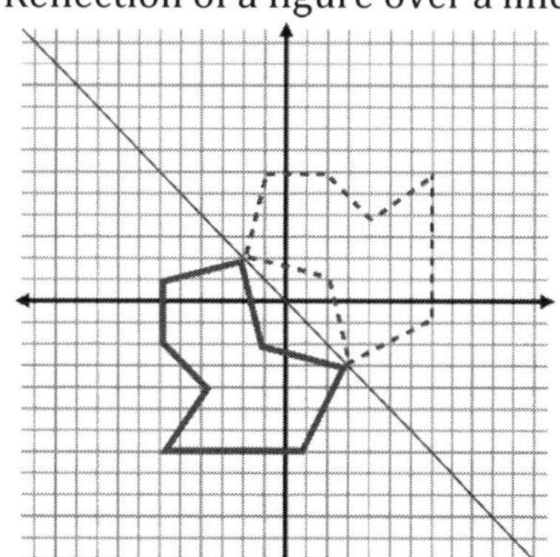

Reflection of a figure over a point

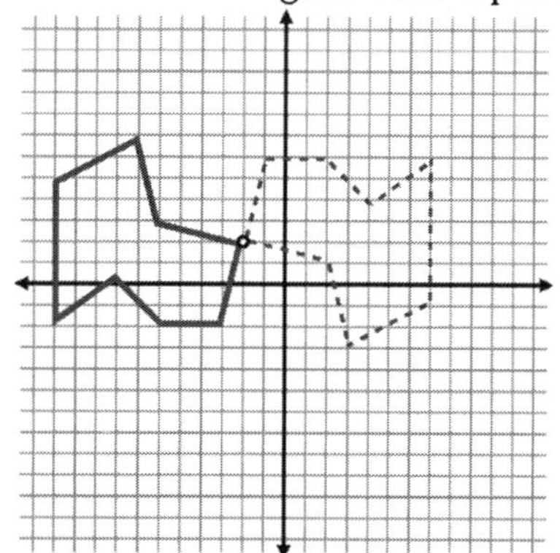

Review Video: Reflection
Visit mometrix.com/academy and enter code: 955068

The side of a triangle opposite the right angle is called the **hypotenuse**. The other two sides are called the legs. The Pythagorean theorem states a relationship among the legs and hypotenuse of a right triangle: ($a^2 + b^2 = c^2$), where a and b are the lengths of the legs of a right triangle, and c is the length of the hypotenuse. Note that this formula will only work with right triangles.

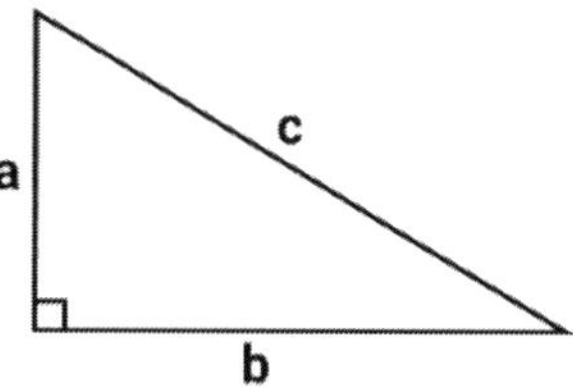

Review Video: Pythagorean Theorem
Visit mometrix.com/academy and enter code: 906576

In the diagram below, angle C is the right angle, and side c is the hypotenuse. Side a is the side opposite to angle A and side b is the side opposite to angle B. Using ratios of side lengths as a means to calculate the sine, cosine, and tangent of an acute angle only works for right triangles.

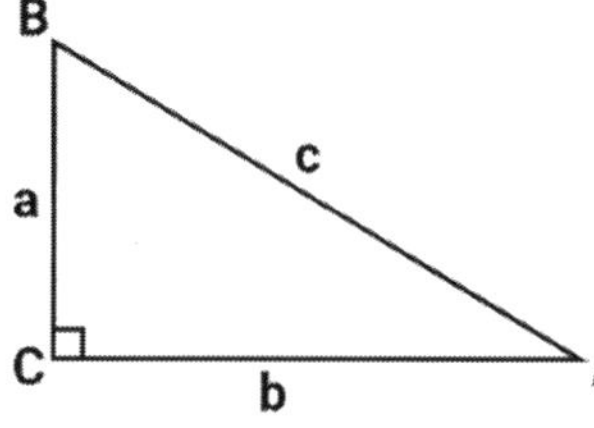

$$\sin A = \frac{\text{opposite side}}{\text{hypotenuse}} = \frac{a}{c} \qquad \csc A = \frac{1}{\sin A} = \frac{\text{hypotenuse}}{\text{opposite side}} = \frac{c}{a}$$

$$\cos A = \frac{\text{adjacent side}}{\text{hypotenuse}} = \frac{b}{c} \qquad \sec A = \frac{1}{\cos A} = \frac{\text{hypotenuse}}{\text{adjacent side}} = \frac{c}{b}$$

$$\tan A = \frac{\text{opposite side}}{\text{adjacent side}} = \frac{a}{b} \qquad \cot A = \frac{1}{\tan A} = \frac{\text{adjacent side}}{\text{opposite side}} = \frac{b}{a}$$

Laws of Sines and Cosines

The **law of sines** states that $\frac{\sin A}{a} = \frac{\sin B}{b} = \frac{\sin C}{c}$, where A, B, and C are the angles of a triangle, and a, b, and c are the sides opposite their respective angles. This formula will work with all triangles, not just right triangles.

The **law of cosines** is given by the formula $c^2 = a^2 + b^2 - 2ab(\cos C)$, where a, b, and c are the sides of a triangle, and C is the angle opposite side c. This is a generalized form of the Pythagorean theorem that can be used on any triangle.

Review Video: Law of Sines
Visit mometrix.com/academy and enter code: 206844

Review Video: Law of Cosines
Visit mometrix.com/academy and enter code: 158911

A **quadrilateral** is a closed two-dimensional geometric figure that has four straight sides. The sum of the interior angles of any quadrilateral is 360°.

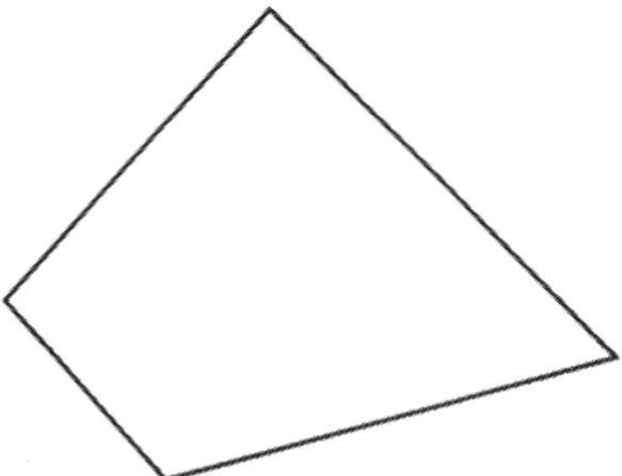

Review Video: Diagonals of Parallelograms, Rectangles, and Rhombi
Visit mometrix.com/academy and enter code: 320040

Kite

A **kite** is a quadrilateral with two pairs of adjacent sides that are congruent. A result of this is perpendicular diagonals. A kite can be concave or convex and has one line of symmetry.

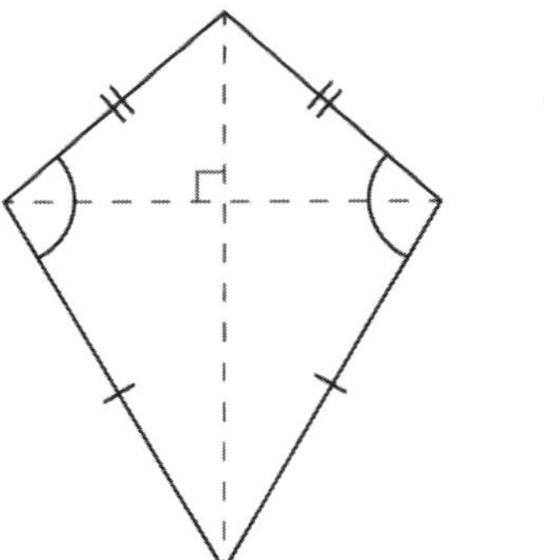

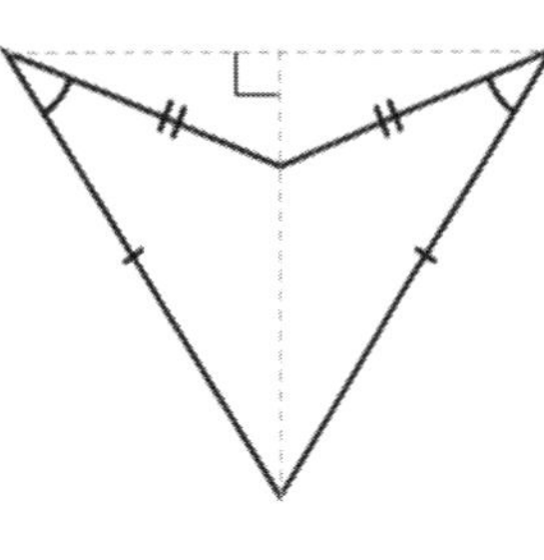

TRAPEZOID

Trapezoid: A trapezoid is defined as a quadrilateral that has at least one pair of parallel sides. There are no rules for the second pair of sides. So, there are no rules for the diagonals and no lines of symmetry for a trapezoid.

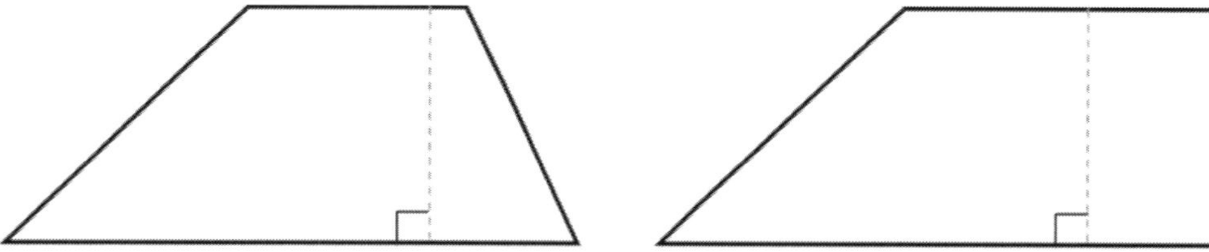

The **area of a trapezoid** is found by the formula $A = \frac{1}{2}h(b_1 + b_2)$, where h is the height (segment joining and perpendicular to the parallel bases), and b_1 and b_2 are the two parallel sides (bases). Do not use one of the other two sides as the height unless that side is also perpendicular to the parallel bases.

The **perimeter of a trapezoid** is found by the formula $P = a + b_1 + c + b_2$, where a, b_1, c, and b_2 are the four sides of the trapezoid.

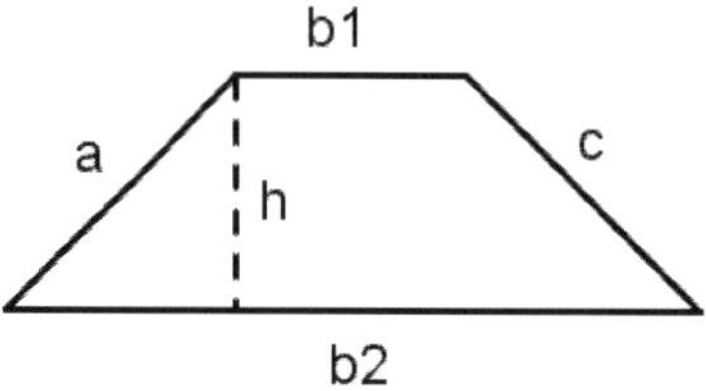

Review Video: Area and Perimeter of a Trapezoid
Visit mometrix.com/academy and enter code: 587523

Isosceles trapezoid: A trapezoid with equal base angles. This gives rise to other properties including: the two nonparallel sides have the same length, the two non-base angles are also equal, and there is one line of symmetry through the midpoints of the parallel sides.

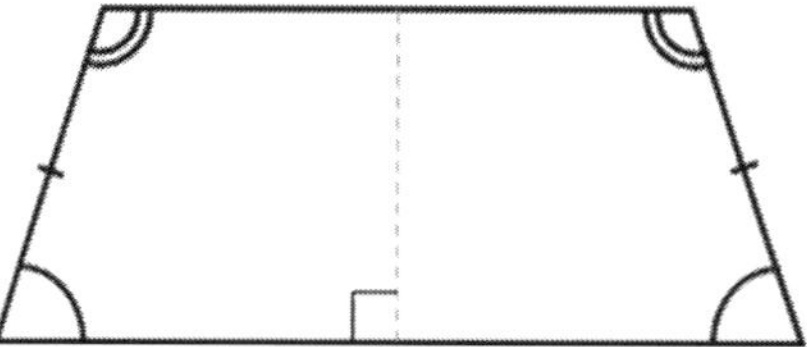

PARALLELOGRAM

A **parallelogram** is a quadrilateral that has two pairs of opposite parallel sides. As such it is a special type of trapezoid. The sides that are parallel are also congruent. The opposite interior angles are always congruent, and the consecutive interior angles are supplementary. The diagonals of a parallelogram divide each other. Each diagonal divides the parallelogram into two congruent triangles. A parallelogram has no line of symmetry, but does have 180-degree rotational symmetry about the midpoint.

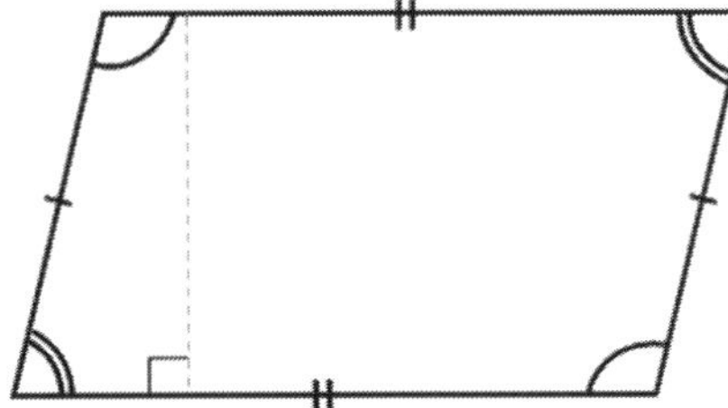

The **area of a parallelogram** is found by the formula $A = bh$, where b is the length of the base, and h is the height. Note that the base and height correspond to the length and width in a rectangle, so this formula would apply to rectangles as well. Do not confuse the height of a parallelogram with the length of the second side. The two are only the same measure in the case of a rectangle.

The **perimeter of a parallelogram** is found by the formula $P = 2a + 2b$ or $P = 2(a + b)$, where a and b are the lengths of the two sides.

Review Video: Area and Perimeter of a Parallelogram
Visit mometrix.com/academy and enter code: 718313

RECTANGLE

A **rectangle** is a quadrilateral with four right angles. All rectangles are parallelograms and trapezoids, but not all parallelograms or trapezoids are rectangles. The diagonals of a rectangle are congruent. Rectangles have two lines of symmetry (through each pair of opposing midpoints) and 180-degree rotational symmetry about the midpoint.

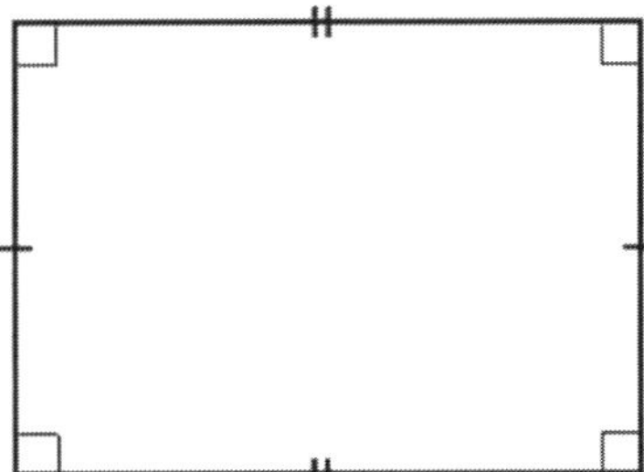

The **area of a rectangle** is found by the formula $A = lw$, where A is the area of the rectangle, l is the length (usually considered to be the longer side) and w is the width (usually considered to be the shorter side). The numbers for l and w are interchangeable.

The **perimeter of a rectangle** is found by the formula $P = 2l + 2w$ or $P = 2(l + w)$, where l is the length, and w is the width. It may be easier to add the length and width first and then double the result, as in the second formula.

Rhombus

A **rhombus** is a quadrilateral with four congruent sides. All rhombuses are parallelograms and kites; thus, they inherit all the properties of both types of quadrilaterals. The diagonals of a rhombus are perpendicular to each other. Rhombi have two lines of symmetry (along each of the diagonals) and 180° rotational symmetry. The **area of a rhombus** is half the product of the diagonals: $A = \frac{d_1 d_2}{2}$ and the perimeter of a rhombus is: $P = 2\sqrt{(d_1)^2 + (d_2)^2}$.

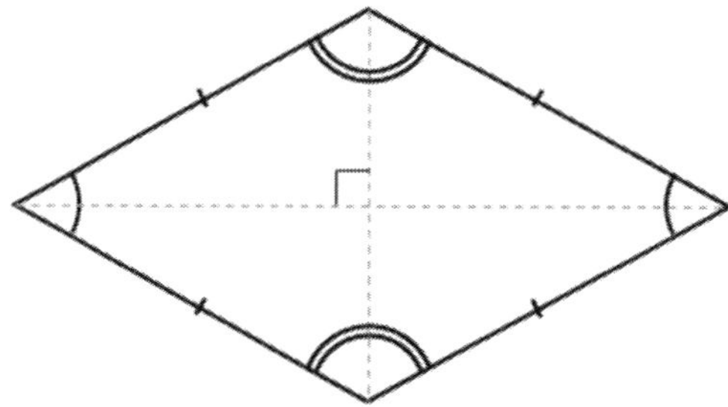

Square

A **square** is a quadrilateral with four right angles and four congruent sides. Squares satisfy the criteria of all other types of quadrilaterals. The diagonals of a square are congruent and perpendicular to each other. Squares have four lines of symmetry (through each pair of opposing midpoints and along each of the diagonals) as well as 90° rotational symmetry about the midpoint.

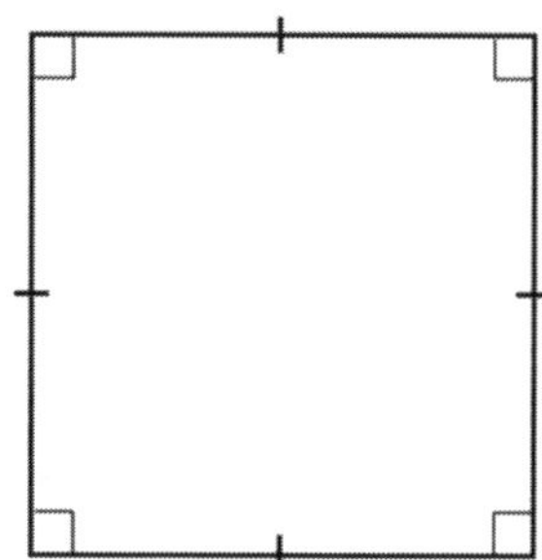

The **area of a square** is found by using the formula $A = s^2$, where s is the length of one side. The **perimeter of a square** is found by using the formula $P = 4s$, where s is the length of one side. Because all four sides are equal in a square, it is faster to multiply the length of one side by 4 than to add the same number four times. You could use the formulas for rectangles and get the same answer.

Review Video: Area and Perimeter of Rectangles and Squares
Visit mometrix.com/academy and enter code: 428109

HIERARCHY OF QUADRILATERALS

The hierarchy of quadrilaterals is as follows:

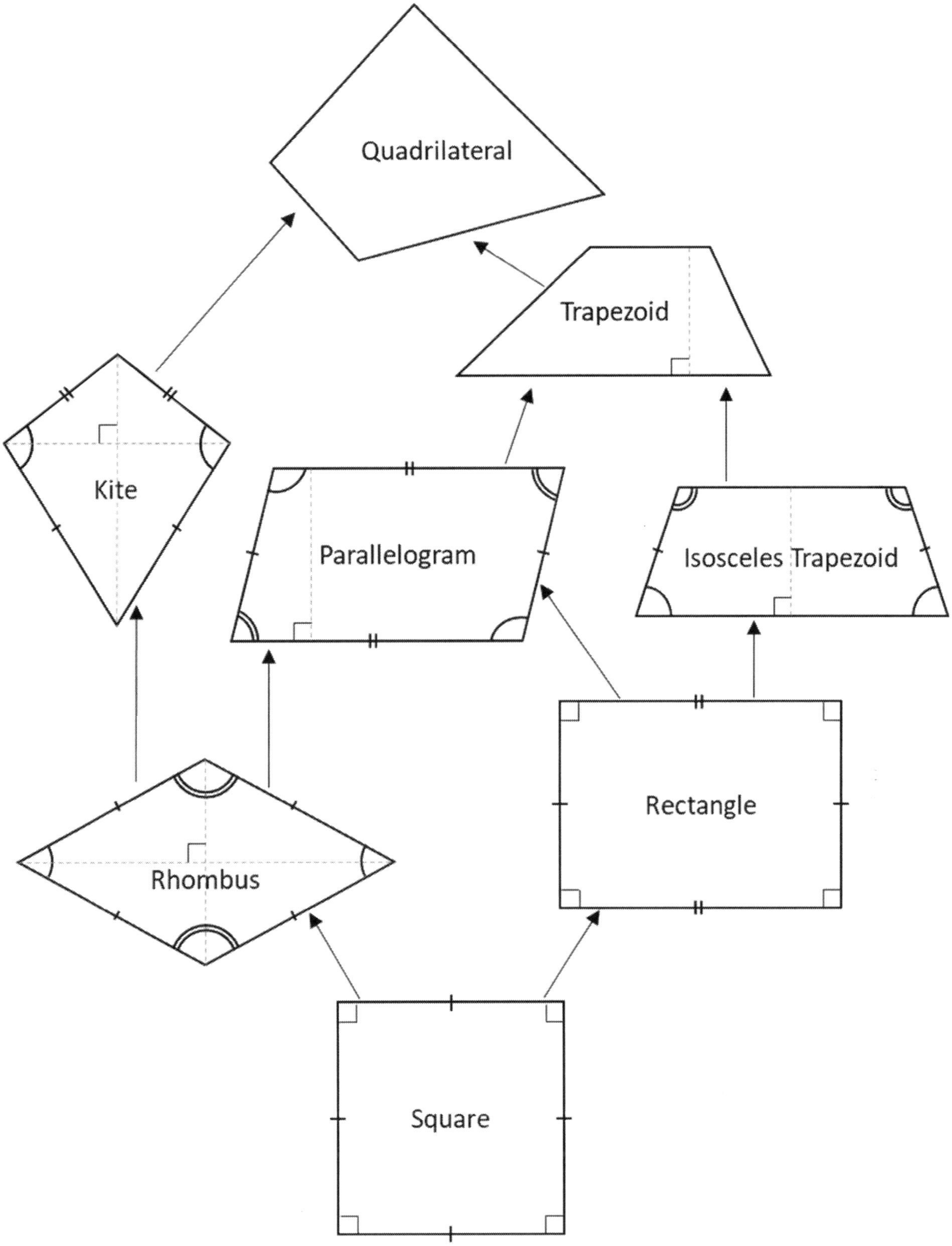

Quadrilateral

Trapezoid

Kite

Parallelogram

Isosceles Trapezoid

Rectangle

Rhombus

Square

The **center** of a circle is the single point from which every point on the circle is **equidistant**. The **radius** is a line segment that joins the center of the circle and any one point on the circle. All radii of a circle are equal. Circles that have the same center but not the same length of radii are **concentric**. The **diameter** is a line segment that passes through the center of the circle and has both endpoints on the circle. The length of the diameter is exactly twice the length of the radius. Point O in the diagram below is the center of the circle, segments $\overline{OX}$, $\overline{OY}$, and $\overline{OZ}$ are radii; and segment $\overline{XZ}$ is a diameter.

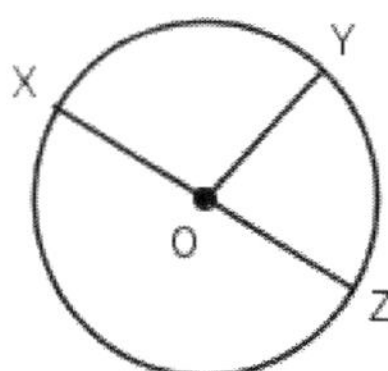

Review Video: Points of a Circle
Visit mometrix.com/academy and enter code: 420746

Review Video: Diameter, Radius, and Circumference
Visit mometrix.com/academy and enter code: 448988

The **area of a circle** is found by the formula $A = \pi r^2$, where r is the length of the radius. If the diameter of the circle is given, remember to divide it in half to get the length of the radius before proceeding.

The **circumference** of a circle is found by the formula $C = 2\pi r$, where r is the radius. Again, remember to convert the diameter if you are given that measure rather than the radius.

Review Video: Area and Circumference of a Circle
Visit mometrix.com/academy and enter code: 243015

Inscribed and Circumscribed Figures

These terms can both be used to describe a given arrangement of figures, depending on perspective. If each of the vertices of figure A lie on figure B, then it can be said that figure A is **inscribed** in figure B, but it can also be said that figure B is **circumscribed** about figure A. The following table and examples help to illustrate the concept. Note that the figures cannot both be circles, as they would be completely overlapping and neither would be inscribed or circumscribed.

Given	Description	Equivalent Description	Figures
Each of the sides of a pentagon is tangent to a circle	The circle is inscribed in the pentagon	The pentagon is circumscribed about the circle	
Each of the vertices of a pentagon lie on a circle	The pentagon is inscribed in the circle	The circle is circumscribed about the pentagon	

ARCS

An **arc** is a portion of a circle. Specifically, an arc is the set of points between and including two points on a circle. An arc does not contain any points inside the circle. When a segment is drawn from the endpoints of an arc to the center of the circle, a sector is formed. A **minor arc** is an arc that has a measure less than 180°. A **major arc** is an arc that has a measure of at least 180°. Every minor arc has a corresponding major arc that can be found by subtracting the measure of the minor arc from 360°. A **semicircle** is an arc whose endpoints are the endpoints of the diameter of a circle. A semicircle is exactly half of a circle.

Arc length is the length of that portion of the circumference between two points on the circle. The formula for arc length is $s = \frac{\pi r \theta}{180^{\circ}}$, where s is the arc length, r is the length of the radius, and θ is the angular measure of the arc in degrees, or $s = r\theta$, where θ is the angular measure of the arc in radians (2π radians $= 360$ degrees).

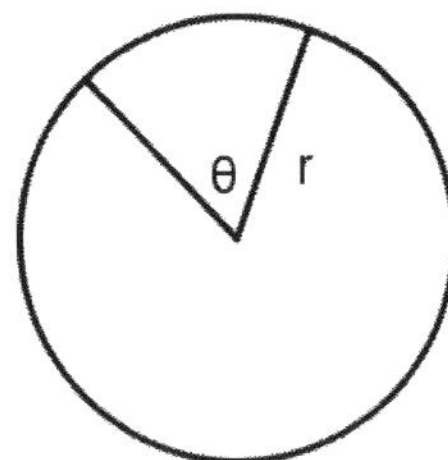

ANGLES OF CIRCLES

A **central angle** is an angle whose vertex is the center of a circle and whose legs intercept an arc of the circle. The measure of a central angle is equal to the measure of the minor arc it intercepts.

An **inscribed angle** is an angle whose vertex lies on a circle and whose legs contain chords of that circle. The portion of the circle intercepted by the legs of the angle is called the intercepted arc. The measure of the intercepted arc is exactly twice the measure of the inscribed angle. In the following diagram, angle ABC is an inscribed angle. $\widehat{AC} = 2(\text{m}\angle ABC)$.

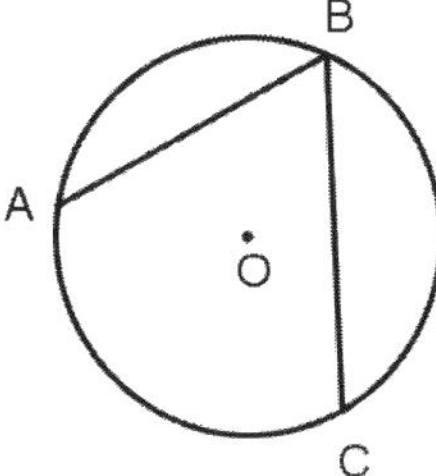

Arithmetic Reasoning and Math Knowledge

Any angle inscribed in a semicircle is a right angle. The intercepted arc is 180°, making the inscribed angle half that, or 90°. In the diagram below, angle ABC is inscribed in semicircle ABC, making angle ABC equal to 90°.

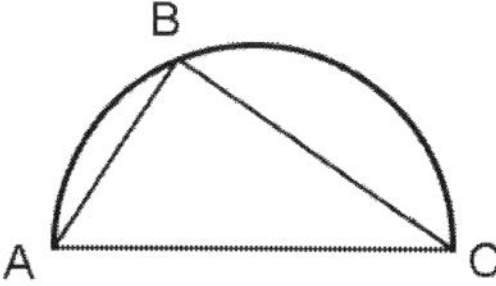

Review Video: Arcs and Angles of Circles
Visit mometrix.com/academy and enter code: 652838

Secants, Chords, and Tangents

A **secant** is a line that intersects a circle in two points. The segment of a secant line that is contained within the circle is called a **chord**. Two secants may intersect inside the circle, on the circle, or outside the circle. When the two secants intersect on the circle, an inscribed angle is formed. When two secants intersect inside a circle, the measure of each of two vertical angles is equal to half the sum of the two intercepted arcs. Consider the following diagram where $m\angle AEB = \frac{1}{2}(\widehat{AB} + \widehat{CD})$ and $m\angle BEC = \frac{1}{2}(\widehat{BC} + \widehat{AD})$.

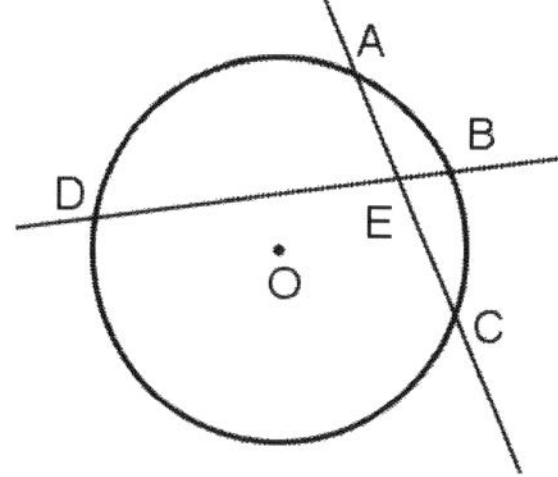

When two secants intersect outside a circle, the measure of the angle formed is equal to half the difference of the two arcs that lie between the two secants. In the diagram below, $m\angle AEB = \frac{1}{2}(\widehat{AB} - \widehat{CD})$.

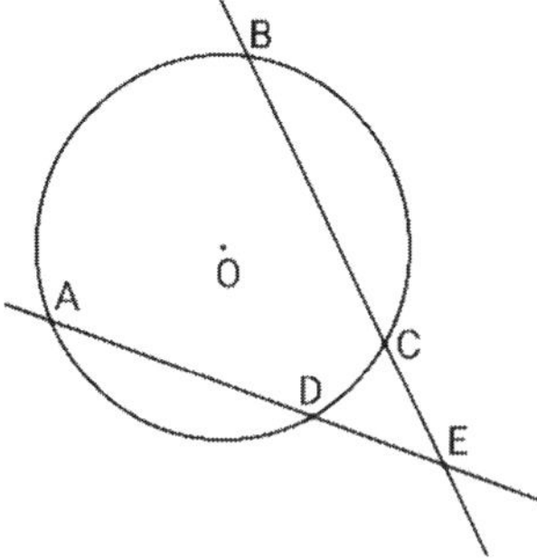

A **tangent** is a line in the same plane as a circle that touches the circle in exactly one point. The point at which a tangent touches a circle is called the **point of tangency**. While a line segment can be tangent to a circle as part of a line that is tangent, it is improper to say a tangent can be simply a line segment that touches the circle in exactly one point.

In the diagram below, $\overleftrightarrow{EB}$ is a secant and contains chord $\overline{EB}$, and $\overleftrightarrow{CD}$ is tangent to circle A. Notice that $\overline{FB}$ is not tangent to the circle. $\overline{FB}$ is a line segment that touches the circle in exactly one point, but if the segment were extended, it would touch the circle in a second point. In the diagram below, point B is the point of tangency.

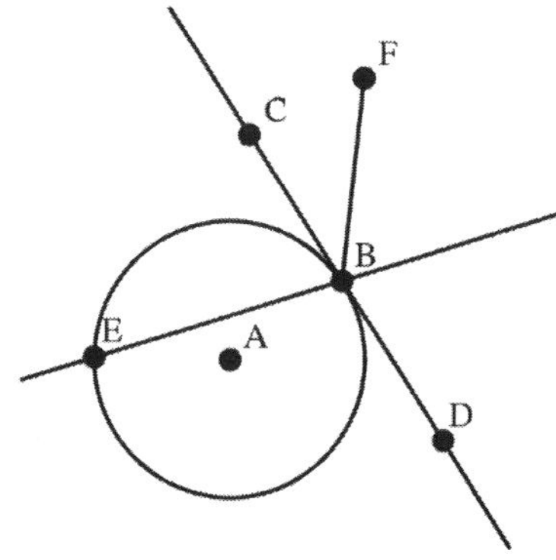

Review Video: Secants, Chords, and Tangents
Visit mometrix.com/academy and enter code: 258360

Review Video: Tangent Lines of a Circle
Visit mometrix.com/academy and enter code: 780167

SECTORS

A **sector** is the portion of a circle formed by two radii and their intercepted arc. While the arc length is exclusively the points that are also on the circumference of the circle, the sector is the entire area bounded by the arc and the two radii.

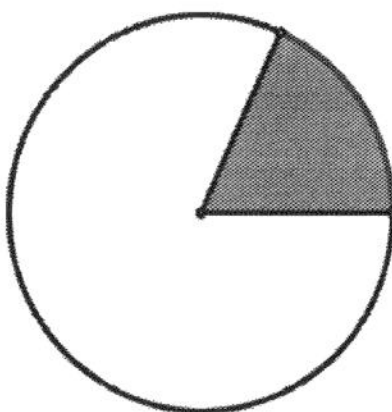

The **area of a sector** of a circle is found by the formula, $A = \frac{\theta r^2}{2}$, where A is the area, θ is the measure of the central angle in radians, and r is the radius. To find the area with the central angle in degrees, use the formula, $A = \frac{\theta \pi r^2}{360}$, where θ is the measure of the central angle and r is the radius.

SOLIDS

The **surface area of a solid object** is the area of all sides or exterior surfaces. For objects such as prisms and pyramids, a further distinction is made between base surface area (B) and lateral surface area (LA). For a prism, the total surface area (SA) is $SA = LA + 2B$. For a pyramid or cone, the total surface area is $SA = LA + B$.

Arithmetic Reasoning and Math Knowledge

The **surface area of a sphere** can be found by the formula $A = 4\pi r^2$, where r is the radius. The volume is given by the formula $V = \frac{4}{3}\pi r^3$, where r is the radius. Both quantities are generally given in terms of π.

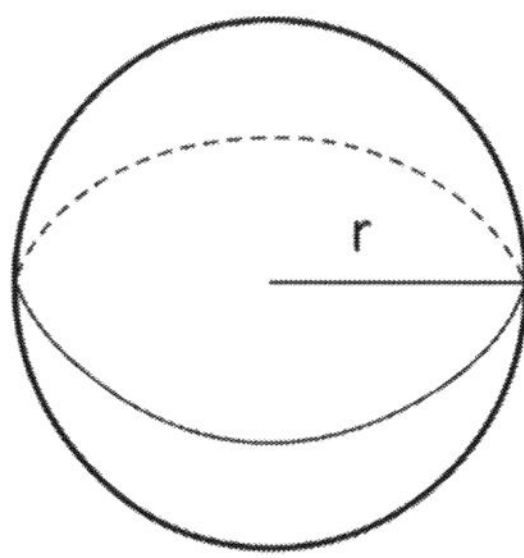

Review Video: Volume and Surface Area of a Sphere
Visit mometrix.com/academy and enter code: 786928

Review Video: How to Calculate the Volume of 3D Objects
Visit mometrix.com/academy and enter code: 163343

The **volume of any prism** is found by the formula $V = Bh$, where B is the area of the base, and h is the height (perpendicular distance between the bases). The surface area of any prism is the sum of the areas of both bases and all sides. It can be calculated as $SA = 2B + Ph$, where P is the perimeter of the base.

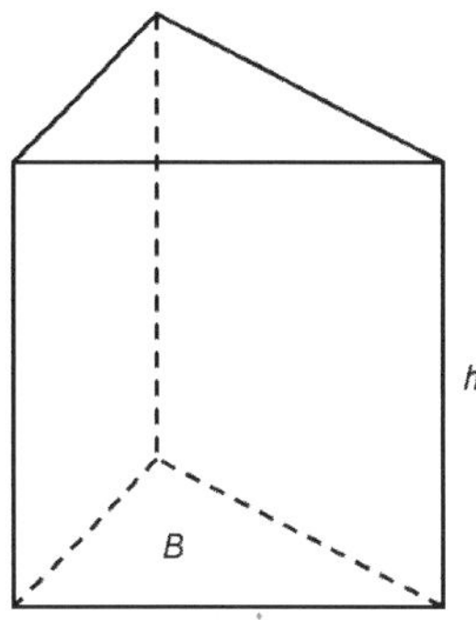

Review Video: Volume and Surface Area of a Prism
Visit mometrix.com/academy and enter code: 420158

For a **rectangular prism**, the volume can be found by the formula $V = lwh$, where V is the volume, l is the length, w is the width, and h is the height. The surface area can be calculated as $SA = 2lw + 2hl + 2wh$ or $SA = 2(lw + hl + wh)$.

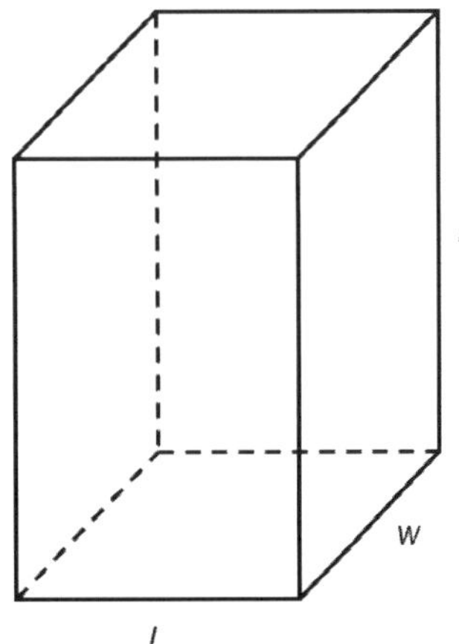

Review Video: Volume and Surface Area of a Rectangular Prism
Visit mometrix.com/academy and enter code: 282814

The **volume of a cube** can be found by the formula $V = s^3$, where s is the length of a side. The surface area of a cube is calculated as $SA = 6s^2$, where SA is the total surface area and s is the length of a side. These formulas are the same as the ones used for the volume and surface area of a rectangular prism, but simplified since all three quantities (length, width, and height) are the same.

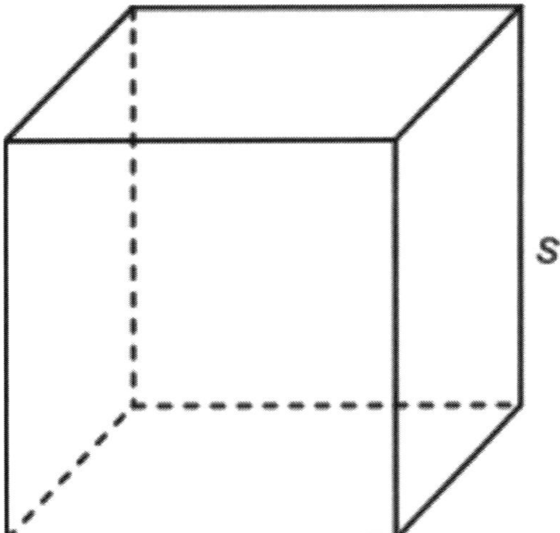

Review Video: Volume and Surface Area of a Cube
Visit mometrix.com/academy and enter code: 664455

The **volume of a cylinder** can be calculated by the formula $V = \pi r^2 h$, where r is the radius, and h is the height. The surface area of a cylinder can be found by the formula $SA = 2\pi r^2 + 2\pi rh$. The first term is the base area multiplied by two, and the second term is the perimeter of the base multiplied by the height.

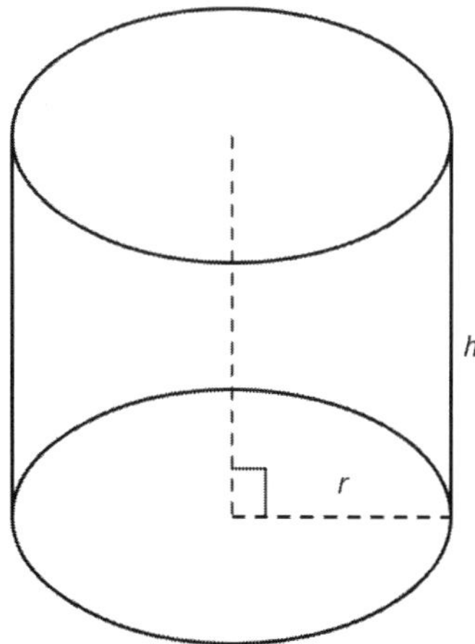

Review Video: Volume and Surface Area of a Right Circular Cylinder
Visit mometrix.com/academy and enter code: 226463

The **volume of a pyramid** is found by the formula $V = \frac{1}{3}Bh$, where B is the area of the base, and h is the height (perpendicular distance from the vertex to the base). Notice this formula is the same as $\frac{1}{3}$ times the volume of a prism. Like a prism, the base of a pyramid can be any shape.

Finding the **surface area of a pyramid** is not as simple as the other shapes we've looked at thus far. If the pyramid is a right pyramid, meaning the base is a regular polygon and the vertex is directly over the center of that polygon, the surface area can be calculated as $SA = B + \frac{1}{2}Ph_s$, where P is the perimeter of the base, and h_s is the slant height (distance from the vertex to the midpoint of one side of the base). If the pyramid is irregular, the area of each triangle side must be calculated individually and then summed, along with the base.

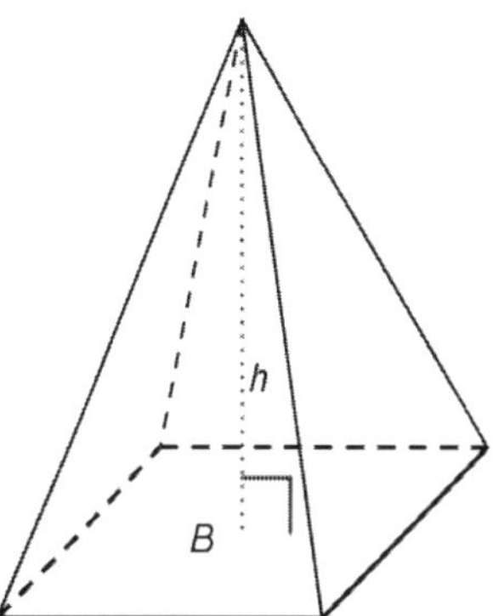

Review Video: Finding the Volume and Surface Area of a Pyramid
Visit mometrix.com/academy and enter code: 621932

The **volume of a cone** is found by the formula $V = \frac{1}{3}\pi r^2 h$, where r is the radius, and h is the height. Notice this is the same as $\frac{1}{3}$ times the volume of a cylinder. The surface area can be calculated as $SA = \pi r^2 + \pi rs$, where s is the slant height. The slant height can be calculated using the Pythagorean theorem to be $\sqrt{r^2 + h^2}$, so the surface area formula can also be written as $SA = \pi r^2 + \pi r\sqrt{r^2 + h^2}$.

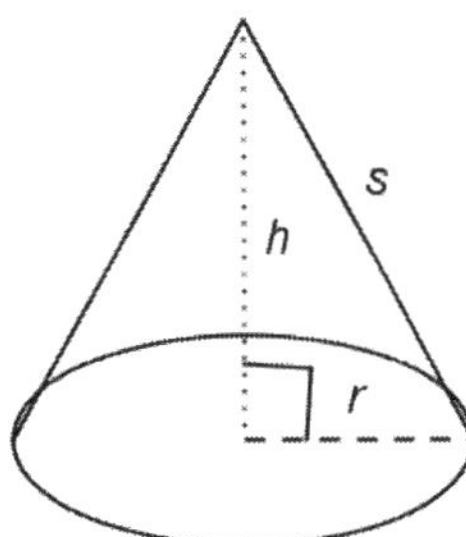

Review Video: Volume and Surface Area of a Right Circular Cone
Visit mometrix.com/academy and enter code: 573574

Word Knowledge

What Do Word Knowledge Questions Look Like?

Word knowledge questions follow a very simple format. You will be given a word and you must select the word that is closest in meaning to the given word, from the choices given.

How Can I Prepare?

Unfortunately, there is no easy way to prepare for this section. The questions test your vocabulary and if you don't have a very large vocabulary, this will probably be one of your harder sections to prepare for. The best way to build a large, long-lasting vocabulary is to read extensively, but you may not have time for that if your test is soon. Cramming with vocabulary lists is one way to build up a short-term vocabulary. Learning common prefixes and suffixes is another valuable use of your limited time. Whether or not you decide you need to add to your vocabulary before the test, there are a few strategies you can use to get the most out of the words you already know.

What Strategies Can I Use?

Nearly and Perfect Synonyms

You must determine which of the provided choices has the best similar definition as a certain word. **Nearly similar** may often be more correct, because the goal is to test your understanding of the nuances, or little differences, between words. A perfect match may not exist, so don't be concerned if your answer choice is not a complete synonym. Focus upon edging closer to the word. Eliminate the words that you know aren't correct first. Then narrow your search. Cross out the words that are the least similar to the main word until you are left with the one that is the most similar.

Prefixes

Take advantage of every clue that the word might include. Prefixes and suffixes can be a huge help. Usually, they allow you to determine a word's basic meaning. *Pre-* means before, *post-* means after, *pro-* is positive, *de-* is negative. From these prefixes and suffixes, you can get an idea of the general meaning of the word and look for its opposite. Be sure to watch out for traps, though. Just because *con* is the opposite of *pro*, doesn't necessarily mean *congress* is the opposite of *progress*!

Positive vs. Negative

Many words can be easily determined to be a positive word or a negative word. Words such as despicable, gruesome, and bleak are all **negative**. Words such as ecstatic, praiseworthy, and magnificent are all **positive**. You will be surprised at how many words can be viewed as either positive or negative. Once that is determined, you can quickly eliminate any other words with an opposite meaning and focus on those that have the same characteristic, whether positive or negative.

Word Strength

Part of the challenge is determining the most nearly similar word. This is particularly true when two words seem to be similar. When analyzing a word, determine how strong it is. For example, stupendous and good are both positive words.

However, stupendous is a much stronger positive adjective than good. Also, towering or gigantic are stronger words than tall or large. Search for an answer choice that is similar and also has the same strength. If the main word is weak, look for similar words that are also weak. If the main word is strong, look for similar words that are also strong.

TYPE AND TOPIC

Another key is what type of word is the main word. If the main word is an adjective describing height, then look for the answer to be an adjective describing height as well. Match both the type and topic of the main word. The **type** refers to the parts of speech, whether the word is an adjective, adverb, noun, or verb. The **topic** refers to what sort of definition or thing the word refers to, such as sizes or fashion styles.

FORM A SENTENCE

Many words seem more natural in a sentence. *Specious* reasoning, *irresistible* force, and *uncanny* resemblance are just a few of the word combinations that usually go together. When faced with an uncommon word that you barely understand, try to put the word in a sentence that makes sense. It will help you to understand the word's meaning. Once you have a good descriptive sentence that utilizes the main word properly, plug in the answer choices and see if the sentence still has the same meaning with each answer choice. The answer choice that maintains the meaning of the sentence is correct!

USE REPLACEMENTS

Using a sentence is a great help because it puts the word into a proper perspective. Since the exam actually gives you a sentence, you don't always have to create your own (though in many cases the sentence won't be helpful). Read the provided sentence, picking out the main word. Then read the sentence again and again, each time replacing the main word with one of the answer choices. The correct answer should "sound" right and fit.

Example: The desert landscape was desolate. Desolate means

a. Cheerful
b. Creepy
c. Excited
d. Forlorn

After reading the example sentence, begin replacing "desolate" with each of the answer choices. Does "the desert landscape was cheerful, creepy, excited, or forlorn" sound right? Deserts are typically hot, empty, and rugged environments, probably not *cheerful*, or *excited*. While *creepy* might sound right, that word would be more appropriate for a haunted house. But "the desert landscape was forlorn" has a certain ring to it and would be correct. *Forlorn* means abandoned or lonely, *desolate* similarly means empty, bleak, or barren. Both of these words make sense when used to convey the lonely feeling one may experience when looking at an empty desert landscape.

ELIMINATE SIMILAR CHOICES

If you don't know the word, don't worry. Remember that there is only one correct answer choice. If you can find a common relationship between a set of answer choices, then you know they are wrong. Find the answer choice that does not have a common relationship to the other answer choices and it will be the correct answer.

Example: Laconic most nearly means

a. Wordy
b. Talkative
c. Expressive
d. Quiet

In this example, the first three choices are all similar. Even if you don't know that laconic means the same as quiet, you know that "quiet" must be correct, because the other three choices are all virtually the same. They are all the same, so they must all be wrong. The one that is different must be correct. So, don't worry if you don't know a word. Focus on the answer choices that you do understand and see if you can identify similarities. Even identifying two words that are similar will allow you to eliminate those two answer choices. Because they are similar, they are either both right or both wrong, and since they can't both be right, they must both be wrong.

Example: He worked slowly, moving the leather back and forth until it was ____.

a. Rough
b. Hard
c. Stiff
d. Pliable

In this example the first three choices are all similar. *Hard* and *stiff* are both synonyms, and *rough*, while not quite a synonym, is not the opposite of *hard* or *stiff*. Even without knowing what pliable means, it has to be correct, because you know the other three answer choices mean similar things.

Adjectives Give it Away

Words mean things and are added to sentences for a reason. Adjectives in particular may be the clue to determining which answer choice is correct.

Example: The brilliant scientist made several discoveries that were

a. Dull
b. Dazzling

Look at the adjectives first to help determine what makes sense. A "brilliant" or smart scientist would make dazzling discoveries, rather than dull ones. Without that simple adjective, no answer choice is clear.

Use Logic

Ask yourself questions about each answer choice to see if they are logical.

Example: In the distance, the deep pounding resonance of the drums could be

a. Seen
b. Heard

Would resonating pounding be seen or would resonating pounding be heard?

The Trap of Familiarity

Don't just choose a word because you recognize it. On difficult questions, you may only recognize one or two words. The exam doesn't have "make-believe words" on it, so don't think that just because you only recognize one word means that word must be correct. If you don't recognize most of the words, then focus on the ones that you do recognize. Are any of them correct? Try your best to determine if they fit the sentence. If any of them do, you have your answer, but if not, eliminate them and guess from among the remaining options.

Practice Questions

1. Sketch most nearly means

a. Skip
b. Scope
c. Draw
d. Drain
e. Drip

2. The child was frightened by the movie.

a. Scared
b. Entertained
c. Amused
d. Saddened
e. Delighted

3. Sever most nearly means

a. Hard
b. Cut
c. Add
d. Soft
e. Change

4. Her prediction was accurate.

a. False
b. Funny
c. Planned
d. Assumed
e. Correct

5. Taunt most nearly means

a. Truant
b. Tried
c. Tight
d. Tease
e. Tired

6. Her concern for him was sincere.

a. Intense
b. Genuine
c. Brief
d. Misunderstood
e. Repetitive

7. Disclose most nearly means

a. Reveal
b. Return
c. Near
d. Hide
e. Conceal

8. He <u>sprinted</u> down the road.

a. Crawled
b. Walked
c. Hurried
d. Ran
e. Drove

9. The naughty child was <u>disciplined</u>.

a. Upset
b. Punished
c. Hidden
d. Bad
e. Surprised

10. <u>Seize</u> most nearly means

a. Grab
b. Release
c. Tell
d. Fight
e. Give

Practice Answers

1. C: To sketch something is to draw something. Saying somebody was planning to sketch a landscape and saying they were going to draw a landscape conveys the same meaning.

2. A: To say somebody is frightened is the same as saying they are scared or afraid.

3. B: To sever something is to cut something. For example, to say that somebody severed all ties with someone else means that they have cut those ties. It can also be used to describe the cutting of objects. For example, saying someone severed a rope with a knife means they cut the rope.

4. E: Describing something as accurate and describing it as correct conveys the same meaning. For example, saying somebody accurately predicted something is the same as saying they correctly predicted something.

5. D: To taunt somebody is to tease them. To say somebody taunted another person conveys the same meaning as saying somebody teased another person. Usually, teasing and taunting is understood to be a mean practice.

6. B: To say something is sincere means that it is genuine or real. For example, saying someone showed sincere concern means that their concern was genuine, not fake.

7. A: To disclose something is to reveal something. For example, saying somebody disclosed something they had been hiding is the same as saying they revealed it.

8. D: To sprint is to run. Saying that somebody sprinted to their destination and saying they ran to their destination conveys the same meaning.

9. B: To discipline someone for their undesirable actions or behaviors is to punish them. Saying a child was disciplined for his actions and saying he was punished conveys the same meaning.

10. A: To seize something is to take hold of it or grab it. For example, saying the woman seized the man's arm is the same as saying she grabbed it.

Reading Comprehension

What Do Reading Comprehension Questions Look Like?

The questions in this section will follow the typical format of reading comprehension questions on standardized tests. You'll be given a passage to read, several paragraphs in length, and then be shown several questions about the passage. Each question will have five possible answers to choose from; only one answer will be correct.

What Are They Testing?

The questions in this section are testing your ability to read and understand written material. Most people taking the AFOQT will have a level of reading ability that's quite a bit higher than the reading ability of the average American, and the passages in this section will reflect that fact. They will tend to be written on the level of articles in academic and scientific publications, and not at the level of articles one reads in most magazines or newspapers, or on most websites.

However, don't take this to mean that you'll need any specialized scientific or technical knowledge to do well on these questions; you won't. Each passage, while written on a higher level than average, and possibly on a scientific or technical subject, will assume no specialized knowledge on the part of the reader about the subject matter.

Some questions will test your ability to remember or quickly locate facts in the passage, and these questions will generally not use the same words or phrases used in the passage. Other questions will require you to make judgments about what you've read, such as choosing a statement the author would agree or disagree with, perceiving the author's main point, or detecting the author's purpose in writing the passage.

How Can I Prepare?

The vast majority of Americans engage in very little reading these days, beyond texts and social media. Needless to say, that kind of reading won't suffice to prepare you for the AFOQT. Even if you do some legitimate reading from time to time, odds are that you read much less than the average aspiring Air Force officer of 30 years ago did, and you too likely need to brush up on your reading comprehension skills.

In either case, you'll want to set aside regular practice sessions where you read higher level reading passages than you're used to and ask yourself a lot of questions after each passage.

- What is the author's main point?
- What kind of statements would the author be likely to agree with or disagree with?
- Is the passage educational, persuasive, argumentative, etc.?
- What are some of the secondary points the author makes?
- Is the article fact based, or merely stating an opinion?
- Has the author made a good case?
- If you think he has, what do you base this on?
- If not, where is his argument or article weak?

Libraries have a lot of great resources you can take advantage of to help you improve your reading comprehension skills.

Practice Questions

Sample Passage

Historically, the term pilot error has been used to describe an accident in which an action or decision made by the pilot was the cause or a contributing factor that led to the accident. This definition also includes the pilot's failure to make a correct decision or take proper action. From a broader perspective, the phrase human factors related more aptly describes these accidents. A single decision or event does not lead to an accident, but a series of events, and the resultant decisions together form a chain of events leading to an outcome.

In his article *Accident-Prone Pilots*, Dr. Patrick R. Veillette uses the history of Captain Everyman to demonstrate how aircraft accidents are caused more by a chain of poor choices rather than one single poor choice. In the case of Captain Everyman, after a gear-up landing accident, he became involved in another accident while taxiing a Beech 58P Baron out of the ramp. Interrupted by a radio call from the 17-11 dispatcher, Everyman neglected to complete the fuel crossfeed check before taking off. Everyman, who was flying solo, left the right-fuel selector in the cross-feed position. Once aloft and cruising, he noticed a right roll tendency and corrected with aileron trim. He did not realize that both engines were feeding off the left wing's tank, making the wing lighter.

After two hours of flight, the right engine quit when Everyman was flying along a deep canyon gorge. While he was trying to troubleshoot the cause of the right engine's failure, the left engine quit. Everyman landed the aircraft on a river sand bar but it sank into ten feet of water.

Several years later, Everyman flew a de Havilland Twin Otter to deliver supplies to a remote location. When he returned to home base and landed, the aircraft veered sharply to the left, departed the runway, and ran into a marsh 375 feet from the runway. The airframe and engines sustained considerable damage. Upon inspecting the wreck, accident investigators found the nose wheel steering tiller in the fully deflected position. Both the after-takeoff and before-landing checklists required the tiller to be placed in the neutral position. Everyman had overlooked this item.

Now, is Everyman accident prone or just unlucky? Skipping details on a checklist appears to be a common theme in the preceding accidents. While most pilots have made similar mistakes, these errors were probably caught prior to a mishap due to extra margin, good warning systems, a sharp copilot, or just good luck. What makes a pilot less prone to accidents?

The successful pilot possesses the ability to concentrate, manage workloads, and monitor and perform several simultaneous tasks. Some of the latest psychological screenings used in aviation test applicants for their ability to multitask, measuring both accuracy and the individual's ability to focus attention on several subjects simultaneously. The FAA oversaw an extensive research study on the similarities and dissimilarities of accident-free pilots and those who were not. The project surveyed over 4,000 pilots, half of whom had clean records while the other half had been involved in an accident.

Five traits were discovered in pilots prone to having accidents. These pilots:

- Have disdain toward rules.
- Have very high correlation between accidents on their flying records and safety violations on their driving records.
- Frequently fall into the thrill and adventure seeking personality category.
- Are impulsive rather than methodical and disciplined, both in information gathering and in speed and selection of actions to be taken.
- Show a disregard for or under-utilization of outside sources of information, including copilots, flight attendants, flight service personnel, flight instructors, and air traffic controllers.

(Questions on the following page)

1. The primary purpose of the passage is to

a. Criticize Captain Everyman.
b. Advocate for more comprehensive pilot training.
c. Reduce flight accidents.
d. Entertain the reader with a story of pilot incompetence.
e. Describe some characteristics that correlate with flight accidents.

2. Which of the following statements about Captain Everyman is NOT supported by the passage?

a. Captain Everyman is a reckless thrill-seeker.
b. Captain Everyman is easily distracted.
c. Captain Everyman is not methodical in his work.
d. Captain Everyman can fly a variety of aircraft.
e. Captain Everyman does not double-check his work.

3. Why does the author prefer to describe the main cause of accidents as human factors rather than pilot error?

a. Because most accidents are caused by multiple poor decisions rather than a single error.
b. Because most accidents are caused by faulty equipment.
c. Because most accidents can be traced to a single mistake.
d. Because many accidents are caused by miscommunication with the control tower.
e. Because pilots can be subject to criminal charges of negligence.

4. In the fifth paragraph, *prone* most nearly means

a. Immobile
b. Supine
c. Likely to have
d. Lying down
e. Encouraging

5. With which one of the following claims about pilots would the author most likely agree?

a. Pilots should not be allowed to fly solo until they are thirty years old.
b. A good pilot must be able to keep track of many different things simultaneously.
c. Pilots should be restricted to flying one type of plane.
d. Pilots should never fly solo.
e. Some pilots never make mistakes.

Practice Answers

1. E: Describing some characteristics that correlate with flight accidents is the primary purpose of the passage. The author explains how most flight accidents are the result of several mistakes in sequence, and how inattention, inability to multi-task, and carelessness are common characteristics of the accident-prone pilot.

2. A: The passage presents a critical portrait of Captain Everyman, but it never directly suggests that he is a reckless thrill-seeker. The passage does state that this personality type is correlated with flight accidents, but, in the example scenarios, the causes of Captain Everyman's accidents are carelessness and distraction rather than recklessness.

3. A: The author prefers saying that the main cause of accidents is human factors, not simply pilot error, because accidents are rarely the result of a single mistake, but rather are typically caused by a series of mistakes, oversights, or general carelessness over a period of time. The author makes this point in the first paragraph of the passage.

4. C: In the fifth paragraph, *prone* most nearly means *likely to have*. The author is discussing pilots who are accident prone, meaning that they are more likely to have accidents. Prone can also mean *lying down,* or *supine*, but it does not have that meaning in this context.

5. B: The author would most likely agree that a good pilot must be able to keep track of many different things simultaneously. Specifically, the author emphasizes the importance of multi-tasking as a pilot. There is no indication in the passage that age or flying different types of aircraft is correlated with accidents, and there is no argument that pilots should never fly solo. Finally, the author explicitly states that all pilots make mistakes, though some are better than others at correcting them.

Situational Judgment

What Do Situational Judgment Questions Look Like?

All situational judgment questions will have a similar format. Test takers will be given a scenario which requires some action to be taken to solve a problem that has come up, usually involving interpersonal and/or official relationships between an officer and his subordinates and/or his superiors. The test taker will then be shown several possible actions that could be taken, and will be told to select both the **most effective** and the **least effective** of the actions listed.

What Are Situational Judgment Questions Testing?

This is a newer section of the AFOQT, added to make the test a better predictor of success as an Air Force officer. These questions are primarily focused on testing a person in the areas of judgment and self-sufficient decision-making abilities. In order to do well on this section, test takers will need to show that they can lead subordinates and solve problems independently by using their core competencies of resource management, communication, innovation, mentoring, leadership, professionalism, and integrity.

How Can I Prepare?

Situational judgment questions aren't the kind of questions that lend themselves easily to preparation, as there really isn't any material for a person to review and memorize. However, you should keep in mind the qualities listed above (resource management, communication, innovation, mentoring, leadership, professionalism, and integrity) when answering questions. Your answers should reflect these qualities as much as possible. Also, you should avoid choosing any answer which involves going to a superior for advice or help unless there are no other viable options, or discussing a person's shortcomings behind their back no matter their rank. Officers are expected to be resourceful men and women of character.

Physical Science

What Do Physical Science Questions Look Like?

Physical science questions primarily test your understanding of scientific terms. You won't be asked to perform complex physics calculations or balance a chemical reaction. The purpose of this section is to make sure you paid attention in high school science and retained some of the general concepts.

How Can I Prepare?

The best way to prepare for these questions is to brush up on your science terminology and concepts. We've included a glossary of terms here to give you head start, but it's a good idea to find a high school physical science textbook and look through the full glossary in there if you want a more thorough review.

A

Absolute zero: The lowest possible temperature (−273.15 °C).

Atmospheric pressure: The pressure exerted by the gases in the air. Units of measurement are kilopascals (kPa), atmospheres (atm), millimeters of mercury (mmHg) and Torr. Standard atmospheric pressure is 100 kPa, 1atm, 760 mmHg, or 760 Torr.

Atom: The smallest particle of an element; a nucleus and its surrounding electrons.

Atomic mass: The mass of an atom measured in atomic mass units (amu). An atomic mass unit is equal to one-twelfth of the atom of carbon-12. Atomic mass is now more generally used instead of atomic weight. Example: the atomic mass of chlorine is about 35 amu.

Atomic number: Also known as the proton number, it is the number of electrons or the number of protons in an atom. Example: the atomic number of gold is 79.

Atomic weight: A common term used to mean the average molar mass of an element. This is the mass per mole of atoms. Example: the atomic weight of chlorine is about 35 g/mol.

B

Boiling point: The temperature at which a substance undergoes a phase change from a liquid to a gas.

C

Celsius scale (°C): A temperature scale on which the freezing point of water is at 0 degrees and the normal boiling point at standard atmospheric pressure is 100 degrees.

Change of state: A change between two of the three states of matter, solid, liquid and gas. Example: when water evaporates it changes from a liquid to a gaseous state.

Compound: A chemical consisting of two or more elements chemically bonded together. Example: Calcium can combine with carbon and oxygen to make calcium carbonate ($CaCO_3$), a compound of all three elements.

Condensation: The formation of a liquid from a gas. This is a change of state, also called a phase change.

Conduction: (1) the exchange of heat (heat conduction) by contact with another object, or (2) allowing the flow of electrons (electrical conduction).

Convection: The exchange of heat energy with the surroundings produced by the flow of a fluid due to being heated or cooled.

D

Decay (radioactive decay): The way that a radioactive element changes into another element due to loss of mass through radiation. Example: uranium 238 decays with the loss of an alpha particle to form thorium 234.

Density: The mass per unit volume (e.g., g/cm^3).

Diffusion: The slow mixing of one substance with another until the two substances are evenly mixed. Mixing occurs because of differences in concentration within the mixture. Diffusion works rapidly with gases, very slowly with liquids.

Dissolve: To break down a substance in a solution without causing a reaction.

E

Electrical potential: The energy produced by an electrochemical cell and measured by the voltage or electromotive force (emf).

Electron: A tiny, negatively charged particle that is part of an atom. The flow of electrons through a solid material such as a wire produces an electric current.

Element: A substance that cannot be decomposed into a simpler substance by chemical means. Examples: calcium, iron, gold.

Explosive: A substance which, when a shock is applied to it, decomposes very rapidly, releasing a very large amount of heat and creating a large volume of gases as a shock wave.

F

Fluid: Able to flow; either a liquid or a gas.

Freezing point: The temperature at which a substance undergoes a phase change from a liquid to a solid. It is the same temperature as the melting point. At any temperature below this point the substance will freeze.

G

Gamma rays: Waves of radiation produced as the nucleus of a radioactive element rearranges itself into a tighter cluster of protons and neutrons. Gamma rays carry enough energy to damage living cells.

Gas/gaseous phase: A form of matter in which the molecules form no definite shape and are free to move about to uniformly fill any vessel they are put in. A gas can easily be compressed into a much smaller volume.

Group: A vertical column in the Periodic Table. There are eight groups in the table. Their numbers correspond to the number of electrons in the outer shell of the atoms in the group. Example: Group 2 contains beryllium, magnesium, calcium, strontium, barium, and radium.

H

Half-life: The time it takes for the radiation coming from a sample of a radioactive element to decrease by half.

Heat: The energy that is transferred when a substance is at a different temperature to that of its surroundings.

Heat capacity: The ratio of the heat supplied to a substance, compared with the rise in temperature that is produced.

Heat of combustion: The amount of heat given off by a mole of a substance during combustion. This heat is a property of the substance and is the same no matter what kind of combustion is involved. Example: The heat of combustion of carbon is $94.14 \text{ kcal} \times -4.18 \text{ kJ/kcal} = -393.5 \text{ kJ}$.

I

Ion: An atom, or group of atoms, that has gained or lost one or more electrons and so developed an electrical charge. Ions behave differently from electrically neutral atoms and molecules. They can move in an electric field, and they can also bind strongly to solvent molecules such as water. Positively charged ions are called cations; negatively charged ions are called anions. Ions can carry an electrical current through solutions.

Isotope: One of two or more atoms of the same element that have the same number of protons in their nucleus (atomic number), but which have a different number of neutrons (atomic mass). Example: carbon-12 and carbon-14.

K

Kinetic energy: The energy an object has by virtue of its being in motion.

L

Latent heat: The amount of heat that is absorbed or released during the process of changing state between gas, liquid, or solid. For example, heat is absorbed when a substance melts, and it is released again when the substance solidifies.

Liquid/liquid phase: A form of matter that has a fixed volume but no fixed shape.

M

Mass: The amount of matter in an object. In everyday use the word *weight* is often used (somewhat incorrectly) to mean mass.

Matter: Anything that has mass and takes up space.

Melting point: The temperature at which a substance changes state from a solid phase to a liquid phase. It is the same as freezing point. At any temperature above this point the substance will melt.

Metal: A class of elements that is a good conductor of electricity and heat, has a metallic luster, is malleable and ductile, forms cations and has oxides that are bases. Metals are formed as cations held together by a sea of electrons. A metal may also be an alloy of these elements. Example: sodium, calcium, gold.

Mixture: A material that can be separated into two or more substances using physical means. Example: a mixture of copper (II) sulfate and cadmium sulfide can be separated by filtration.

Mole: 1 mole is the amount of a substance which contains Avogadro's number (about 6×10^{23}) of particles. Example: 1 mole of carbon-12 weighs exactly 12 g.

Molecule: A group of two or more atoms held together by chemical bonds. Example: O_2.

N

Neutron: A particle inside the nucleus of an atom that is neutral and has no charge.

Newton (N): The unit of force required to give one kilogram an acceleration of one meter per second every second ($1\ m/s^2$).

Noble gases: The members of Group 8 of the Periodic Table: helium, neon, argon, krypton, xenon, and radon. These gases are almost entirely unreactive.

Nucleus: The small, positively charged particle at the center of an atom. The nucleus is responsible for most of the mass of an atom.

P

Period: A row in the Periodic Table.

Periodic Table: A chart organizing elements by atomic number and chemical properties into groups and periods.

Phase: A particular state of matter. A substance may exist as a solid, liquid or gas and may change between these phases with addition or removal of energy. Examples: ice, liquid and vapor are the three phases of water. Ice undergoes a phase change to water when heat energy is added.

Photon: A parcel of light energy.

Potential energy: The energy an object has by virtue of its position or orientation, most commonly its height above some reference point, or amount of compression as with a spring.

Pressure: The force per unit area measured in Pascals.

Proton: A positively charged particle in the nucleus of an atom that balances out the charge of the surrounding electrons.

R

Radiation: The exchange of energy with the surroundings through the transmission of waves or particles of energy. Radiation is a form of energy transfer that can happen through space; no intervening medium is required (as would be the case for conduction and convection).

S

Solid/solid phase: A rigid form of matter which maintains its shape, whatever its container.

Table Reading

What Are These Questions Testing?

The table reading section tests your ability to quickly and accurately locate information stored in a table. The questions require you to find a particular number in a table given a set of coordinates.

What Is the Question Format?

The questions will be given in groups of around 5 questions, where each group will refer to a table of numbers, with column and row headers. Each question will give an ordered pair of numbers that indicate the location in the table where the correct answer can be found. The ordered pair is given in the form (x, y), where x is the column number and y is the row number.

The questions will be presented like this:

	-3	-2	-1	0	1	2	3
3	41	39	84	77	35	42	37
2	75	57	95	16	93	16	15
1	34	54	50	89	26	19	94
0	66	89	65	23	13	42	20
-1	15	97	86	76	76	58	92
-2	80	92	78	52	90	11	56
-3	88	81	61	79	35	64	52

1. $(\mathbf{3}, -\mathbf{2})$
  a. 56
  b. 39
  c. 64
  d. 11
  e. 92

To answer the question, look at the ordered pair. It indicates that the number you are looking for is in the column labeled 3, and the row labeled -2. In this table, that number is 56, answer choice A.

What Strategies Can I Use to Answer the Questions Quickly and Accurately?

The best way to approach these questions is methodically. Take the first number in the ordered pair and find it on the column headers. Keep your finger on that number while you take the second number of the ordered pair and locate it on the row headers. Put another finger on that number. Drag the first finger straight down the column until you get to the row that your other finger is on. The number at the intersection of the indicated column and row is your answer.

If you find yourself staring at the table for too long trying to be sure that you've selected the right number, you may find it helpful to draw lines on the graph, or take two pieces of scratch paper and line up their edges with the column and row numbers given in the question so that the number you are looking for appears at the corner where the two pieces of paper come together.

WHAT ARE THE COMMON MISTAKES TO AVOID?

Since the process for answering these questions is very straightforward, most errors are the result of trying to go too quickly. The more you practice these sorts of questions, the faster you will be able to accurately answer them. Once you've practiced for a while, you'll be able to get a feel for how fast you can go while accurately answering all the questions. On test day, force yourself to go no faster than this.

One common mistake made on these questions is taking the ordered pair in the question to be ordinal coordinates rather than numbers referencing the column and row labels. For example, suppose a question asks for the ordered pair (1,2). Under the pressure of the test, many people will instinctively go to the first column and second row, and take that number. Don't succumb to pressure on the test. Just follow the procedure and work through the questions at your ideal speed.

Practice Questions

For each question, select the number that appears in the table at the given coordinates. Recall that the first number in the ordered pair gives the column number, and the second gives the row number. For instance, the ordered pair $(0, -2)$ refers to the number in column 0, row -2, which is 84 in the table below.

Use the table below to answer questions 1-5.

	-3	-2	-1	0	1	2	3
3	89	57	70	68	11	95	40
2	85	28	75	82	63	42	58
1	85	20	16	52	62	87	87
0	25	83	78	21	73	11	31
-1	30	72	73	51	91	30	70
-2	16	82	32	84	28	91	63
-3	74	19	96	38	49	17	25

1. $(-1, 1)$

a. 63
b. 84
c. 16
d. 51
e. 87

2. $(-2, 3)$

a. 57
b. 21
c. 25
d. 58
e. 51

3. $(3, -3)$

a. 58
b. 25
c. 89
d. 16
e. 21

4. $(-2, 2)$

a. 28
b. 96
c. 11
d. 72
e. 49

Table Reading

5. $(-1, -2)$

a. 17
b. 95
c. 32
d. 42
e. 25

Use the table below to answer questions 6-10.

	-3	-2	-1	0	1	2	3
3	94	49	12	84	91	92	33
2	23	79	99	97	33	51	22
1	50	92	16	12	74	86	53
0	59	11	55	72	86	29	65
-1	14	66	14	34	16	97	17
-2	27	37	82	52	18	39	43
-3	79	39	96	22	87	98	54

6. $(1, 1)$

a. 28
b. 16
c. 42
d. 73
e. 74

7. $(-2, 1)$

a. 49
b. 92
c. 28
d. 91
e. 57

8. $(0, 2)$

a. 30
b. 25
c. 20
d. 91
e. 97

9. $(3, -3)$

a. 54
b. 82
c. 87
d. 95
e. 20

10. $(-2, -1)$

a. 82
b. 63
c. 52
d. 72
e. 66

Practice Answers

1. C

2. A

3. B

4. A

5. C

6. E

7. B

8. E

9. A

10. E

Instrument Comprehension

What Are These Questions Testing?

These questions are designed to test your familiarity with and understanding of common instruments.

What Is the Question Format?

The question format will vary depending on the types of instruments that the test covers. This section of the book will focus on the compass and the attitude indicator, two instruments commonly used in airplanes.

Test questions related to these instruments will illustrate a compass and an attitude indicator inside an airplane cockpit. Based on the readings of both of these instruments, you will have to determine the position and orientation of the airplane.

How Do I Read the Compass and Attitude Indicator Instruments?

The compass, a relatively intuitive instrument with which many people are familiar, shows which direction a person or vehicle is facing. When a person is facing north, for example, the needle on the compass points toward the "N." If the person is facing a direction between south and southeast, the needle will point between "S" and "SE."

The attitude indicator is an instrument that shows how the nose and wings of a plane are tilted. For most people, the attitude indicator is less intuitive and less familiar than the compass. However, if you imagine yourself actually flying in a plane, the attitude indicator becomes easier to read and understand.

The attitude indicator has two components that illustrate how the nose of an airplane is tilted with respect to the ground: the miniature wings and the horizon bar. The miniature wings represent the actual wings of the aircraft, and the horizon bar represents the horizon, the imaginary line that divides the ground and the sky from the pilot's point of view. When the miniature wings are level with the horizon bar, the plane is level. When the miniature wings are above the horizon bar, the plane is tilted upward, and when the miniature wings are below the horizon bar, the plane is tilted downward. These categories of nose tilt are shown in the drawing below.

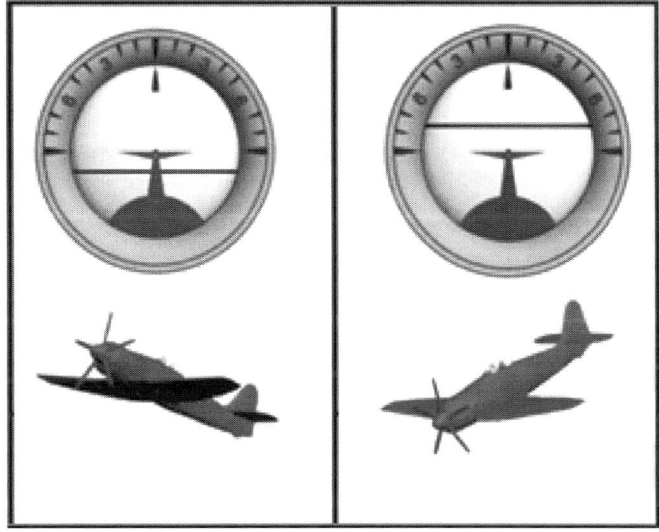

To illustrate how the wings are tilted from side to side, the attitude indicator instrument also has a dial with degree marks representing the bank angle. A needle on the dial indicates the exact bank angle, and the horizon bar is tilted accordingly, as shown in the picture below. If the left wing of the plane is tilted downward, the needle will be to the right of the center of the dial; if the right wing is tilted downward; the needle will be to the left of the center. Note that the tilted horizon bar reflects the pilot's point of view: if the left wing of the plane is tilted downward, the horizon will appear to be tilted in the opposite direction.

To answer the questions on this test, you will have to use information from both the compass and attitude indicator to determine how the plane is oriented. If the plane is flying north, it will appear to fly into the page in the illustrations.

For example, based on the compass and attitude indicator shown below, which of the answer choices represents the orientation of the plane?

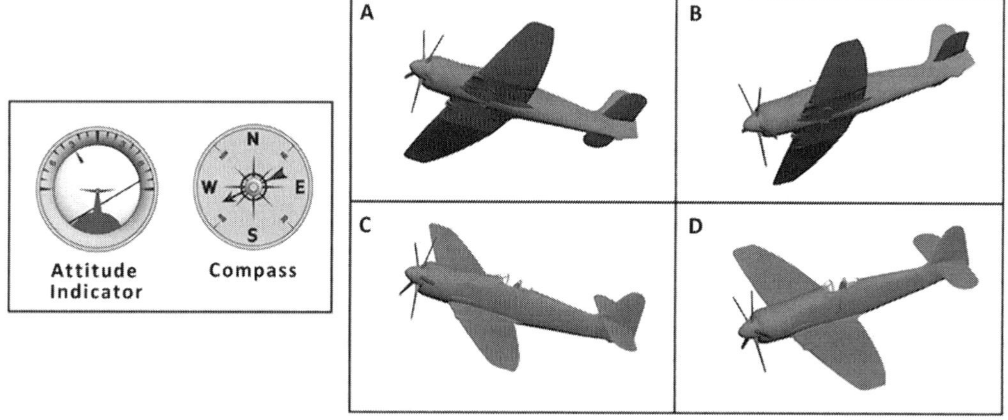

ANSWER: The answer is A. First, notice that the compass is pointing in a west-southwest direction. If a north-flying plane is facing into the page, then a westbound plane will be facing left. The compass indicates that the plane is flying somewhere between west and southwest, so the illustration will show a plane that appears to be facing left and just slightly out of the page.

Second, notice that the miniature wings in the attitude indicator are above the horizon line, and the needle on the dial is to the left of the center. From this information, you know that 1) the nose of the plane is tilted upward, and 2) the left wing of the plane is tilted upward, and the right wing is tilted downward. Because only the plane illustrated in choice A fits this description, it is the correct answer.

How Can I Improve My Ability to Read the Compass and Attitude Indicator?

Most people don't encounter these instruments on an everyday basis, so the best way to improve your ability to read them is simply to do the practice question in this section. However, although the attitude indicator is not commonly found outside of aircraft, you might want to practice using a real compass if you are still having trouble with these questions. You can find a reasonably-priced compass at most outdoor or sporting goods stores.

Practice Questions

1. Which of the answer choices represents the orientation of the plane?

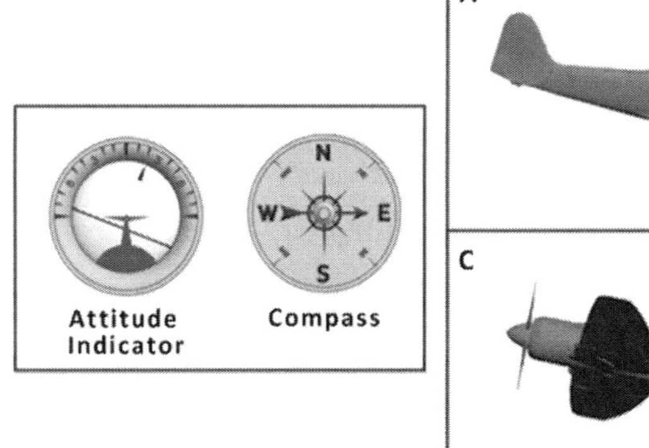

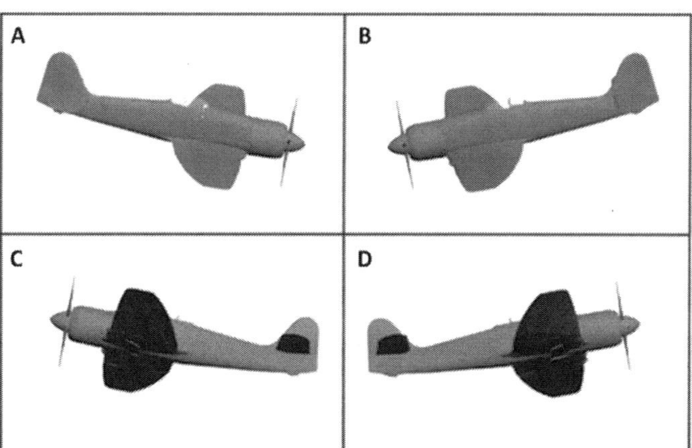

2. Which of the answer choices represents the orientation of the plane?

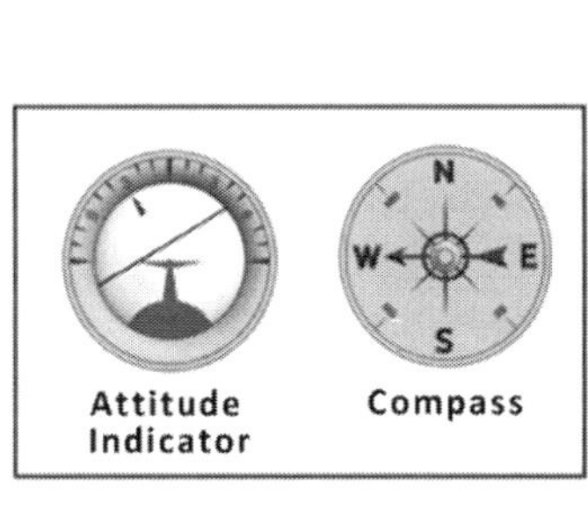

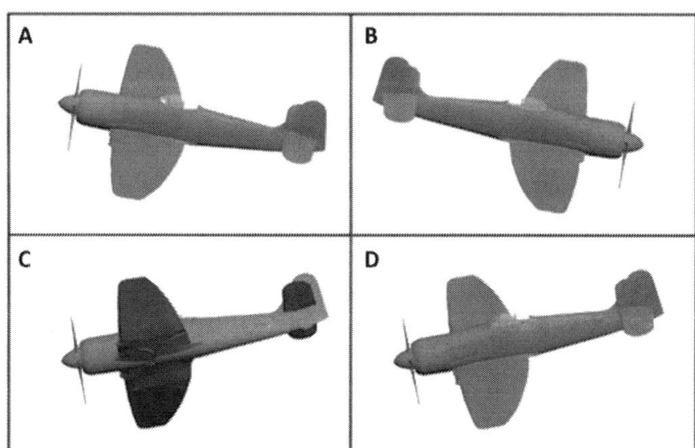

3. Which of the answer choices represents the orientation of the plane?

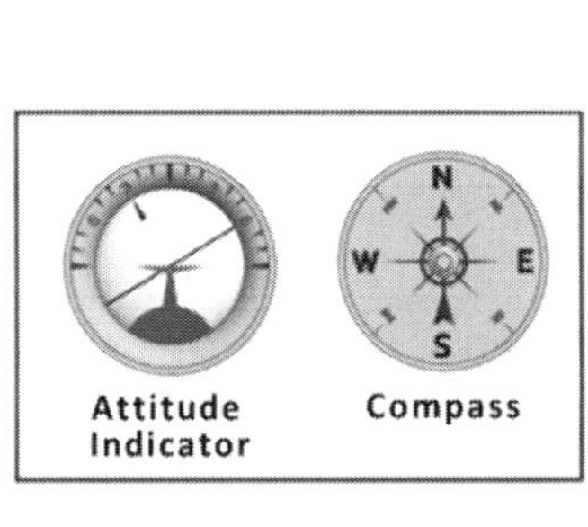

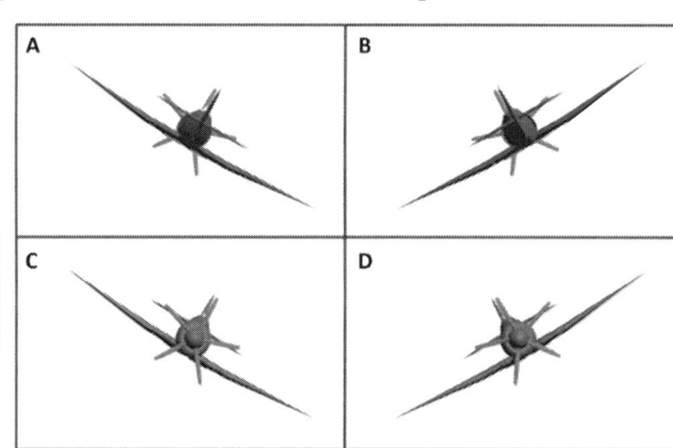

4. Which of the answer choices represents the orientation of the plane?

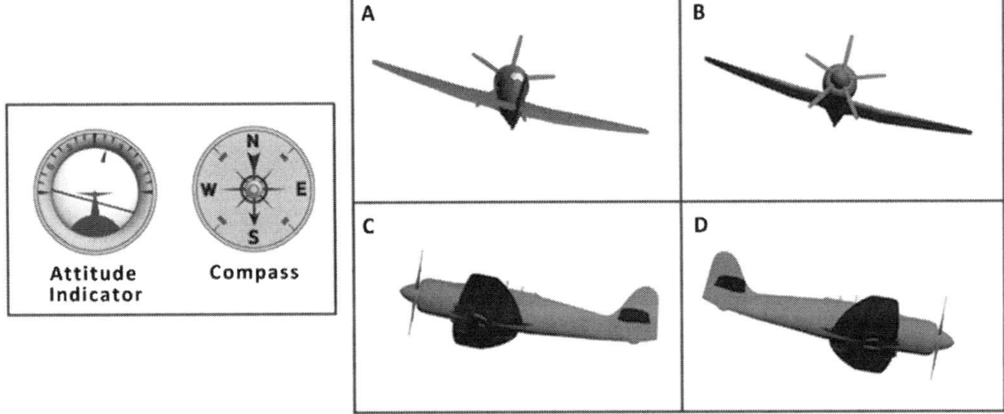

5. Which of the answer choices represents the orientation of the plane?

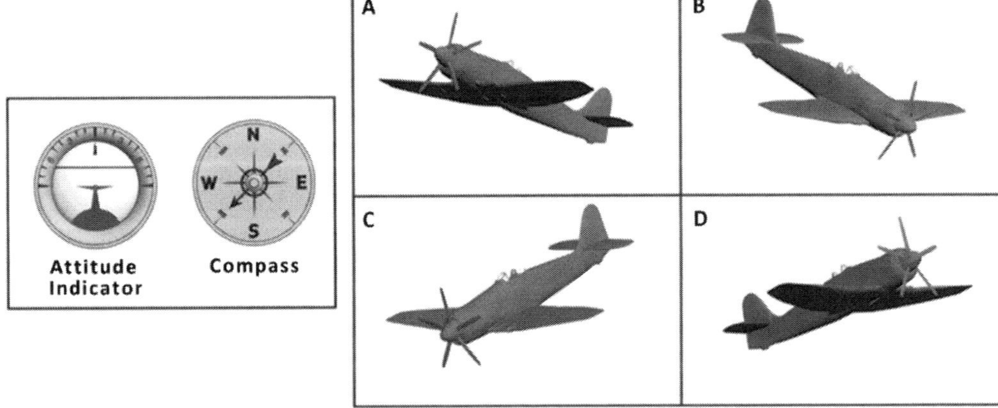

6. Which of the answer choices represents the orientation of the plane?

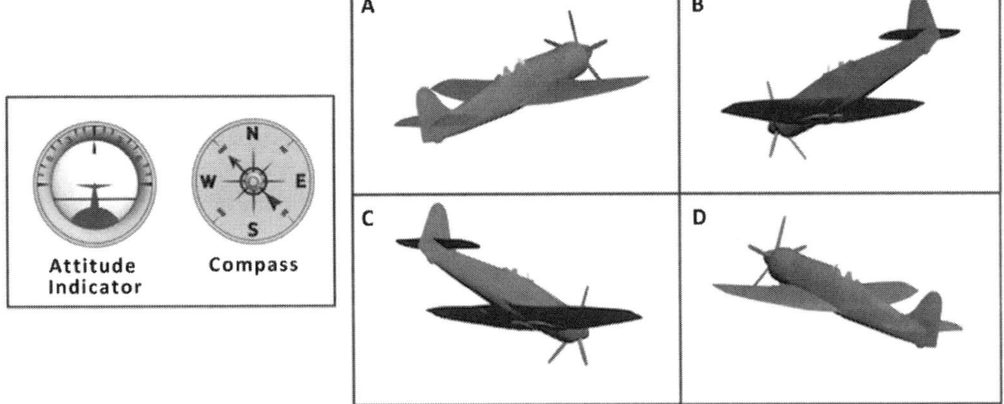

7. **Which of the answer choices represents the orientation of the plane?**

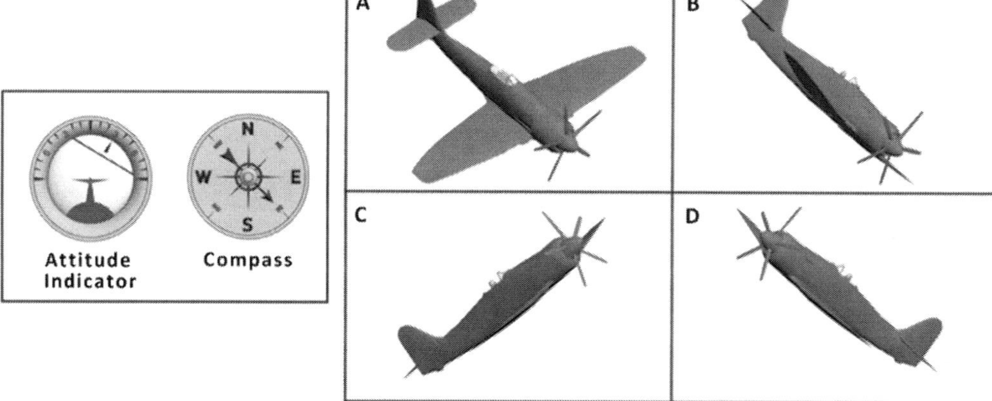

8. **Which of the answer choices represents the orientation of the plane?**

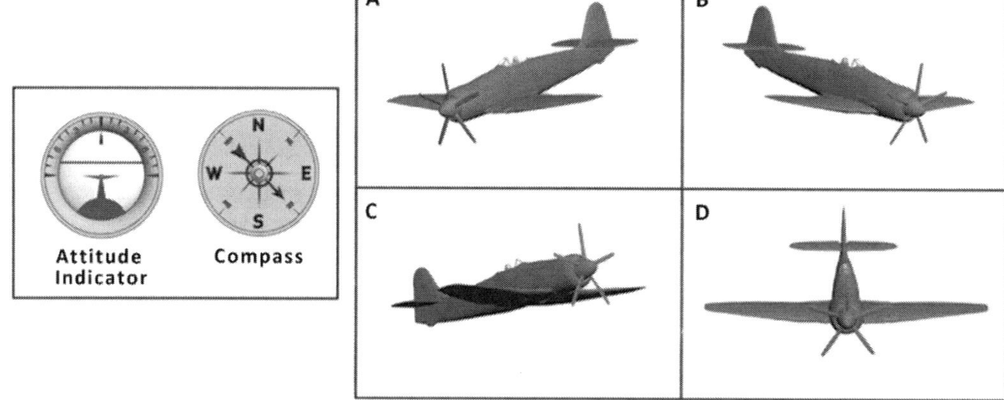

9. **Which of the answer choices represents the orientation of the plane?**

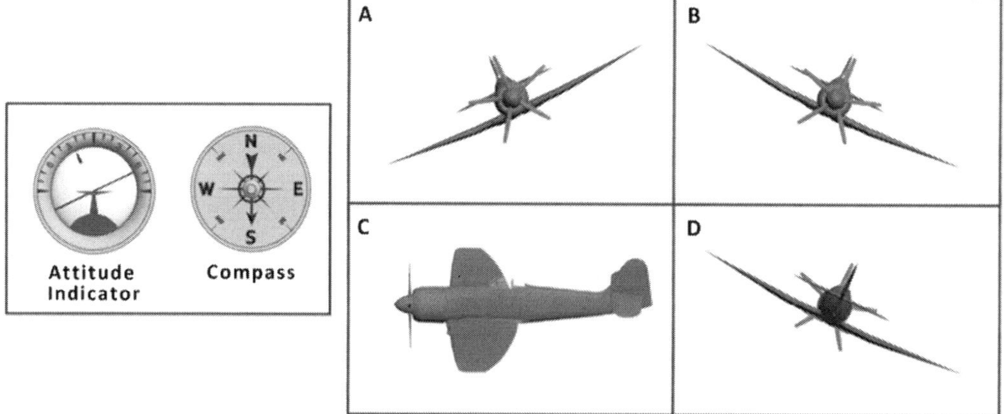

10. Which of the answer choices represents the orientation of the plane?

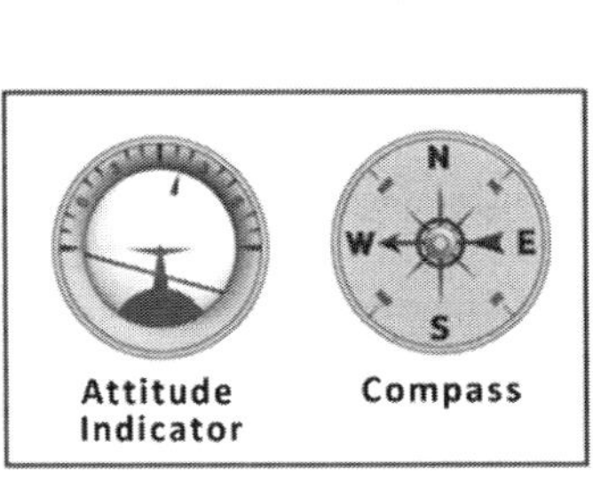

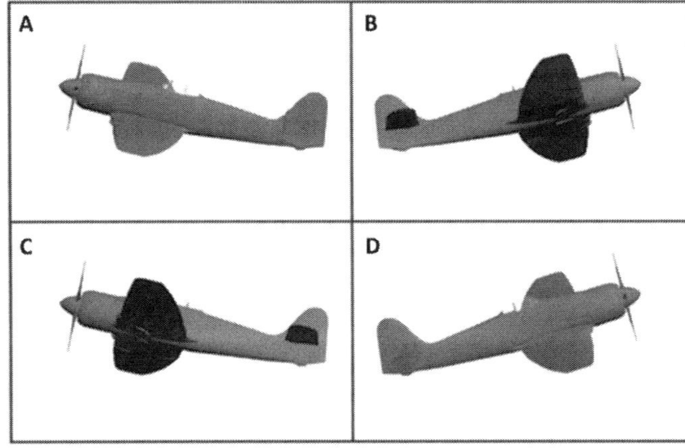

Practice Answers

1. D: The plane is flying east, which eliminates choices B and C. The attitude indicator indicates that the right wing of the plane is tilted upward. Only choice D meets this requirement.

2. C: The plane is facing west, which eliminates choice B. The attitude indicator indicates that the left wing of the plane is facing upward, so the answer is choice C.

3. A: The plane is facing north, which eliminates choices C and D. The attitude indicator indicates that the left wing is tilted upward, so the answer is choice A.

4. B: The answer is B because this is the only answer choice in which the plane is facing south.

5. C: The miniature wings indicate that the nose is tilted downward, which eliminates choices A and D. Of the two remaining choices, the answer must be C because the plane is flying southwest.

6. D: The attitude indicator indicates that the nose is tilted upward, which eliminates choices B and C. In addition, the compass is pointing northwest. Only choice D meets both requirements.

7. B: The compass shows that the plane is flying southeast, so you can eliminate choice D. In addition, the attitude indicator indicates that the nose of the plane is tilted downward, and the right wing of the plane is tilted upward. The only choice that meets both requirements is B.

8. B: The miniature wings in the attitude indicator are below the horizon bar, so the nose of the plane is tilted downward. As explained earlier, a plane that is traveling north is facing into the page. Therefore, a plane that is going southeast will have the orientation shown in choice B.

9. A: Because the compass is pointing south, the plane must appear to fly out of the page, so you can eliminate choices C and D. In addition, the attitude indicator indicates that the plane's left wing is tilted upward. Thus, A is the correct answer.

10. A: The compass indicates that the plane is flying west, which eliminates choices B and D. Also, the attitude indicator indicates that the right wing of the plane is tilted upward. Thus, A is the correct answer.

Block Counting

What Are These Questions Testing?

These questions are designed to test your spatial, geometric, and logical abilities.

What Is the Question Format?

The test will show a drawing of a three-dimensional arrangement of blocks with the same size and shape and ask you to identify how many other blocks a particular block is touching. Typically, the blocks are arranged in irregular shapes, and some of the blocks are hidden. You will have to use spatial intuition and reasoning to determine how many blocks are touching the block in question.

How Do I Know How Many Blocks Are Touching the Particular Block?

First, it is important to know which blocks qualify as "touching" the other block. If at least part of a face of one block touches at least part of a face of another block, those blocks are considered to touch each other. However, if a block shares only a corner or an edge with another block, the two blocks do not touch.

The example below illustrates the difference between touching and non-touching blocks. Block A is touching blocks 1, 2, and 3 because part of a face of block A is touching each of these blocks. However, blocks 4 and 5 do *not* touch block A because they only contact block A at an edge; that is, they share no area with any faces of block A. Therefore, block A is touching three blocks in this picture.

Sometimes, the blocks may be positioned so that certain blocks are hidden from view. In these cases, you will have to use basic spatial intuition and logic to determine the number of blocks touching a particular block.

In the example below, try to figure out how many blocks are touching block A.

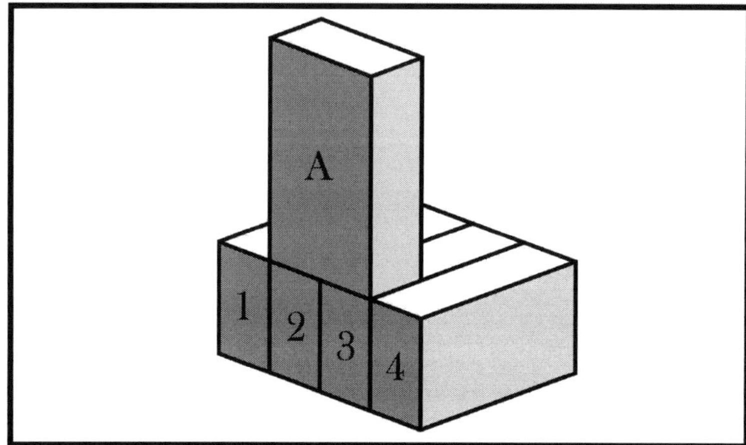

Answer: There are two blocks touching block A. Even though blocks 1 and 4 each share an edge with block A, they do not "touch" block A, as the word is used in the context of the test. Only blocks 2 and 3 actually touch a face of block A, so block A is only touching two blocks.

Are There Any Ways to Make It Easier to Count the Number of Touching Blocks?

Remember that for a block to count as "touching," it must contact a face of that block. Therefore, it might help to count the number of blocks that are touching each face of the block in question.

Try to apply this strategy to the example below, in order to count the number of blocks touching block A.

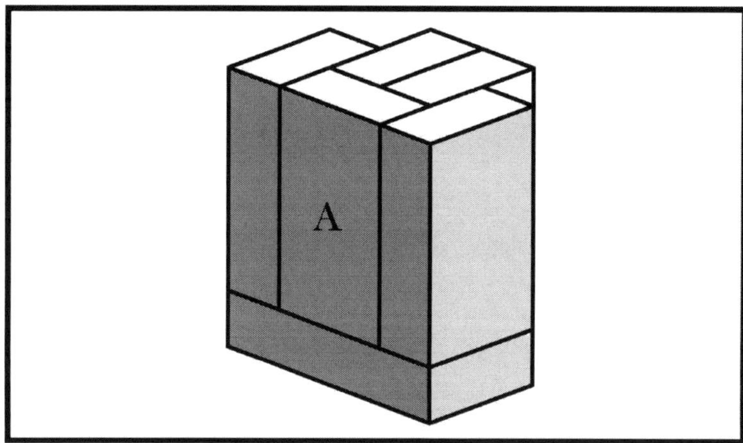

Answer: The back face of block A is touching two blocks. The left face of block A is touching one block, as is the right side. The bottom face is touching one block. Therefore, block A is touching a total of five blocks.

If you are still having trouble with the practice questions, it might help to try to re-create the example problems with a set of rectangular blocks. Practicing with physical blocks will make it easier to visualize hidden blocks when the blocks are drawn on paper.

Practice Questions

The explanations to these problems use terms like "top," "left," and "front" to refer to the faces of the blocks. Because this terminology can be confusing due to the angled view of the block arrangements, the illustration below is provided to help you keep these terms straight.

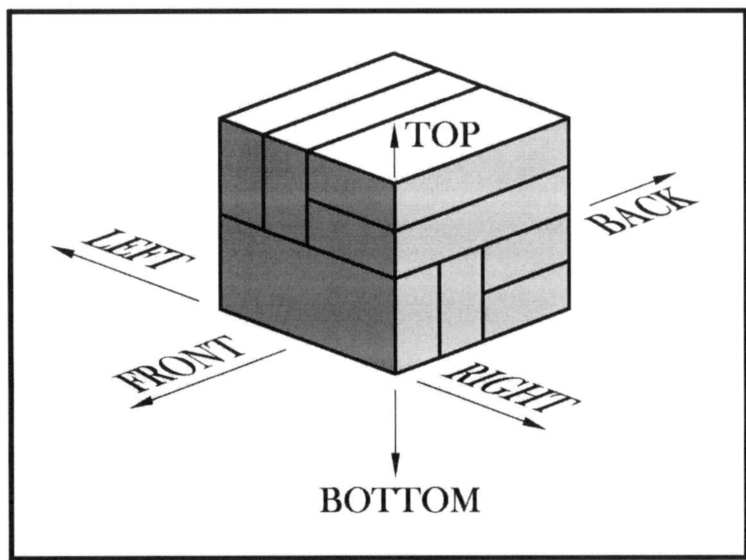

Once you understand these terms, proceed to the practice problems below.

1. How many blocks are touching block 1 in the arrangement below?

2. How many blocks are touching block 2 in the arrangement below?

3. How many blocks are touching block 8 in the arrangement below?

4. How many blocks are touching block 14 in the arrangement below?

5. How many blocks are touching block 18 in the arrangement below?

Practice Answers

1. There are a total of six blocks touching block 1. One block (block #4) is touching the top face of block 1, two blocks are touching the left face, and three blocks are touching the bottom face.

2. There are a total of seven blocks touching block 2. Two blocks are touching the left face of block 2, one block (block 4) is touching the right face, and four blocks are touching the bottom face.

Note that the picture only directly shows two blocks (block 5 and the block in front of it) touching the bottom face of block 2. However, you can deduce from the picture that block 3 and the block in front of it must also touch block 2. Because the width of each block is twice the thickness, the width of block 3 and the block next to it must extend underneath block 2. Therefore, block 2 touches both of these blocks, even if it isn't explicitly shown in the picture.

3. A total of eight blocks are touching block 8. One block is touching the left face, one block is touching the right face, three blocks are touching the bottom face, one block is touching the top face, and two blocks are touching the back face.

4. A total of five blocks are touching block 14. One block (block 11) is touching the left face, and four blocks are touching the top face.

5. A total of nine blocks are touching block 18. Four blocks, including blocks 19 and 17, are touching the front face of block 18, four blocks are touching the back face, and one block is touching the bottom face.

Aviation Information

What Are These Questions Testing?

The aviation information section tests your knowledge of basic aviation information. This includes a variety of things including aircraft terminology, the basic physics involved in flight, and common airport information.

How Can I Improve My Ability to Answer These Questions?

Since these are all knowledge-based questions, you can improve your success rate here by reading up on aircraft operation and airport information. The section below is an overview of the basics in these areas.

Fixed-Wing Aircraft

There are six basic components of a fixed-wing aircraft: wings, fuselage, tail assembly, landing gear, powerplant, and flight controls and control surfaces.

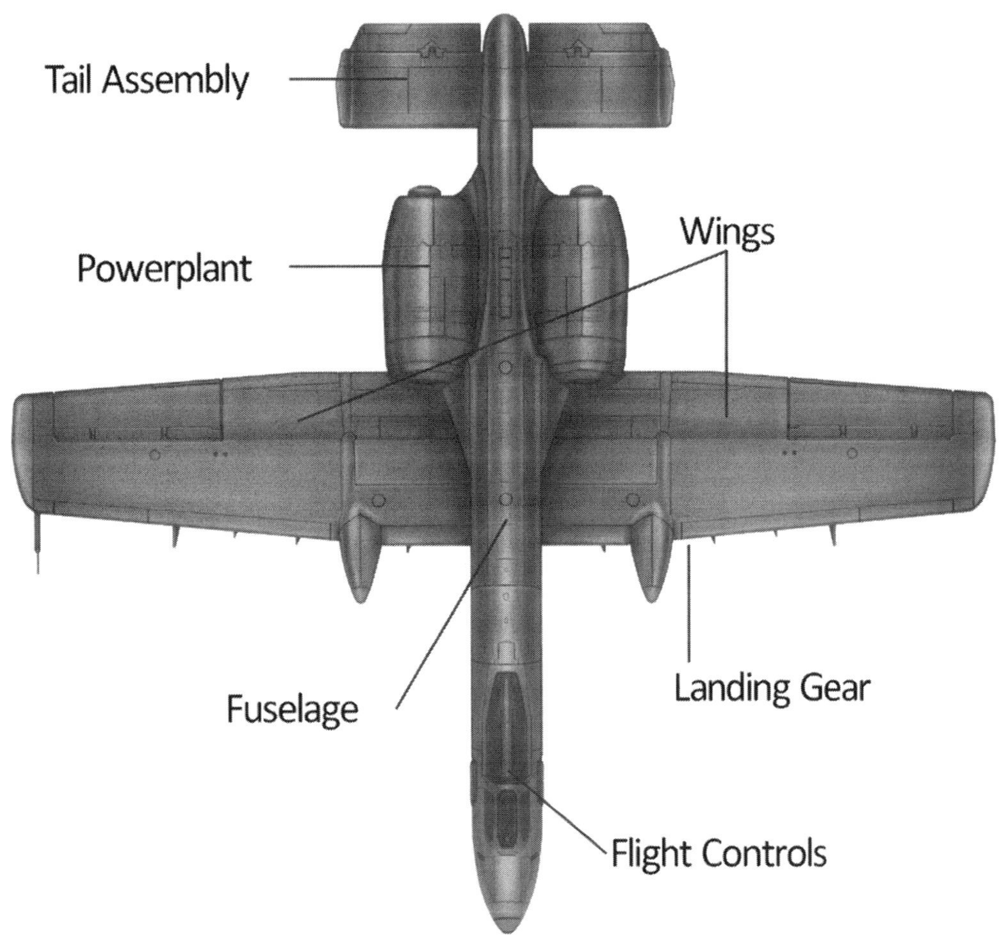

Wings

The **wings** are the primary airfoils of the plane. An airfoil is anything designed to produce lift when it moves through the air. The leading edge of an airfoil is thicker and rounder than the trailing edge, and the top surface of the airfoil has a greater curve than the bottom. The result is that air flows more quickly over the top of the wing, and the greater air pressure beneath pushes the wing, and thus the plane, upwards.

The wings connect to either side of the fuselage. Planes are designated as high-, mid-, and low-wing, depending on where the wings are attached. The wings themselves are described as either cantilever or semi-cantilever. A **cantilever wing** has sufficient internal support structures to keep it steady in its location. A **semi-cantilever wing**, on the other hand, requires additional external support structures. The trailing edge of a wing typically has two control surfaces attached by means of a hinge: **flaps** run from the fuselage to the middle of the wing, and **ailerons** run from the middle of the wing to the tip. By raising and lowering the ailerons, the pilot can roll the plane. The plane will roll when the ailerons are pointed in opposite directions. When the plane is cruising, however, these control surfaces are aligned with the rest of the wing. During takeoff and landing, both surfaces are extended, which increases the lift. This principle does not apply to aircraft that do not utilize flaps or ailerons for lift or control.

The distance from one wingtip to the other is the **wingspan**, and the distance from the leading edge to the trailing edge is called the **chord**. The chord line runs through the wing from leading edge to trailing edge: it divides the wing into upper and lower surfaces. The **mean camber** line runs along the inside of the wing, such that the parts of the wing above and below it are equal in thickness. The camber is the curvature of the airfoil: if an airfoil is heavily curved, it has a **high camber**. The thickness of a wing is measured at its greatest point. The shape of the wings when viewed from overhead is known as the **planform**.

When the wings are not attached parallel to the horizontal plane, the angle they make with the horizontal plane is called the **dihedral angle**. A positive dihedral wing angle (wings angling above the horizontal plane) keeps the plane stable when it rolls, as it will encourage the plane to return to its original position. This does diminish the maneuverability of the plane, which is why the wings of fighter jets are usually horizontal or even pointed slightly downwards (**anhedral**).

The shape of the wings has a major influence on the handling, maneuverability, and speed of the plane. Today's planes generally have a straight, sweep, or delta shape. **Straight wings** may be rectangular, elliptical (rounded), or tapered. They are commonly found on sailplanes, gliders, and other low-speed aircraft.

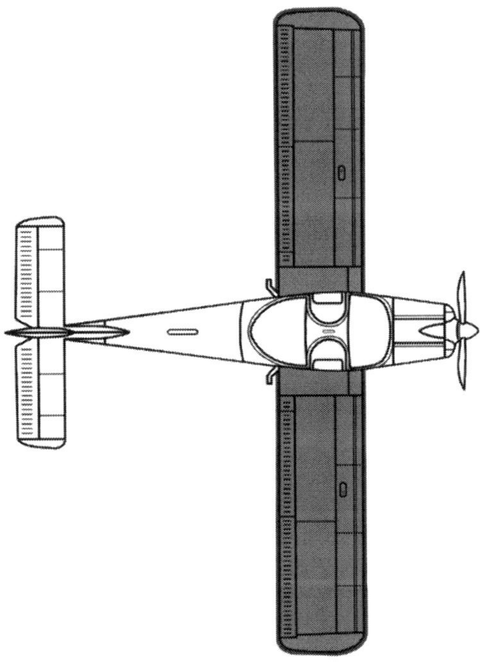

A **swept wing** can help provide better handling at high speeds, but makes the plane slightly less stable at low speeds. Since most modern aircraft are designed to operate at high speeds, this is the most commonly used wing style. Swept wings may also decrease drag and delay critical Mach. Wings may be swept forward or back, though forward-swept wings are rarely seen. In general, a higher angle of sweep is used for planes that are meant to travel faster and be more maneuverable; however, more extreme sweeps require much greater speeds for takeoff and landing.

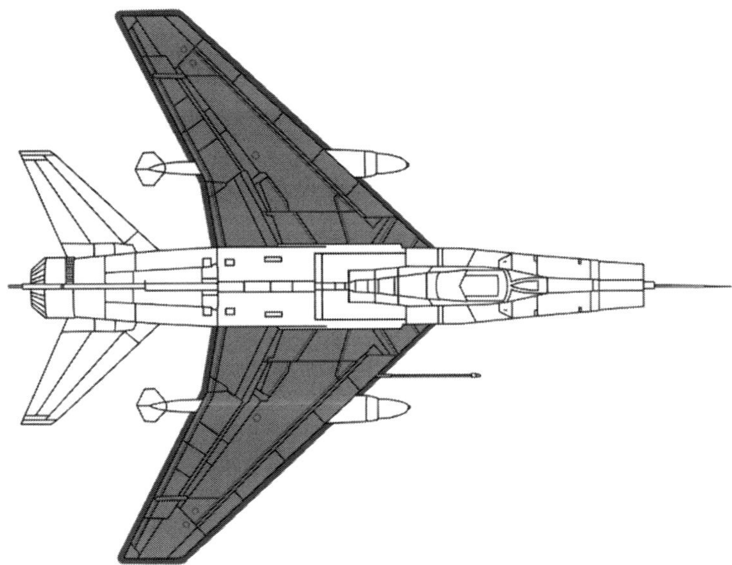

The **delta wing** shape is triangular, so that the leading edge of the wing has a high sweep angle while the trailing edge is mostly, if not completely, straight. A delta shape enables the plane to travel but also requires very high takeoff and landing speeds. Many of the earliest supersonic aircraft used the delta wing shape, as did the space shuttles.

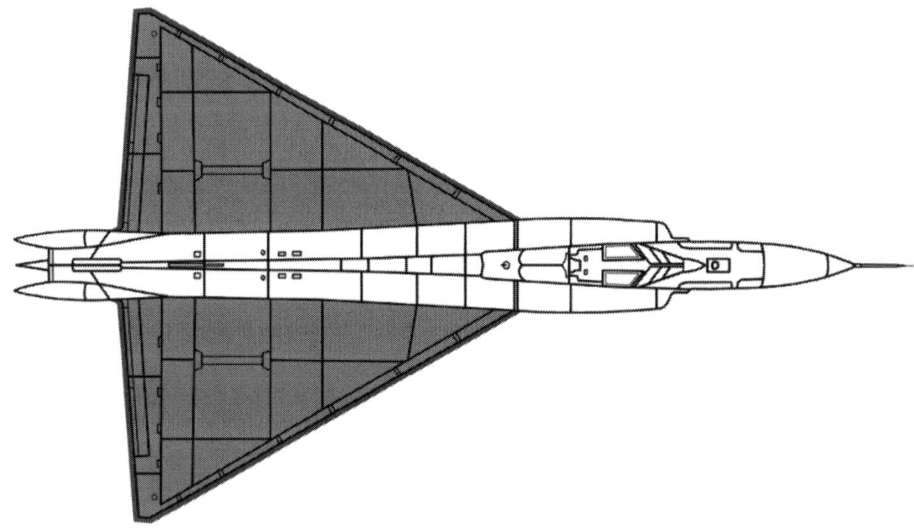

Fuselage

The **fuselage** is the main body of the airplane. The basic features of the fuselage are the cockpit, cabin, cargo area, and attachment points for external components, like the wings and landing gear. Some planes designed for specific purposes may not have all of these components; for instance, a fighter jet will not have a cabin for passengers or a cargo area, since it needs to be light and maneuverable. The fuselage may be described as either **truss** or **monocoque**, depending on whether its strength is created by triangular arrangements of steel or aluminum tubing or by bulkheads, stringers, and formers. A **stringer** is a support structure that runs the length of the fuselage, while a **former** runs perpendicular.

Tail Assembly

The **tail assembly**, or empennage, includes the vertical and horizontal stabilizers, elevators, rudders, and trim tabs. The **stabilizers** are fixed (non-adjustable) surfaces that extend from the back end of the fuselage. The **elevators** are positioned along the trailing edges of the horizontal stabilizers; the pilot can move them to raise or lower the nose of the plane. The **rudders** are connected to the trailing edge of the vertical stabilizer and are used to move the nose of the plane to the left or right, typically in combination with the ailerons. The **trim tabs** are movable surfaces that extend off the trailing edges of the rudder, elevators, and ailerons and are used to make smaller adjustments.

Landing Gear

The **landing gear** usually consists of three sets of wheels used for takeoffs and landings, though some planes have special non-wheel landing gear for landing on snow or water. Landing gear is commonly retractable, meaning that it is pulled up inside the plane during flight to reduce drag. In a typical arrangement, wheel sets are positioned either under each wing or on the sides of the fuselage, with the third wheel set being under the nose or the tail. The most common arrangement on modern aircraft is the **tricycle** arrangement, which has the third wheel set under the nose, but having the third wheel set under the tail is still known as the **conventional** arrangement. Whether located under the tail or the nose, the third wheel will typically be able to rotate so that the plane can turn while traveling on the ground. The addition of extra wheels to each set allows the plane to handle a greater weight.

Powerplant

In aviation, the **powerplant** is the part of the plane that supplies the thrust. A jet engine operates by compressing the air that comes in the front, burning it along with fuel, and then blasting it out the back. There are different methods for compressing the air, but most jet engines do so by slowing it down with a set of small rotating blades. This greatly increases the air pressure at the front of the engine. The compressed air is then forced into a different section, where it is mixed with fuel and burned. As it then expands, it is pushed at great force through a series of turbines, the turning of which moves the compressor blades at the front of the engine, supplying both power and air. The exhausted air then passes out the back of the engine, which propels the plane forward. Some jet engines have afterburners, which feed extra fuel into the area between the turbines and the rear exhaust, increasing forward thrust.

In a propeller plane, on the other hand, the powerplant is the propellers and the engine. The propellers have tilted blades, which push air backwards and thereby push the plane forward. There are two types of propeller: fixed-pitch or variable-pitch. The blade angle of a **fixed-pitch propeller** cannot be adjusted by the pilot. **Variable-pitch propellers** allow the pilot, usually indirectly via the plane's control systems, to adjust the pitch of the propeller blades to alter the amount of thrust being generated. Some variable-pitch propellers are designed to operate only at a single rotational speed, allowing the engine to be much simpler and more efficient, so the amount of thrust is controlled entirely by the pitch of the blades. These are known as **constant-speed propellers**.

The engines of a propeller plane turn the **crankshafts**, which turn the propellers. The engines also are responsible for powering the plane's electrical system. The location of the engines on a propeller plane may vary. Single-engine planes typically have their engines in front of the fuselage, while multi-engine planes usually have their engines underneath the wings. Some multi-engine planes have engines in both locations.

Flight Envelope

During flight, there are four forces a pilot must manage: lift, weight, thrust, and drag. These forces act downward (weight), upward (lift), forward (thrust), and backward (drag). These forces are fundamental for understanding both how flight works and the range of permissible flight conditions aircraft can tolerate. A **flight envelope** is a graphical representation that helps pilots and aircraft designers operate and calculate the limits of an aircraft within various flight parameters to ensure safe and efficient flight.

Weight

The **weight** of a plane is the primary force that must be overcome for flight to take place. The force of gravity on a given object is the same, regardless of orientation, though it varies slightly with large changes in altitude.

Aviation experts distinguish between different types of weight. The basic weight includes the aircraft and any internal or external equipment that will remain a part of the plane during flight. The **operating weight** is the basic weight plus the crew and any other nonexpendable items not included in the basic weight. The **gross weight** is the total weight of the aircraft and all contents at any given time. The weight of the airplane when it has no usable fuel is called the **zero-fuel weight**.

Lift

In order to overcome gravity, the plane must generate **lift**. Lift is the upward force of air pressure on the aircraft, primarily the wings, that allows it to achieve and maintain altitude. In order to generate lift, the plane typically must be traveling forward at considerable speed.

If the wing tilts too far back the airflow may stop over the wing's upper surface, which will result in a rapid loss of altitude and often control of the plane. This is known as a stall, and it may be avoided by decreasing the angle of attack, so that normal airflow over the top of the wing is not interrupted.

Thrust

The speed required for generating lift is provided by the aircraft's **thrust**. It ensures that the aircraft is able to continue moving forward at sufficient speed to generate lift. As was discussed in the previous section, thrust is generated by the powerplant of the aircraft, usually one or more jet engines or propellers.

Drag

An aircraft's thrust is countered by **drag**, the resistance to forward movement provided by the air that the aircraft is traveling through. At anything above normal walking or running speeds, air resistance is a noticeable hindrance to motion, and it only increases as airspeed goes up. The primary implication that this has on aircraft is that the faster the aircraft goes, the more thrust is required just to overcome the drag and maintain a constant speed.

Drag is usually categorized in two basic ways: parasite drag and induced drag. **Parasite drag** is the combined value of several types of drag like form, skin friction, and interference which are all non-lift producing components. **Induced drag**, on the other hand, is drag that results from the wings generating lift. Part of the process of generating lift involves the wings redirecting the oncoming air downward (think Newton's third law), and this causes additional drag.

Atmospheric Conditions

The flight envelope is significantly affected by the atmospheric conditions, primarily the density of the surrounding air and the speed and direction of any wind. The density is in turn determined by the temperature, pressure, and humidity of the air. Lower temperatures, higher pressures, and lower humidity are all associated with higher density air. Denser air will produce greater lift, but will also produce more drag. Air pressure is most closely associated with altitude. In general, pressure decreases with altitude, so as you go higher up, the pressure of the surrounding air decreases.

With regard to wind, flying into the wind (**headwind**) has a similar type of impact to flying in denser air, though of much greater magnitude. In a headwind, the aircraft will have a higher speed relative to the surrounding air, which means it will experience greater drag and lift forces. Similarly, if the aircraft is flying the same direction as the wind (**tailwind**), it will have a lower speed relative to the surrounding air, and will experience reduced drag and lift.

Flight Concepts and Terminology

Flight Attitude

The flight attitude is described in terms of three axes, all of which meet at the plane's center of mass.

The **longitudinal** axis is the axis that extends from the center forward toward the nose and rearward toward the tail. The **lateral** axis extends from the center out to the right and left, perpendicular to the longitudinal axis. Typically, the lateral axis passes through (over/under) the wings. Both of these axes are in the horizontal plane when the aircraft is level. The **vertical** axis meanwhile extends straight upward and downward from the aircraft's center, perpendicular to the horizontal plane of the other two axes. The motion of the aircraft can be described in relation to these axes: Rotation about the longitudinal axis is called **roll**; rotation about the lateral axis is called **pitch**; rotation about the vertical axis is called **yaw**. In turn, these three types of motion are controlled by three sets of flight control surfaces. Roll is controlled by the ailerons, pitch by the elevators, and yaw by the rudder. This information is summarized in the table below, and is expanded upon in the following section.

Axis	Motion	Control surface
Longitudinal	Roll	Ailerons
Lateral	Pitch	Elevators
Vertical	Yaw	Rudder

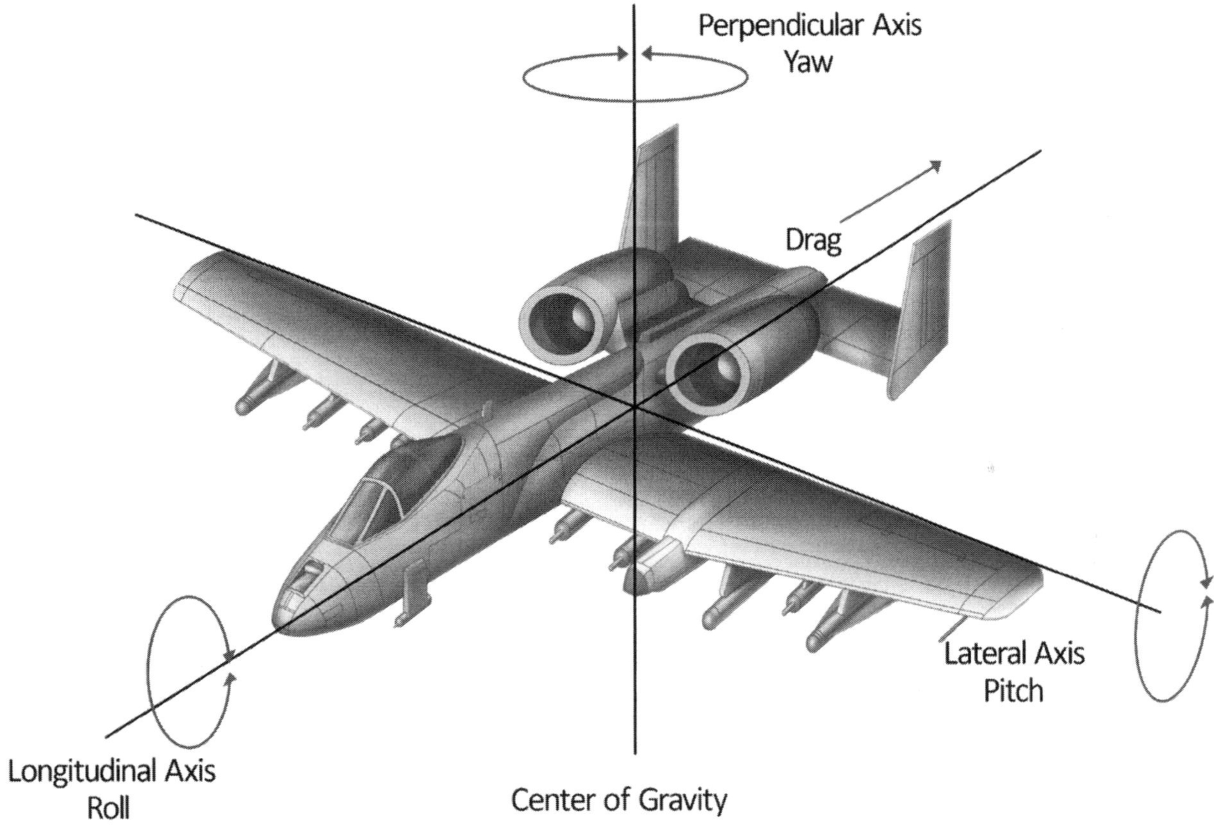

Flight Controls

Flight controls are divided into primary and secondary groups.

Primary

The **primary flight control surfaces** are the ailerons, rudder, and elevator.

The **ailerons** are responsible for the roll, or movement around the longitudinal axis. The ailerons extend from the trailing edges of the wings as shown in the figure below. They can be manipulated by the pilot to cause the wing to either dip below or elevate above the horizontal plane.

The joystick, also known as the yoke (or control wheel), controls the roll of the aircraft. By pushing the stick (or turning the wheel) to the left, the pilot raises the left aileron and lowers the right aileron, causing the left wing to dip and the right wing to elevate.

The **elevators** control the plane's pitch, or movement around the lateral axis. They are attached to the trailing edges of the horizontal stabilizers at the rear of the aircraft. Depending on the design of the plane, there may be one elevator that extends across the length of the horizontal stabilizer, or there may be two elevators, divided by the vertical stabilizer, as shown in the figure below. Some aircraft may have a combined control surface that acts as both an elevator and a stabilizer known as a stabilator. It moves as a single unit to control pitch and maintain stability.

The joystick also controls the pitch of the aircraft. By pulling the stick back, the pilot raises the elevators, causing the tail of the plane to experience downward force, thus raising the nose of the plane. Pushing the stick forward will have the opposite effect on the elevators and will result in the nose of the plane dropping as the tail is pushed upward.

The **rudder** is a large flap attached by a hinge to the vertical stabilizer. It controls the motion of the plane around its vertical axis. The rudder can swing to the right or the left, causing the plane to turn (yaw) in either direction.

The rudder is controlled with two pedals: when the pilot pushes on the right pedal, the rudder swings out to the right, causing leftward pressure on the tail of the aircraft. This results in the nose of the plane turning to the right. Similarly, if the pilot pushes on the left pedal, the rudder will swing to the left, causing the tail to move right, and the nose to turn left.

The pilot also controls the amount of power or thrust being produced by the engines by manipulating the **throttle**. It is considered a primary flight control because the pilot must manage the thrust to ensure that the plane will be able to accomplish its intended maneuvers. With all three of the primary control surfaces, it is important to remember that the speed of the aircraft relative to the surrounding air determines the magnitude of the aircraft's response to the control. A plane that is traveling at 300 mph will roll much more quickly than one that is traveling at 200 mph in response to the same amount of aileron manipulation. The same is true of the other two types of motion.

Flight maneuvers usually involve the use of multiple controls. To make a proper turn, for instance, the pilot will need to employ the rudder, ailerons, and elevators. The bank is established by raising and lowering the ailerons, and the rudder pedals counteract any adverse yaw that occurs. Adverse yaw is the drifting of the nose caused by the extra drag on the downward-pointing aileron. Also, because extra lift is needed during a turn, the pilot must increase the angle of attack by applying downward elevator pressure. The amount of back elevator pressure required will be in proportion to the sharpness of the turn. This will be discussed in greater detail in the section on flight maneuvers.

SECONDARY

The **secondary flight control surfaces** include the flaps and leading-edge devices, spoilers, and trim systems.

The **flaps** are connected to the trailing edges of the wings; they are raised or lowered to adjust the lift or drag. The retractable flaps on modern airplanes make it possible to cruise at a high speed and land at a low speed. On the opposite end of the wing, **leading-edge devices** accomplish much the same purpose, they can increase camber, lift, or airflow, depending on the device. Both flaps and leading-edge devices reduce stall speed. There are a number of different leading-edge devices: fixed slats, moveable slats, and leading-edge flaps.

Spoilers are attached to the wings of some airplanes in order to diminish the lift and increase the drag. Spoilers can also be useful for roll control, in part because they reduce adverse yaw. This is accomplished by raising the spoiler on the side of the turn. This reduces the lift and creates more drag on that side, which causes that wing to drop and the plane to bank and yaw to that side. If both of the spoilers are raised at the same time, the plane can descend without increasing its speed. Raising the spoilers also improves the performance of the brakes, because they eliminate lift and push the plane down onto its wheels.

Trim systems exist mainly to ease the work of the pilot. They are attached to the trailing edges of one or more of the primary control surfaces. Small aircraft often have a single trim tab attached to the elevator. This tab is adjusted with a small wheel or crank, and its position is displayed in the cockpit. When the tab is deflected upwards, the trailing edge of the elevator is forced downward and the tail is pushed up, which lowers the nose of the plane.

Typically, a pilot first will achieve the desired pitch, power, attitude, and configuration, and then use the trim tabs to resolve the remaining control pressures. There are control pressures generated by any change in the flight condition, so trimming is necessary after any change. Trimming is complete when the pilot has eliminated any heaviness in the nose or tail of the plane.

Flight Maneuvers

The four basic maneuvers in flight are straight-and-level flight, turning, climbing, and descending. As the name suggests, **straight-and-level flight** involves keeping the aircraft headed in a particular direction at a particular altitude. Maintaining straight-and-level flight requires frequent adjustment, much the same way as the driver of a car has to make frequent adjustments to maintain a straight path on a windy day or when driving on a rough uneven road.

Making a smooth **turn** requires the use of all four primary controls: the throttle is set to achieve a speed suitable to the desired type of turn, the ailerons bank the wings and the elevators raise the nose to establish the rate of turn, and the rudder is employed to counter any undesired yaw resulting from the effects of the other controls or to introduce desired yaw.

There are three classes of turn: shallow, medium, and deep. A **shallow turn** has a bank of less than 20 degrees. At angles this shallow, most planes will tend to try to stabilize themselves back to a level angle, so the pilot must maintain some pressure on the stick to ensure that the plane doesn't pull out of the bank prematurely. A **medium turn** has a bank of roughly 20 to 45 degrees. Most planes will tend to stay in a medium bank until the pilot makes an adjustment. Finally, a **steep turn** is one in which the bank is greater than 45 degrees. For angles this steep, most planes will tend to try to increase the banking angle even further unless the pilot counters that tendency by maintaining some pressure on the stick in a stabilizing direction.

While the pilot is getting the plane to the desired bank angle, he will also be pulling back on the stick to ensure that the nose of the plane does not dip during the bank. This also serves to increase the rate at which the plane turns its heading. In general, the steeper the bank, the more sharply the pilot must pull back on the stick to maintain altitude. Because the lowered aileron on the raised wing generally creates more drag than the raised aileron on the lowered wing, the airplane tends to yaw in the direction opposite to the turn. For this reason, the pilot must at the same time apply rudder pressure in the direction of the turn.

To initiate a **climb**, an aircraft's nose is angled upward so that it gains altitude. Several things that remain constant while the aircraft is flying level change when the nose of the plane is raised. The two most significant are the effective angle of gravity and the angle of attack of the wings.

When the aircraft is level, gravity acts entirely in the direction of the vertical axis of the plane. When the plane angles upward, the force of gravity, which still acts straight down like before, now has a component in the longitudinal direction, since the rear of the plane is now pointed slightly toward the ground. Additionally, since raising the noise of the aircraft increases the angle of attack of the wings, the amount of drag the aircraft experiences goes up considerably during a climb. This means that, in order to maintain flight, the thrust must now overcome both an increased amount of drag and part of the force of gravity.

If the nose of the aircraft is raised too quickly or without a sufficient increase in thrust to account for the changing flight conditions, the aircraft may **stall**. The most common cause of a stall is when an aircraft exceeds its critical angle of attack and there is not enough airflow over the airfoil to create sufficient lift to generate continuous flight. To correct a stall, the pilot must angle the nose of the aircraft steeply downward and increase the throttle to generate enough airspeed in the forward direction so that the control surfaces are effective in controlling the flight of the plane again, and pull out of the dive. As should be apparent from this description, recovering from a stall involves significant loss of altitude, which makes stalling at low altitudes extremely dangerous.

There are a few different styles of controlled **descent**, but they all involve manipulation of the same two factors: pitch and thrust. By angling the nose of the plane downward, the pilot reduces the angle of attack of the wings and consequently reduces the amount of lift generated by the wings. This causes the plane to lose altitude. Similarly, by pulling back on the throttle, the pilot reduces the amount of thrust being generated, which in turn reduces the plane's air speed and the amount of lift generated by the wings, also resulting in a loss of altitude.

A **glide** is a controlled descent in which little or no engine power is used, and the plane drifts downward at a regular pace. The pilot manages a glide by balancing the forces of lift and gravity as they act on the plane.

When a pilot is executing a **landing**, the nose of the plane will actually be angled upward, but the throttle will be pulled far back to ensure that the plane continues its descent all the way to the ground.

Helicopters

In many ways, the operation of a helicopter is based on the same fundamentals as airplane flight. A helicopter is subject to the same four fundamental forces of lift, weight, thrust, and drag. Unlike an airplane, however, a helicopter applies most of its thrust vertically. When a helicopter flies at a constant speed in a stable horizontal path, the lift is equal to the weight and the forward thrust is equal to the drag. The helicopter will increase its horizontal speed if the thrust is greater than the drag, and will increase its altitude if the lift is greater than the weight. If the helicopter is hovering (i.e., not moving at all), there is no drag or forward thrust; only gravity and vertical thrust or lift, which are balanced.

The manner in which a helicopter generates lift is considerably different from that of an airplane. Whereas a plane derives its lift from the natural flow of air over the wing, the helicopter spins its "wing" rapidly and at a variable angle, giving it a variety of options for angles of attack. Because the main rotor of the helicopter is being torqued with such great force, it exerts the same amount of torque back on the fuselage of the helicopter but in the opposite direction (Newton's third law again). This necessitates a tail rotor to provide the force required to the keep the fuselage from spinning around while in flight. This function of the tail rotor is called **torque control**. Manipulation of the tail rotor is also used to change the heading of the helicopter.

Helicopter Controls

Piloting a helicopter requires the use of three controls: the cyclic (stick), the collective, and the directional control system. The **cyclic** controls the longitudinal and lateral movement of the helicopter by adjusting the tilt of the main rotor. Moving the stick forward tilts the rotor forward, which in turn pushes the helicopter forward.

The **collective** is a tube running up from the cockpit floor to the left of the pilot. It has a handle that may be raised or lowered to affect the pitch, as well as a throttle that wraps around the handle and can be used to alter the engine torque. The collective controls the angle of the main rotor blades. If the handle is pulled up, the leading edge of the rotor blade lifts relative to the trailing edge.

The **directional control system** is a pair of pedals the pilot uses to alter the pitch of the tail rotor blades. Pressing one or the other of the pedals will cause the tail rotor to exert more or less force on the fuselage, which will in turn affect the heading of the helicopter.

A helicopter pilot must use all three of the controls at the same time. The cyclic and collective adjust the action of the main rotor, which must be compensated for with adjustment to the tail rotor. For instance, if the speed of the main rotor increases during a climb, the pilot will need to increase the amount of force generated by the tail rotor to ensure the fuselage does not begin to rotate.

If the helicopter loses engine power for some reason, the pilot will need to rely on **autorotation**, or the spinning of the rotors that is generated by airflow rather than the engine. The amount of torque on the fuselage will be smaller during autorotation, but it will still be enough to require the use of the tail rotor.

Unique Forces

A helicopter generates some other forces that distinguish it from an airplane. **Translational lift** is extra lift a helicopter experiences when traveling in a forward direction.

The **Coriolis force** is another physical phenomenon related to helicopters. The Coriolis force is the increase in rotational speed that occurs when the weight of a spinning object moves closer to the rotation center. In the case of a helicopter, having a greater portion of the weight closer to the base of the blade will cause the rotor to move faster, or to require less power to move at the same rotational speed.

If the main rotor increases the flow of air over the rear part of the main rotor disc, then the rear part will have a smaller angle of attack. The result of this will be less lift in the rear part of the rotor disc. This is called the **transverse flow effect**. However, when a force is applied to a spinning disc, the effects will occur ninety degrees later. This phenomenon is known as **gyroscopic precession**.

Airport Information

At an **airport**, the areas controlled by the aircraft traffic controller are called the **movement areas** (or maneuvering areas). These include the runways and taxiways. **Runways** may be composed of all different materials, ranging from grass and dirt to asphalt and concrete. At a general aviation airport, the runways may be as little as 800 feet long and 26 feet wide, while an international airport may have runways that are 18,000 feet long and 260 feet across. The markings on a runway are white and usually outlined in black so that they may be better seen. **Taxiways** and areas not meant to be traveled by aircraft are marked in yellow.

There are three basic types of runways: visual, nonprecision instrument, and precision instrument. **Visual runways** are typical of small airports: they have no markings, though the boundaries and center lines may be indicated in some way. They are called visual runways because the pilot must be able to see the ground in order to land. It is not possible to land a plane on a visual runway with only the use of instruments.

With a **nonprecision instrument runway**, a pilot may be able to make his approach using instruments. Specifically, this sort of runway can provide feedback on the horizontal position of the plane as it nears. Nonprecision instrument runways are commonly found at small and medium airports. These runways may have threshold markings, centerlines, and designators. These runways may also have a special mark, called an aiming point, between 1000 and 1500 feet long along the centerline of the runway.

Medium and large airports will have **precision instrument runways**, which give the pilot feedback on both horizontal and vertical position when the plane is on instrument approach. A precision instrument runway includes thresholds, designators, centerlines, aiming points, blast pads, stopways, and touchdown zone marks every 500 feet from the 500-foot to the 3000-foot mark.

Runways are named according to their **direction** on the compass, ranging from 01 to 36. So, for instance, due south would be runway 18 ("one-eight"), and due west would be runway 27 ("two-seven"). In North America, the runways are named in accordance with magnetic north, rather than geographic (grid) north. Of course, a runway may have two names, one for each direction in which it is used. The same runway may be referred to as runway 05 ("zero-five") or runway 23 ("two-three") depending on the direction it is being used on a given day. In most cases, fixed-wing aircraft take off and land against the wind, because the extra amount of air over the wing will increase lift (and reduce the required ground speed).

In the event that **multiple runways** travel in the same direction, they will be distinguished from each other by their relative positions according to an observer on approach from the appropriate direction: left or right runway if there are only two; left, right, or center runway if there are three. Of course, a runway that is on the right when travelling in one direction will be on the left when it is being used in the opposite direction.

In most cases, **runway lights** are operated by the airport control tower. There are a number of different components to a runway lighting system. A Runway Centerline Lighting System is a line of white lights mounted every fifty feet along the centerline. When the approaching plane gets within 3000 feet of the runway, the lights begin to blink red and white; when the plane gets within 1000 feet, the lights become solid red. Precision instrument runways have runway end lights and edge lights. Runway end lights run the width of both ends of the runway: from the ground these lights appear red, while they appear green from above. Runway edge lights run the length of the runway on both sides. This lighting typically changes color as well when the plane gets within a certain distance of the front end of the runway. There are similar lights marking the boundaries of taxiways. An Approach Lighting System is a set of strobe lights and/or lightbars that indicate the end of the runway from which descending aircraft should arrive. Runway end identification lights are synchronized lights that flash at the runway thresholds. At some airports these lights face in every direction, while at others they only face the direction from which planes approach. Runway end identification lights are useful when the runway doesn't stand out from the surrounding area, or when visibility is poor.

Some big airports also have **Visual Approach Slope Indicators**, which give the incoming pilot useful information. In a typical VASI system, white lights indicate the lower glide path limits, and red lights indicate the upper. The VASI should be visible for twenty miles at night and for three to five miles during the day under normal conditions. An effective VASI should keep the plane clear of obstructions so long as it remains within approximately ten degrees of the extended runway centerline and within four nautical miles of the runway threshold.

Practice Questions

1. What would be the name of a runway that the pilot approaches while heading due east?

a. Runway 1
b. Runway 9
c. Runway 27
d. Runway E
e. Runway B

2. Which part of a fixed-wing airplane supplies the thrust?

a. Tail assembly
b. Control surfaces
c. Fuselage
d. Landing gear
e. Powerplant

3. What is the path of the chord line on a wing?

a. From leading edge to trailing edge, through the wing
b. From leading edge to trailing edge, along the surface of the wing
c. Along the inside of the wing, such that the upper and lower wings are equal in thickness
d. From one wingtip to the other
e. From wingtip to fuselage

4. Which of the following statements about a medium bank is true?

a. A plane will tend to level out from a medium bank unless there is input from the pilot.
b. A plane that is put into a medium bank will tend to increase its bank unless the ailerons are applied.
c. A medium bank is between ten and thirty degrees.
d. A medium bank is between thirty and fifty degrees.
e. A plane will tend to remain in a medium bank until the pilot makes an adjustment.

5. Which of the following is NOT one of the four basic maneuvers in flight?

a. Turn
b. Spin
c. Straight-and-level flight
d. Climb
e. Descent

Practice Answers

1. B: The name of a runway pointing due east would be Runway 9 in the United States. In other countries, it is possible to have a leading zero before a single digit runway. In that case, it would be named Runway 09. The names of runways are based on the compass. A runway pointing due south would be Runway 18, and a runway pointing due west would be Runway 27. Of course, every runway will be called by two names, depending on which direction planes are traveling on it. Runway 9 will become Runway 27 when the planes travel west rather than east. When the names of runways are spoken, each digit in the name is stated individually. So, Runway 24 would be spoken, "Runway Two-Four" rather than "Runway Twenty-four."

2. E: The powerplant supplies the thrust for a fixed-wing aircraft. The powerplant may be a jet engine or an engine and a set of propellers. Thrust is the force that propels the plane forward.

3. A: The chord line runs through the wing from the leading edge to the trailing edge. This line divides the upper and lower surfaces of the wing. This is one of the key elements of wing design. The distance from one wingtip to the other, meanwhile, is called the wingspan. The mean camber line runs along the inside of the wing, such that the upper and lower wings are equal in thickness.

4. E: A plane will tend to remain in a medium bank until the pilot makes an adjustment. A medium bank is between 20 and 45 degrees. A shallow bank, on the other hand, is less than 20 degrees, and requires the assistance of the ailerons to maintain itself. A steep bank is greater than 45 degrees. When a plane enters a steep bank, it will tend to increase the bank unless the ailerons are used to prevent this. Turning occurs because of the forces that act on a banked wing. The plane will be pushed in a direction perpendicular to the wings.

5. B: Spin is not one of the four basic maneuvers in flight. Straight-and-level flight, turn, climb, and descent are the four basic flight maneuvers. Straight-and-level flight occurs when the plane maintains a constant altitude and is pointed in the same direction. Of course, maintaining the same altitude and direction requires a number of adjustments. Turns are made by banking the wings in the direction of the turn. For example, turning to the right requires lowering the right wing. A climb requires raising the nose of the plane and increasing the power from the engine. Finally, there are a few types of descent. A plane may descend with its nose up, down, or level.

Self-Description Inventory

The final section of the AFOQT is a self-description inventory, or basically a personality test. You will be shown a series of statements and you will have to decide how well those statements describe you. There are no right or wrong answers to the questions in this section, so don't spend a lot of thinking about them. Your first instinct will usually be the most accurate assessment of yourself.

AFOQT Practice Test #1

Want to take this practice test in an online interactive format?
Check out the online resources page, which includes interactive practice questions and much more: **mometrix.com/resources719/afoqt-27353**

Verbal Analogies

1. *Chastise* is to *reprimand* as *impetuous* is to

a. Punish
b. Rash
c. Considered
d. Poor
e. Calm

2. *Arm* is to *humerus* as *leg* is to

a. Ulna
b. Clavicle
c. Femur
d. Mandible
e. Metacarpal

3. *Multiplication* is to *division* as *product* is to

a. Quotient
b. Divisor
c. Integer
d. Dividend
e. Multiplier

4. *Wear* is to *sweater* as *eat* is to

a. Shirt
b. Top hat
c. Asparagus
d. Looks
e. Mouth

5. *Money* is to *impecunious* as *food* is to

a. Famished
b. Nauseated
c. Distracted
d. Antagonistic
e. Impoverished

6. ***Denigrate*** **is to** ***malign*** **as** ***demur*** **is to**

a. Protest
b. Defer
c. Slander
d. Benumb
e. Belittle

7. ***Obeisance*** **is to** ***deference*** **as** ***munificent*** **is to**

a. Benevolent
b. Magnificent
c. Squalid
d. Generous
e. Avarice

8. ***Goat*** **is to** ***nanny*** **as** ***pig*** **is to**

a. Shoat
b. Ewe
c. Cub
d. Sow
e. Calf

9. ***Cache*** **is to** ***reserve*** **as** ***dearth*** **is to**

a. Stockpile
b. Paucity
c. Cudgel
d. Dirge
e. Somber

10. ***Arable*** **is to** ***farmable*** **as** ***asylum*** **is to**

a. Famine
b. Danger
c. Arid
d. Fertile
e. Refuge

11. ***Myriad*** **is to** ***few*** **as** ***stationary*** **is to**

a. Peripatetic
b. Many
c. Several
d. Halted
e. Parked

12. ***House*** **is to** ***mansion*** **as** ***bottle*** **is to**

a. Flagon
b. Container
c. Vessel
d. Pot
e. Flask

13. *Dictionary* is to *definition* as *thesaurus* is to

a. Pronunciations
b. Synonyms
c. Explanations
d. Pronouns
e. Definitions

14. *Abstruse* is to *esoteric* as *adamant* is to

a. Yielding
b. Stubborn
c. Keen
d. Forthright
e. Flexible

15. *Bees* is to *hive* as *cattle* is to

a. Swarm
b. Pod
c. Herd
d. Flock
e. Pack

16. *Latitude* is to *longitude* as *parallel* is to

a. Strait
b. Line
c. Equator
d. Aquifer
e. Meridian

17. *Prevention* is to *deterrence* as *incitement* is to

a. Excitement
b. Provocation
c. Request
d. Disregard
e. Disgust

18. *Value* is to *worth* as *measure* is to

a. Gauge
b. Allowance
c. Demerit
d. Insignificance
e. Large

19. *Enervate* is to *energize* as *espouse* is to

a. Oppose
b. Wed
c. Equine
d. Epistolary
e. Marry

20. ***Hammer*** **is to** ***carpenter*** **as** ***stethoscope*** **is to**

a. Patient
b. Hearing
c. Heartbeat
d. Doctor
e. Pedometer

21. ***Armoire*** **is to** ***bedroom*** **as** ***desk*** **is to**

a. Chair
b. Office
c. Computer
d. Work
e. Building

22. ***Plankton*** **is to** ***whales*** **as** ***bamboo*** **is to**

a. Predators
b. Grasses
c. Pandas
d. Fast-growing
e. China

23. ***Tundra*** **is to** ***arctic*** **as** ***savanna*** **is to**

a. Prairie
b. Lush
c. Tropic
d. Georgia
e. Jungle

24. ***Thirsty*** **is to** ***parched*** **as** ***hungry*** **is to**

a. Famished
b. Fed
c. Satiated
d. Satisfied
e. Full

25. ***Felicity*** **is to** ***sadness*** **as** ***ignominy*** **is to**

a. Shame
b. Slander
c. Crime
d. Indict
e. Honor

Arithmetic Reasoning

1. A man earns $15.23 per hour and gets a raise of $2.34 per hour. What is his new hourly rate of pay?

a. $12.89
b. $15.46
c. $17.57
d. $23.40
e. $35.64

2. Half of a 140-acre forest is cut down to make way for development. How many acres is the remaining forest?

a. 70
b. 80
c. 90
d. 100
e. 120

3. A farmer has 360 cows. He decides to sell 45. Shortly after, he purchases 85 more cows. How many cows does he have?

a. 230
b. 315
c. 400
d. 490
e. 530

4. Four friends go shopping. They purchase items that cost $6.65 and $159.23. If they split the cost evenly, how much will each friend have to pay?

a. $26.64
b. $39.81
c. $41.47
d. $55.30
e. $82.95

5. Five workers each earn $135/day. What is the total amount earned by the five workers for one day of work?

a. $675
b. $700
c. $725
d. $750
e. $775

6. In a town, the ratio of men to women is 2 : 1. If the number of women in the town is doubled, what will be the new ratio of men to women?

a. 1 : 2
b. 1 : 1
c. 2 : 1
d. 3 : 1
e. 4 : 1

7. If one gallon of paint can paint 3 rooms, how many rooms can be painted with 28 gallons of paint?

a. 10
b. 25
c. 56
d. 84
e. 92

8. One worker has an office that is 20 feet long. Another has an office that is 6 feet longer. What is the combined length of both offices?

a. 26 feet
b. 36 feet
c. 46 feet
d. 56 feet
e. 66 feet

9. A girl scores a 99 on her math test. On her second test, her score drops by 15. On the third test, she scores 5 points higher than she did on her second. What was the girl's score on the third test?

a. 79
b. 84
c. 89
d. 99
e. 104

10. Giselle is selling notebooks at the school store. She earns $45.00 for selling 30 notebooks. How much is Giselle charging for each notebook?

a. $135.00
b. $3.00
c. $1.25
d. $3.50
e. $1.50

11. What is the perimeter of a rectangular room that is 35 feet long and 88 feet wide?

a. 158 feet
b. 246 feet
c. 1,540 square feet
d. 3,080 feet
e. 3,080 square feet

12. A man buys two shirts. One is $7.50 and the other is $3.00. A 6% tax is added to his total. How much does he pay in all?

a. $10.50
b. $11.13
c. $14.58
d. $16.80
e. $18.21

13. In a drawing that contains both circles and squares, there are 16 more circles than squares. The total number of circles and squares is 36. How many squares are there in the drawing?

a. 10
b. 16
c. 18
d. 24
e. 26

14. A woman has $450 in a bank account. She earns 0.5% interest on her end-of-month balance. How much interest will she earn for the month?

a. $0.50
b. $2.25
c. $4.28
d. $4.73
e. $6.34

15. What is the volume of a rectangular tissue box that is 9 inches long by 4 inches wide and 5 inches tall?

a. 180 square inches
b. 180 cubic inches
c. 45 square inches
d. 45 cubic inches
e. 36 square inches

16. A woman weighing 250 pounds goes on a diet. During the first week, she loses 3% of her body weight. During the second week, she loses 2% of her new body weight. At the end of the second week, how many pounds has she lost in all?

a. 10
b. 12.35
c. 12.5
d. 15
e. 17.5

17. A recipe calls for 2 cups of water for every 6 cups of flour. Josie wants to make a smaller batch using only 2 cups of flour. How much water should she use?

a. $\frac{1}{2}$ cup
b. 2 cups
c. $\frac{2}{3}$ cup
d. $2\frac{2}{3}$ cups
e. 12 cups

18. A woman must earn $250 in the next four days to pay a traffic ticket. How much will she have to earn each day?

a. $45.50
b. $62.50
c. $75.50
d. $100.50
e. $125.00

19. If one side of a cube is 5 cm long, what is the volume of the cube?

a. 15 cm^3
b. 65 cm^3
c. 105 cm^3
d. 125 cm^3
e. 225 cm^3

20. Four workers at a shelter agree to care for the dogs over a holiday. If there are 48 dogs, how many must each worker look after?

a. 8
b. 10
c. 12
d. 14
e. 16

21. If 1 inch on a map represents 60 feet, how many yards apart are two points if the distance between the points on the map is 10 inches?

a. 1,800 yards
b. 600 yards
c. 300 yards
d. 200 yards
e. 2 yards

22. A man goes to the mall with $50.00. He spends $15.64 in one store and $7.12 in a second store. How much does he have left?

a. $27.24
b. $32.76
c. $34.36
d. $42.80
e. $57.12

23. Two women have credit cards. One earns 3 points for every dollar she spends. The other earns 6 points for every dollar she spends. If they each spend $5.00, how many combined total points will they earn?

a. 15
b. 30
c. 45
d. 60
e. 75

24. At the gym, 30% of the equipment consists of cardio machines. Of the cardio machines, 40% are treadmills. What percentage of the equipment at the gym consists of treadmills?

a. 1.2%
b. 10%
c. 12%
d. 67%
e. 70%

25. Snack boxes are taken on a school field trip. Each snack box holds either pretzels, chips, or a granola bar. If $\frac{1}{3}$ of the snack boxes contain pretzels and $\frac{1}{4}$ contains chips, which fraction of the snack boxes contain granola bars?

a. $\frac{1}{12}$
b. $\frac{5}{12}$
c. $\frac{1}{2}$
d. $\frac{7}{12}$
e. $\frac{5}{7}$

Word Knowledge

Select the answer choice that is closest in meaning to the given word.

1. SPOILED

a. Ruined
b. Splendid
c. Told
d. Believed
e. Hated

2. OATH

a. Delivery
b. Promise
c. Statement
d. Criticism
e. Threat

3. INQUIRE

a. Invest
b. Ask
c. Tell
d. Release
e. Inquest

4. COMPREHEND

a. Learn
b. Speak
c. Understand
d. Appreciate
e. Commemorate

5. APPARENT

a. Clear
b. Occasional
c. Angry
d. Applied
e. Father

6. SILENCE

a. Darkness
b. Excitement
c. Quiet
d. Mood
e. Quaint

7. ABSOLUTELY

a. Assuredly
b. Rapidly
c. Never
d. Weakly
e. completely

8. MODIFIED

a. Checked
b. Shortened
c. Considered
d. Changed
e. Lengthened

9. DELICATE

a. Fragile
b. Sturdy
c. Loud
d. Soft
e. Lovely

10. FESTIVITIES

a. Commitments
b. Celebrations
c. Crowds
d. Dates
e. Funeral

11. EXHAUSTED

a. Excited
b. Tired
c. Worried
d. Energized
e. Animated

12. CLEANSED

a. Examined
b. Washed
c. Touched
d. Dried
e. Motivated

13. BATTLED

a. Fought
b. Attempt
c. Bold
d. Saw
e. Excited

14. WANDERED

a. Looked
b. Shopped
c. Roamed
d. Searched
e. Lived

15. ABRUPTLY

a. Homely
b. Commonly
c. Wisely
d. Ugly
e. Suddenly

16. TRICKED

a. Conned
b. Begged
c. Convinced
d. Nagged
e. Criticized

17. EXTREMELY

a. Almost
b. Slightly
c. Very
d. Clearly
e. Happily

18. DOUBTFUL

a. Uncertain
b. Panicked
c. Pondering
d. Indifferent
e. Confused

19. PECULIAR

a. Original
b. Novel
c. Dull
d. Strange
e. Awesome

20. COURTEOUS

a. Handsome
b. Polite
c. Inconsiderate
d. Odd
e. Unrelenting

21. TROUBLED

a. Relieved
b. Satisfied
c. Bothered
d. Relaxed
e. Persistent

22. PERSPIRATION

a. Sweat
b. Work
c. Help
d. Advice
e. Job

23. TREMBLED

a. Spoke
b. Shook
c. Wept
d. Ducked
e. Cowered

24. ADHERED

a. Stuck
b. Went
c. Spoke
d. Altered
e. Stunk

25. TIDY

a. Furnished
b. Warm
c. Locked
d. Neat
e. Inviting

Mathematics Knowledge

1. A chest is filled with large gold and silver coins, weighing a total of 30 pounds. If each gold coin weighs 12 ounces, each silver coin weighs 8 ounces, and there are 50 coins in all, how many gold coins does the chest contain? (There are 16 ounces in a pound.)

a. 10 coins
b. 15 coins
c. 20 coins
d. 30 coins
e. 45 coins

2. If $3x - 30 = 45 - 2x$, what is the value of x?

a. 5
b. 10
c. 15
d. 20
e. 25

3. If $x = -3$, calculate the value of the following expression.

$$3x^3 + (3x + 4) - 2x^2$$

a. -104
b. -58
c. 0
d. 58
e. 104

4. What is the area of a square that has a perimeter of 8 cm?

a. 2 cm^2
b. 4 cm^2
c. 32 cm^2
d. 64 cm^2
e. 160 cm^2

5. Which of the following expressions is equivalent to $(3x^{-2})^3$?

a. $9x^{-6}$
b. $9x^6$
c. $27x^{-4}$
d. $27x^{-6}$
e. $27x^{-8}$

6. What is $16x^2 - 64$ written in factored form?

a. $(4x + 4)(4x + 4)$
b. $(4x - 4)(4x + 8)$
c. $(4x + 8)(4x - 8)$
d. $(8x + 8)(2x - 8)$
e. $(2x + 4)(8x + 16)$

7. If $x + y = 9$ and $x + 2y = 13$, what is the simultaneous solution?

a. $x = 4, y = 5$
b. $x = 8, y = 1$
c. $x = -4, y = -5$
d. $x = 5, y = 4$
e. $x = -1, y = -9$

8. Simplify the following expression.

$$(3x^2 7x^7) + (2y^3 9y^{12})$$

a. $21x^{14} + 18y^{26}$
b. $10x^9 + 11y^{15}$
c. $21x^{14} + 18y^{15}$
d. $21x^9 + 18y^{15}$
e. $10x^{14} + 11y^{26}$

9. A triangle has a base measuring 12 cm and a height of 12 cm. What is its area?

a. 24 cm^2
b. 56 cm^2
c. 72 cm^2
d. 144 cm^2
e. 288 cm^2

10. If $\frac{x}{3} + 27 = 30$, what is the value of x?

a. 3
b. 6
c. 9
d. 12
e. 27

11. If $\frac{x}{3} + 7 = 35$, what is the value of x?

a. 9.33
b. 14
c. 84
d. 126
e. 168

12. Which of the following expressions is equivalent to $3\left(\frac{6x-3}{3}\right) - 3(9x + 9)$?

a. $-3(7x + 10)$
b. $-3x + 6$
c. $(x + 3)(x - 3)$
d. $3x^2 - 9$
e. $15x - 9$

13. Simplify the following expression.

$$\frac{50x^{18}t^6w^3z^{20}}{5x^5t^2w^2z^{19}}$$

a. $10x^{13}t^3wz$
b. $10x^{13}t^4wz$
c. $10x^{12}t^4wz$
d. $10x^{13}t^4wz^2$
e. $10x^{12}t^3w^2z^2$

14. Which statement is true?

a. A triangle can have three obtuse angles.
b. A triangle can have three acute angles.
c. A triangle can have three right angles.
d. A triangle can have four acute angles.
e. A triangle can have a 200-degree angle.

15. If $x = 4$ and $y = 2$, what is the value of the following expression?

$$3xy - 12y + 5x$$

a. -4
b. 10
c. 12
d. 20
e. 24

16. The cost, in dollars, of shipping x computers to California for sale is $3,000 + 100x$. The amount received when selling these computers is $400x$ dollars. What is the least number of computers that must be shipped and sold so that the amount received is at least equal to the shipping cost?

a. 10 computers
b. 15 computers
c. 20 computers
d. 25 computers
e. 30 computers

17. Solve for x by factoring.

$$x^2 - 13x + 42 = 0$$

a. $x = 6,7$
b. $x = -6,-7$
c. $x = 6,-7$
d. $x = -6,7$
e. $x = 7$

18. If $x^2 - 5 = 20$, what is one possible value of x?

a. 5
b. 10
c. 12.5
d. 15
e. 25

19. Solve for x in the following inequality.

$$\frac{1}{4}x - 25 \geq 75$$

a. $x \geq 400$
b. $x \leq 400$
c. $x \geq 50$
d. $x \leq 25$
e. $x \geq 25$

20. In the following inequality, solve for q.

$$-3q + 12 \geq 4q - 30$$

a. $q \geq 6$
b. $q = 6$
c. $q \neq 6$
d. $q \leq 6$
e. q does not exist

21. Simplify the following expression.

$$(3x + 5)(4x - 6)$$

a. $12x^2 - 38x - 30$
b. $12x^2 + 2x - 30$
c. $12x^2 - 2x - 1$
d. $12x^2 + 2x + 30$
e. $12x^2 + 7x - 30$

22. Solve the following equation for x.

$$72 \div 8 = x - 17$$

a. 8
b. 9
c. 17
d. 21
e. 26

23. A rectangle has a width of 7 cm and a length of 9 cm. What is its perimeter?

a. 16 cm
b. 32 cm
c. 48 cm
d. 62 cm
e. 64 cm

24. If $\frac{2}{3}x + 10 = 16$, what is the value of x?

a. 6
b. 7
c. 8
d. 9
e. 10

25. Simplify the following expression: $6x + 2y - 3 + 4x + 5y + 6$

a. $10x + 7y + 3$
b. $24x + 7y + 9$
c. $17xy + 3$
d. $2x + 7y + 3$
e. $24x + 10y - 18$

Reading Comprehension

Passage 1

Air is a gas which means it can be compressed or expanded. When air is compressed, a greater amount of air can occupy a fixed volume. Conversely, when pressure on a fixed amount of air is decreased, the air expands and occupies a greater volume. That is, the original column of air at a lower pressure has a lower density. In fact, density is directly proportional to pressure. If the pressure is doubled, the density is doubled, and if the pressure is lowered, so is the density. This statement is true only at a constant temperature.

Increasing the temperature of a substance decreases its density. Conversely, decreasing the temperature increases the density. Thus, the density of air varies inversely with temperature. This statement is true only at a constant pressure. In the atmosphere, both temperature and pressure decrease with altitude and have conflicting effects upon density. However, the fairly rapid drop in pressure as altitude is increased usually has the dominant effect. Hence, pilots can expect the density to decrease with altitude.

The preceding paragraphs are based on the presupposition of perfectly dry air. In reality, it is never completely dry. The small amount of water vapor suspended in the atmosphere is typically considered negligible under most circumstances, but in certain tropical conditions, it can make a measurable difference. Water vapor is lighter than air; consequently, moist air is lighter than dry air. Therefore, as the water content of the air increases, the air becomes less dense, increasing density altitude and decreasing performance. It is lightest or least dense when, in a given set of conditions, it contains the maximum amount of water vapor.

Humidity, also called relative humidity, refers to the amount of water vapor contained in the atmosphere and is expressed as a percentage of the maximum amount of water vapor the air can hold. This amount varies with the temperature; warm air can hold more water vapor, while colder air can hold less. Perfectly dry air that contains no water vapor has a relative humidity of zero percent, while saturated air that cannot hold any more water vapor has a relative humidity of 100 percent. Humidity alone is usually not considered an essential factor in calculating density altitude and aircraft performance; however, it does contribute.

The higher the temperature, the greater amount of water vapor that the air can hold. When comparing two separate air masses, the first warm and moist (both qualities making air lighter) and the second cold and dry (both qualities making it heavier), the first must be less dense than the second. Pressure and temperature have a great influence on aircraft performance because of their effect upon density. There is no rule-of-thumb or chart used to compute the effects of humidity on density altitude, but expect a decrease in overall performance in high humidity conditions.

1. The primary purpose of the passage is to

a. Explain the qualities of air that may affect flight
b. Explain g-force and how it works
c. Describe the constituent elements of air
d. Explain humidity
e. Describe the ideal air conditions for flight

2. In the second paragraph, *inversely* most nearly means

a. Severely
b. Incredibly
c. In the opposite direction
d. In an unrelated fashion
e. Concurrently

3. If the air temperature drops while a plane is gaining altitude, the pilot can expect

a. The density of the air to increase
b. The humidity of the air to increase
c. The air pressure to increase
d. The density of the air to decrease
e. Aircraft performance to decrease

4. With which one of the following claims about air quality would the author most likely agree?

a. Pilots never need to pay attention to relative humidity.
b. For a pilot, the density of air is more important than the relative humidity.
c. Completely dry air is very rare.
d. Aircraft performance is unrelated to humidity.
e. The best conditions for flying are very hot and humid.

5. What is the most likely reason why there is no chart for assessing the effects of humidity on density altitude?

a. Humidity does not affect density altitude.
b. It is impossible to measure humidity.
c. Humidity does not affect flight performance very much.
d. Humidity varies a great deal in relatively small areas.
e. Density altitude never varies.

Passage 2

The climb performance of an aircraft is affected by certain variables. The conditions of the aircraft's maximum climb angle or maximum climb rate occur at specific speeds, and variations in speed will produce variations in climb performance. There is sufficient latitude in most aircraft that small variations in speed from the optimum do not produce large changes in climb performance, and certain operational considerations may require speeds slightly different from the optimum. Of course, climb performance would be most critical with high gross weight, at high altitude, in obstructed takeoff areas, or during malfunction of a powerplant. Then, optimum climb speeds are necessary.

Weight has a very pronounced effect on aircraft performance. If weight is added to an aircraft, it must fly at a higher angle of attack (AOA) to maintain a given altitude and speed. This increases the induced drag of the wings, as well as the parasite drag of the aircraft. Increased drag means that additional thrust is needed to overcome it, which in turn means that less reserve thrust is available for climbing. Aircraft designers go to great effort to minimize the weight since it has such a marked effect on the factors pertaining to performance.

A change in an aircraft's weight produces a twofold effect on climb performance. First, a change in weight will change the drag and the power required. This alters the reserve power available, which in turn, affects both the climb angle and the climb rate. Secondly, an increase in weight will reduce the maximum rate of climb, but the aircraft must be operated at a higher climb speed to achieve the smaller peak climb rate.

An increase in altitude also will increase the power required and decrease the power available. Therefore, the climb performance of an aircraft diminishes with altitude. The speeds for maximum rate of climb, maximum angle of climb, and maximum and minimum level flight airspeeds vary with altitude. As altitude is increased, these various speeds finally converge at the absolute ceiling of the aircraft. At the absolute ceiling, there is no excess of power and only one speed will allow steady, level flight. Consequently, the absolute ceiling of an aircraft produces zero rate of climb. The service ceiling is the altitude at which the aircraft is unable to climb at a rate greater than 100 feet per minute (fpm). Usually, these specific performance reference points are provided for the aircraft at a specific design configuration.

In discussing performance, it frequently is convenient to use the terms power loading, wing loading, blade loading, and disk loading. Power loading is expressed in pounds per horsepower and is obtained by dividing the total weight of the aircraft by the rated horsepower of the engine. It is a significant factor in an aircraft's takeoff and climb capabilities. Wing loading is expressed in pounds per square foot and is obtained by dividing the total weight of an airplane in pounds by the wing area (including ailerons) in square feet. It is the airplane's wing loading that determines the landing speed. Blade loading is expressed in pounds per square foot and is obtained by dividing the total weight of a helicopter by the area of the rotor blades. Blade loading is not to be confused with disk loading, which is the total weight of a helicopter divided by the area of the disk swept by the rotor blades.

6. Which of the following would be the best title for this passage?

a. The Importance of Weight
b. Climb Performance and You
c. Power Loading, Wing Loading, and Disk Loading
d. Influences on Climb Performance
e. Achieving Maximum Climb Angle

7. In the second paragraph, *pronounced* most nearly means

a. Selective
b. Intoned
c. Detrimental
d. Spoken
e. Noticeable

8. Which of the following is NOT one of the effects of increased weight on flight performance?

a. Diminished reserve power
b. Decreased climb rate
c. Lower angle of attack required to maintain altitude
d. Diminished maximum rate of climb
e. Increased drag

9. With which one of the following claims about climb performance would the author most likely agree?

a. Optimal climb performance can be achieved even with heavy cargo.
b. At the end of a long journey, a plane will have a higher maximum rate of climb.
c. A plane can handle any amount of weight, though climb performance will be affected.
d. Pilots have no influence over climb performance.
e. The climb performance of a two-engine plane will remain the same even if one engine fails.

10. If a helicopter weighs two tons and its rotor blades cover an area of five hundred square feet, what is its disc loading measure?

a. 8 pounds per square foot
b. 125 square foot-pounds
c. 0.125 tons per square foot
d. 4 metric tons
e. 8 ton-feet

Passage 3

The aerodynamic properties of an aircraft generally determine the power requirements at various conditions of flight, while the powerplant capabilities generally determine the power available at various conditions of flight. When an aircraft is in steady, level flight, a condition of equilibrium must prevail. An unaccelerated condition of flight is achieved when lift equals weight, and the powerplant is set for thrust equal to drag. The power required to achieve equilibrium in constant-altitude flight at various airspeeds is depicted on a power required curve. The power required curve illustrates the fact that at low airspeeds near the stall or minimum controllable airspeed, the power setting required for steady, level flight is quite high.

Flight in the region of normal command means that while holding a constant altitude, a higher airspeed requires a higher power setting, and a lower airspeed requires a lower power setting. The majority of aircraft flying (climb, cruise, and maneuvers) is conducted in the region of normal command.

Flight in the region of reversed command means flight in which a higher airspeed requires a lower power setting, and a lower airspeed requires a higher power setting to hold altitude. It does not imply that a decrease in power will produce lower airspeed. The region of reversed command is encountered in the low speed phases of flight. Flight speeds below the speed for maximum endurance (lowest point on the power curve) require higher power settings with a decrease in airspeed. Since the need to increase the required power setting with decreased speed is contrary to the normal command of flight, the regime of flight speeds between the speed for minimum required power setting and the stall speed (or minimum control speed) is termed the region of reversed command. In the region of reversed command, a decrease in airspeed must be accompanied by an increased power setting in order to maintain steady flight.

An airplane performing a low airspeed, high pitch attitude power approach for a short-field landing is an example of operating in the region of reversed command. If an unacceptably high sink rate should develop, it may be possible for the pilot to reduce or stop the descent by applying power. But without further use of power, the airplane would probably stall or be incapable of flaring for the landing. Merely lowering the nose of the airplane to regain flying speed in this situation, without the use of power, would result in a rapid sink rate and corresponding loss of altitude.

If during a soft-field takeoff and climb, for example, the pilot attempts to climb out of ground effect without first attaining normal climb pitch attitude and airspeed, the airplane may inadvertently enter the region of reversed command at a dangerously low altitude. Even with full power, the airplane may be incapable of climbing or even maintaining altitude. The pilot's only recourse in this situation is to lower the pitch attitude in order to increase airspeed, which will inevitably result in a loss of altitude. Airplane pilots must give particular attention to precise control of airspeed when operating in the low flight speeds of the region of reversed command.

11. The primary purpose of the passage is to

a. Instruct pilots on proper airspeed.
b. Discuss the interrelationships of airspeed, power, and pitch attitude.
c. Explain reversed command.
d. Discuss the physics of flight at low airspeeds.
e. Persuade the reader to fly faster aircraft.

12. In the fifth paragraph, *inadvertently* most nearly means

a. Unintentionally
b. Indirectly
c. Sequentially
d. Primarily
e. Eventually

13. In which region of command does most flight occur?

a. Inverse command
b. Normal command
c. Direct command
d. Reverse command
e. Decreased command

14. With which one of the following statements about flight would the author most likely agree?

a. As speed increases, the power required to descend decreases.
b. As speed increases, the power required to descend remains constant.
c. As speed decreases, the power required to climb remains constant.
d. As speed increases, the power required to maintain altitude increases.
e. As speed decreases, the power required to maintain altitude increases.

15. Which of the following would be the best title for this passage?

a. How to Avoid Reversed Command
b. Normal Command Flight
c. Learning to Fly
d. Power Requirements During Flight
e. Reversed Command and the Modern Pilot

Passage 4

In many cases, the landing distance of an aircraft will define the runway requirements for flight operations. The minimum landing distance is obtained by landing at some minimum safe speed, which allows sufficient margin above stall and provides satisfactory control and capability for a go-around. Generally, the landing speed is some fixed percentage of the stall speed or minimum control speed for the aircraft in the landing configuration. As such, the landing will be accomplished at some particular value of lift coefficient and angle of attack (AOA). The exact values will depend on the aircraft characteristics but, once defined, the values are independent of weight, altitude, and wind.

To obtain minimum landing distance at the specified landing speed, the forces that act on the aircraft must provide maximum deceleration during the landing roll. The forces acting on the aircraft during the landing roll may require various procedures to maintain landing deceleration at the peak value.

A distinction should be made between the procedures for minimum landing distance and an ordinary landing roll with considerable excess runway available. Minimum landing distance will be obtained by creating a continuous peak deceleration of the aircraft; that is, extensive use of the brakes for maximum deceleration. On the other hand, an ordinary landing roll with considerable excess runway may allow extensive use of aerodynamic drag to minimize wear and tear on the tires and brakes. If aerodynamic drag is sufficient to cause deceleration, it can be used in deference to the brakes in the early stages of the landing roll; i.e., brakes and tires suffer from continuous hard use, but aircraft aerodynamic drag is free and does not wear out with use.

The use of aerodynamic drag is applicable only for deceleration to 60 or 70 percent of the touchdown speed. At speeds less than 60 to 70 percent of the touchdown speed, aerodynamic drag is so slight as to be of little use, and braking must be utilized to produce continued deceleration. Since the objective during the landing roll is to decelerate, the powerplant thrust should be the smallest possible positive value (or largest possible negative value in the case of thrust reversers). In addition to the important factors of proper procedures, many other variables affect the landing performance. Any item that alters the landing speed or deceleration rate during the landing roll will affect the landing distance.

The effect of gross weight on landing distance is one of the principal items determining the landing distance. One effect of an increased gross weight is that a greater speed will be required to support the aircraft at the landing AOA and lift coefficient. For an example of the effect of a change in gross weight, a 21 percent increase in landing weight will require a ten percent increase in landing speed to support the greater weight.

When minimum landing distances are considered, braking friction forces predominate during the landing roll and, for the majority of aircraft configurations, braking friction is the main source of deceleration.

The minimum landing distance will vary in direct proportion to the gross weight. For example, a ten percent increase in gross weight at landing would cause a:

- Five percent increase in landing velocity
- Ten percent increase in landing distance

A contingency of this is the relationship between weight and braking friction force.

The effect of wind on landing distance is large and deserves proper consideration when predicting landing distance. Since the aircraft will land at a particular airspeed independent of the wind, the principal effect of wind on landing distance is the change in the groundspeed at which the aircraft touches down. The effect of wind on deceleration during the landing is identical to the effect on acceleration during the takeoff.

The effect of pressure altitude and ambient temperature is to define density altitude and its effect on landing performance. An increase in density altitude increases the landing speed but does not alter the net retarding force. Thus, the aircraft at altitude lands at the same indicated airspeed as at sea level but, because of the reduced density, the true airspeed is greater. Since the aircraft lands at altitude with the same weight and dynamic pressure, the drag and braking friction throughout the landing roll have the same values as at sea level. As long as the condition is within the capability of the brakes, the net retarding force is unchanged, and the deceleration is the same as with the landing at sea level. Since an increase in altitude does not alter deceleration, the effect of density altitude on landing distance is due to the greater true airspeed.

16. The main purpose of the passage is to

a. Give some examples of near accidents during landing.
b. Improve landing skills.
c. Explain the effects of varying pressure altitudes.
d. Advocate safer protocols for landing.
e. Describe the factors that influence landing distance.

17. Why will a pilot rely on aerodynamic drag when making a normal landing?

a. To increase the rate of deceleration
b. To avoid wearing down the brakes and tires
c. To avoid unnecessary turbulence
d. To mitigate a large gross weight
e. To simplify landing procedures

18. In the fifth paragraph, *principal* most nearly means

a. Most important
b. Easiest
c. Moral
d. First
e. Value

19. Why must a heavier plane land at a higher speed?

a. To diminish fuel supplies and thereby decrease gross weight
b. To encourage a stall just before landing
c. To avoid hitting the runway with too much force
d. To improve handling on the runway
e. To allow for the longest landing distance

20. With which one of the following claims about landing performance would the author most likely agree?

a. Many landings occur without any use of the brakes.
b. Ambient temperature has no effect on minimum landing distance.
c. Gross weight and minimum landing distance are positively correlated.
d. Runway length is less important than gross weight in determining the appropriate airspeed during landing.
e. Minimum landing distance is generally consistent for aircraft of the same size.

Passage 5

For over 25 years, the importance of good pilot judgment, or aeronautical decision-making (ADM), has been recognized as critical to the safe operation of aircraft, as well as accident avoidance. The airline industry, motivated by the need to reduce accidents caused by human factors, developed the first training programs based on improving ADM. Crew resource management (CRM) training for flight crews is focused on the effective use of all available resources: human resources, hardware, and information supporting ADM to facilitate crew cooperation and improve decision-making. The goal of all flight crews is good ADM and the use of CRM is one way to make good decisions.

Research in this area prompted the Federal Aviation Administration (FAA) to produce training directed at improving the decision-making of pilots and led to current FAA regulations that require that decision-making be taught as part of the pilot training curriculum. ADM research, development, and testing culminated in 1987 with the publication of six manuals oriented to the decision-making needs of variously rated pilots.

These manuals provided multifaceted materials designed to reduce the number of decision-related accidents. The effectiveness of these materials was validated in independent studies where student pilots received such training in conjunction with the standard flying curriculum. When tested, the pilots who had received ADM training made fewer inflight errors than those who had not received ADM training. The differences were statistically significant and ranged from about 10 to 50 percent fewer judgment errors. In the operational environment, an operator flying about 400,000 hours annually demonstrated a 54 percent reduction in accident rate after using these materials for recurrency training.

Contrary to popular opinion, good judgment can be taught. Tradition held that good judgment was a natural by-product of experience, but as pilots continued to log accident-free flight hours, a corresponding increase of good judgment was assumed. Building upon the foundation of conventional decision-making, ADM enhances the process to decrease the probability of human error and increase the probability of a safe flight. ADM provides a structured, systematic approach to analyzing changes that occur during a flight and how these changes might affect a flight's safe outcome. The ADM process addresses all aspects of decision-making in the flight deck and identifies the steps involved in good decision-making.

Steps for good decision-making are:

1. Identifying personal attitudes hazardous to safe flight
2. Learning behavior modification techniques
3. Learning how to recognize and cope with stress
4. Developing risk assessment skills
5. Using all resources
6. Evaluating the effectiveness of one's ADM skills

Risk management is an important component of ADM. When a pilot follows good decision-making practices, the inherent risk in a flight is reduced or even eliminated. The ability to make good decisions is based upon direct or indirect experience and education.

Consider automotive seat belt use. In just two decades, seat belt use has become the norm, placing those who do not wear seat belts outside the norm, but this group may learn to wear a seat belt by either direct or indirect experience.

For example, a driver learns through direct experience about the value of wearing a seat belt when he or she is involved in a car accident that leads to a personal injury. An indirect learning experience occurs when a loved one is injured during a car accident because he or she failed to wear a seat belt.

While poor decision-making in everyday life does not always lead to tragedy, the margin for error in aviation is thin. Since ADM enhances management of an aeronautical environment, all pilots should become familiar with and employ ADM.

21. The primary purpose of the passage is to

a. List the steps in good decision-making.
b. Improve the decision-making abilities of the reader.
c. Outline the relationship between aeronautical decision-making and crew resource management.
d. Discuss aeronautical decision-making.
e. Inspire the reader to make better decisions.

22. According to the passage, how is aviation safety distinguished from other forms of safety?

a. Aviation safety is much simpler than most other areas of safety.
b. Aviation safety is no different than most other areas of safety.
c. Aviation safety is only important to a small percentage of the population.
d. There is a smaller margin for error in aviation.
e. Aviation safety can be systematized.

23. In the third paragraph, conjunction most nearly means

a. Combination
b. Linking word
c. Opposition
d. Collection
e. Organization

24. With which one of the following claims about aeronautical decision-making would the author most likely agree?

a. The body of knowledge about ADM is increasing, and this will have a positive effect on flight safety.
b. Aeronautical decision-making is the responsibility of the pilot alone.
c. Eventually, researchers will establish a perfect set of decision-making tools for pilots.
d. Aeronautical decision-making is the only tool required for flight safety.
e. Aeronautical decision-making has no applications in areas other than flight.

25. When a pilot reads the account of a recent aviation accident, this is an opportunity for a(n)

a. Recertification
b. Direct learning experience
c. Implicit learning experience
d. Reorientation of learning
e. Indirect learning experience

Situational Judgment

SITUATION 1:

You are approached by a senior officer, who requests a private meeting with you. He asks you for your candid opinion on your immediate supervisor, who is a subordinate to the senior officer. You have a generally favorable opinion of the supervisor, but you do have a few complaints about her performance. Specifically, you feel that she does a poor job of running staff meetings.

Possible actions:

a. Decline to meet with the senior officer.
b. Meet with the senior officer, and focus on the ways your supervisor could improve staff meetings.
c. Give your candid opinion of your supervisor, including your criticisms, but emphasizing your overall positive opinion.
d. Write a letter to the senior officer, explaining your opinions about your supervisor.
e. Give the senior officer a glowing report of the supervisor, without mentioning your complaints.

1. Select the MOST EFFECTIVE action in response to the situation.

2. Select the LEAST EFFECTIVE action in response to the situation.

SITUATION 2:

While performing administrative work with another officer, you notice that he is manipulating the numbers on some reports. Specifically, the officer is inflating the amounts of time spent on certain training exercises. These reports are sent on to senior officers, who use them to assess the readiness of the airmen for more sophisticated and complicated missions. If men and women are unprepared for these more difficult missions, there is a greater risk of accident or injury, to themselves or others.

Possible actions:

a. Immediately report this infraction to your superior.
b. Wait until you can acquire clear proof of the data manipulation.
c. Say nothing at present, but keep an eye on this other officer.
d. Write an anonymous letter to the other officer, encouraging him to stop manipulating the data.
e. Go back over the other officer's work, correcting the data as necessary.

3. Select the MOST EFFECTIVE action in response to the situation.

4. Select the LEAST EFFECTIVE action in response to the situation.

SITUATION 3:

You and two of your fellow officers have been selected to interview candidates for a promotion. One of the three candidates (Candidate A) is known to be an old family friend of your commanding officer. During the interviews, Candidate A is, in your opinion, the most impressive. However, Candidate B also seems like an excellent choice for the position. Candidate C performs poorly. One of the other judges votes for Candidate A, and the other votes for Candidate B.

Possible actions:

a. Vote for Candidate B to avoid the appearance of favoritism.
b. Vote for Candidate C so that the decision will be passed on to another round of deliberation.
c. Abstain from voting.
d. Request a new set of candidates.
e. Vote for Candidate A because you feel he is the most qualified.

5. Select the MOST EFFECTIVE action in response to the situation.

6. Select the LEAST EFFECTIVE action in response to the situation.

SITUATION 4:

You attend a meeting with two other officers. During the meeting, these officers get into a heated conflict over a possible change in policy. You have heard that they have a personal antipathy, though you are not aware of its origins. They ask you to settle their dispute.

Possible actions:

a. Ignore the request, and instead lecture the two officers on the need for cooperation and goodwill in the military.
b. Take the side of the officer who you believe will be the most help to you in the future.
c. Refuse to take a side, citing the obvious personal differences between the two officers.
d. Select the option that you think is best, leaving aside everything you know about their personal conflict.
e. Take the side of the officer you like better.

7. Select the MOST EFFECTIVE action in response to the situation.

8. Select the LEAST EFFECTIVE action in response to the situation.

SITUATION 5:

You are asked to collaborate on an important project with an officer from a different unit. This officer is very close to retirement and appears to have lost interest in his work. Consequently, he puts very little effort into the work you two are supposed to be sharing.

Possible actions:

a. Request a different partner for the project.
b. Inform your senior officer of the situation.
c. Do your best on your work, but accept that the project probably will fail because of the poor attitude of your collaborator.
d. Do your work and the work that was supposed to be done by your partner, since the most important thing is the successful completion of the project.
e. Express your frustrations directly to your collaborator, emphasizing that the success of this project is very important to you, and agree upon a fair division of labor.

9. Select the MOST EFFECTIVE action in response to the situation.

10. Select the LEAST EFFECTIVE action in response to the situation.

SITUATION 6:

While working in a field office, you observe that one of your colleagues is being severely overworked. Despite doing an excellent job and working more than the required number of hours, she is unable to keep up with the amount of paperwork being sent to her by other offices. Her commanding officers do not seem to be aware that she is being asked to do an unfair amount of work.

Possible actions:

a. Assign one of your subordinates to assist your overworked colleague.
b. Request a meeting with your overworked colleague's commanding officer, and describe the problem to him.
c. Ignore the problem, since it does not relate to your work.
d. Express your sympathy with your overworked colleague.
e. Help your overworked colleague whenever you finish your own work.

11. Select the MOST EFFECTIVE action in response to the situation.

12. Select the LEAST EFFECTIVE action in response to the situation.

SITUATION 7:

You have become suspicious that one of your junior officers is trying to undermine your work. This junior officer is very competent and very ambitious. You have even heard from other officers that this junior officer wants to take over your job. You have not yet mentioned your suspicion directly to the junior officer.

Possible actions:

a. Meet with the junior officer and explain that you expect his full cooperation and support.
b. Publicly reprimand and humiliate the junior officer.
c. Ignore the situation, in the hopes that it will resolve itself.
d. Report this insubordination to your commanding officer.
e. Ask one of your fellow officers to talk with the junior officer and try to improve the situation.

13. Select the MOST EFFECTIVE action in response to the situation.

14. Select the LEAST EFFECTIVE action in response to the situation.

SITUATION 8:

You are extremely busy with paperwork, but a senior officer asks you to complete a set of special reports in addition to your normal work. You do not think it will be possible for you to complete this extra assignment without sacrificing the quality of your work. However, you would like to impress your senior officer by fulfilling his request.

Possible actions:

a. Tell the senior officer that you are too busy to complete extra projects.
b. Accept the extra work and resolve to complete it quickly no matter what.
c. Ask the senior officer if you can have a few days to decide whether you will complete the extra work.
d. Accept the extra work, but have a junior staff member complete it for you.
e. Decline the extra work, but offer to pass it along to another qualified member of your team.

15. Select the MOST EFFECTIVE action in response to the situation.

16. Select the LEAST EFFECTIVE action in response to the situation.

SITUATION 9:

Over the past few months, you have noticed that office supplies are being used at a much greater pace than is usual. There is no clear reason for this, but you have begun to suspect that one of your fellow officers is taking office supplies home with her at night. You have no specific evidence to support your claims, but the office supplies seem to be disappearing after shifts in which this officer is alone with access to the supply closet.

Possible actions:

a. Ignore the situation, since you know that you are not personally responsible for the thefts.
b. Tell a senior officer about your suspicions.
c. Confront the officer with your suspicions and ask for an explanation.
d. Set up a hidden surveillance camera so that you can catch the officer stealing supplies.
e. Ask some of your fellow officers if they have noticed any suspicious behavior.

17. Select the MOST EFFECTIVE action in response to the situation.

18. Select the LEAST EFFECTIVE action in response to the situation.

SITUATION 10:

You have been working in the same unit for the past two years. Although you have been successful, you are beginning to get burnt out, and you are thinking about requesting a transfer. You contact some friends and colleagues in other units, trying to determine whether you would like it there. After a few weeks, you realize that rumors about your interest in a transfer have begun to spread throughout your unit.

Possible actions:

a. In a letter to your senior officer, acknowledge the truth of the rumors and request a transfer.
b. Deny the rumors publicly, but continue to pursue a transfer.
c. Ignore the rumors, but refocus on your work with your current unit.
d. Acknowledge the rumors and refocus on your work with your current unit.
e. Request a leave of absence so that you can decide how to handle the situation.

19. Select the MOST EFFECTIVE action in response to the situation.

20 Select the LEAST EFFECTIVE action in response to the situation.

Situation 11:

You have been asked to attend a meeting between the senior officers in your unit and a group of local community leaders. The meeting has been called because of rumors that your military base will be shut down due to budgetary constraints. The community leaders are willing to lobby on behalf of the base, so long as they receive assurances that the military leadership will cooperate with them on some local initiatives. Specifically, the community leaders would like the airmen to help coordinate disaster relief efforts when necessary. At one point, a community leader turns to you and asks for your opinion on the subject.

Possible actions:

a. Answer the question, but mention only the potential positive consequences of the proposal.
b. Try to answer the question as honestly and completely as possible, but remind the community leader that you are only a junior officer.
c. Answer the question thoroughly, even though you have little direct knowledge of the situation.
d. Remind the community leader that you are a junior officer and cannot give your opinion.
e. Decline to answer the question, and instead refer it to one of the senior officers.

21. Select the MOST EFFECTIVE action in response to the situation.

22. Select the LEAST EFFECTIVE action in response to the situation.

Situation 12:

Another officer in your section is granted a week-long leave to visit his sick grandmother. However, during this period you discover through social media that the officer is actually on a beach vacation with his girlfriend, hundreds of miles from the hospital where his grandmother was supposedly being treated.

Possible actions:

a. Tell the officer that he has been dishonest and unethical, and that you will have to report any future episodes of this nature.
b. Ignore the situation, since it does not really involve you.
c. Tell the officer that you will agree to keep his misbehavior a secret if he will do your weekly reports.
d. Immediately notify your commanding officer in person.
e. Anonymously forward the evidence of the officer's misbehavior to your commanding officer.

23. Select the MOST EFFECTIVE action in response to the situation.

24. Select the LEAST EFFECTIVE action in response to the situation.

SITUATION 13:

One of the airmen in your unit has displayed a marked decline in her performance over the past month. She appears frustrated and burnt out with her normal duties. She is one of the more popular members of the unit, so her negative attitude has a bad influence on her fellow airmen.

Possible actions:

a. Convene a meeting of the entire unit, and use this as a chance to single out the airman for her poor performance.
b. Meet with the airman and offer whatever help you can give to improve her performance, while emphasizing the effect that her behavior has on the other airmen.
c. Reassign the airman to a different unit so that her bad attitude doesn't continue to affect the other airmen.
d. Do nothing, in the hopes that the situation will improve without your influence.
e. Inform your senior officer about the situation.

25. Select the MOST EFFECTIVE action in response to the situation.

26. Select the LEAST EFFECTIVE action in response to the situation.

SITUATION 14:

You are about to transfer to a new unit, where you will have duties in areas where you have little experience. A week before you are due to make the transfer, you receive an email from the senior officer in charge of your new unit. She reminds you that you will be entering her unit at a very important time for them, because they will be leading a set of training exercises for highly-skilled airmen. She wants to make sure that you are ready to contribute immediately to the success of the unit, and that you will not need a great deal of assistance to complete your work.

Possible actions:

a. Do not respond to the email, and assume that you will be able to move into your new role seamlessly.
b. Thank the senior officer for her message, and do some internet research on your new duties.
c. Request that the transfer be canceled, and remain with your original unit.
d. Email the senior officer back, requesting a personal meeting where you can get more information about how to make a good transition to your new role.
e. Ask one of the other officers in your new unit if he will quietly bring you up to speed when you arrive.

27. Select the MOST EFFECTIVE action in response to the situation.

28. Select the LEAST EFFECTIVE action in response to the situation.

SITUATION 15:

One of your responsibilities is to keep a set of officers briefed on some confidential activities that are taking place at your base. One day, you accidentally send an email containing some information about these confidential activities to an officer who has not received the security clearance.

Possible actions:

a. Notify your supervisor of your mistake and let him resolve the situation.
b. Immediately send a second email to the improper recipient, requesting that he or she destroy the email. Inform your supervisors of your mistake.
c. Send a second email to the improper recipient, claiming that your email account has been hacked and that he should disregard any earlier messages.
d. Wait to see if there will be any negative consequences of your mistake.
e. Ask your supervisor if the improper recipient could be given the security clearance retroactively.

29. Select the MOST EFFECTIVE action in response to the situation.

30. Select the LEAST EFFECTIVE action in response to the situation.

SITUATION 16:

After completing your work at the base, you return to your living quarters for the evening. An hour later, you realize that you failed to affix your signature to a set of papers that are to be forwarded on to a different unit for completion. Without your signature, the papers cannot be sent. The content of the papers is not particularly urgent, but the delay will require the other unit officer to stay later than normal at his post.

Possible actions:

a. Wait until your next shift to sign the papers, since they are not considered urgent.
b. Call the base and ask a junior officer to forge your signature so the paperwork can be sent.
c. Call the officer at the other base and explain that the papers will be arriving a little later than expected.
d. Arrive for your next shift a little early and sign the papers first.
e. Return to the base and sign the necessary papers.

31. Select the MOST EFFECTIVE action in response to the situation.

32. Select the LEAST EFFECTIVE action in response to the situation.

SITUATION 17:

Several of the airmen in your unit have yet to complete a basic training module at a nearby base. They have asked to participate in the next training session, but instead, a group of airmen from another unit have been selected. The selected airmen have not been waiting nearly as long as your airmen to complete this training module. You suspect that the director of the training session dislikes you personally, though you have no specific evidence of this.

Possible actions:

a. Request a meeting with the training director, and ask why your airmen have been passed over, emphasizing the importance of this module for their development.
b. Do nothing, in the hopes that the situation will improve on its own.
c. Ask the officer in charge of the other unit if your airmen can attend the training session instead of his.
d. Write a critical letter to the training director and your senior officer, outlining what you perceive as the injustice of the situation.
e. Ask the training director if your airmen can attend the next training session along with the selected airmen.

33. Select the MOST EFFECTIVE action in response to the situation.

34. Select the LEAST EFFECTIVE action in response to the situation.

SITUATION 18:

You have been assigned to draft an important report along with another officer in your unit. It is expected that the report will take approximately one month to complete. However, after about a week of work, the other officer falls ill and is required to go on leave. He is only supposed to be gone for about ten days, but at the end of this period he has not returned and there is no definitive word on when he will. You need the expertise of this officer in order to finish the report.

Possible actions:

a. Wait until the other officer returns from leave, even if it means delaying the report.
b. Ask for an extension, without making excuses for your failure to complete the report on time.
c. Work extra hours to complete the report as best as you can.
d. Tell your commanding officer the situation, and request assistance in completing the report.
e. Order a junior officer to assist you in the completion of the report.

35. Select the MOST EFFECTIVE action in response to the situation.

36. Select the LEAST EFFECTIVE action in response to the situation.

SITUATION 19:

Two months ago, you joined a new unit. The leader of this unit was very welcoming to you and made sure to give you as much assistance as you needed in learning your new duties and responsibilities. However, you are now feeling more comfortable in your role and would like more independence in your work.

Possible actions:

a. Request a meeting with the unit leader, thank him for his assistance, and indicate that you would like to work on your own a bit more.
b. Request that another officer be transferred to your unit so that the unit leader will divert his attention to training this new arrival.
c. Without saying anything directly, try to avoid the unit leader as much as possible.
d. Tell the unit leader's commanding officer that you need the unit leader to give you more space.
e. Keep extensive records of your work so that you can demonstrate your competence to the unit leader.

37. Select the MOST EFFECTIVE action in response to the situation.

38. Select the LEAST EFFECTIVE action in response to the situation.

SITUATION 20:

One of the other officers in your division is going to make an important presentation at the end of the week. He is nervous, but he has done good work in the past and has spent a great deal of time preparing the report. He asks you to look over his work in advance. You notice a few things that need to be changed, but the other officer disagrees with your corrections. You are certain that you are right and that the other officer will be sorry he did not listen to you.

Possible actions:

a. Let your coworker go ahead with the uncorrected presentation, but make yourself look better by mentioning the errors to a senior officer before the presentation.
b. Allow your coworker to go ahead with the presentation as is, without trying to convince him to make the corrections.
c. Discuss the matter with your senior officer, and ask him or her to mandate the corrections.
d. Contrive an excuse to be absent from the presentation.
e. Make every effort to convince your colleague to make the necessary corrections.

39. Select the MOST EFFECTIVE action in response to the situation.

40. Select the LEAST EFFECTIVE action in response to the situation.

SITUATION 21:

You have been working with a new unit for the past six weeks. During that time, you have noticed some inefficiencies in the unit's operations, and you have developed a set of proposals for eliminating them. The majority of your coworkers agree with your proposals, but the senior officer in charge of the unit does not. The senior officer believes that implementing your proposals would be too risky and would undermine the stability of the unit.

Possible actions:

a. Confront your senior officer, using the support of your coworkers as a reason to implement your proposals.
b. Create a detailed and comprehensive report outlining the potential benefits of your proposals. Deliver the report and then obey the senior officer's final decision.
c. Implement your proposals anyway, on the assumption that your senior officer will change his mind once he sees their success.
d. Accept the senior officer's decision and try to succeed within the agreed-upon structure.
e. Accept the senior officer's decision, but keep a running list of the ways your proposals could have improved performance, had they been implemented.

41. Select the MOST EFFECTIVE action in response to the situation.

42. Select the LEAST EFFECTIVE action in response to the situation.

SITUATION 22:

Six months ago, you were assigned a new assistant. Although you have been able to work successfully together, you have developed a personal dislike for this person. In your opinion, he is arrogant and too critical of the other officers. During a meeting with your senior officer, she mentions that she is considering transferring your assistant to another unit. This would represent a step up for him and would make it possible for him to achieve even more promotions in a relatively short time.

Possible actions:

a. Recommend that your assistant receive the promotion, if only to get him away from you.
b. Strongly discourage the senior officer from choosing your assistant so that he will not get a professional reward.
c. Write an anonymous letter to the senior officer, outlining your complaints about your assistant.
d. Strongly discourage the senior officer from choosing your assistant, with an emphasis on his personality flaws.
e. Avoid interfering in the senior officer's decision, but make sure that she is aware of your opinion of your assistant.

43. Select the MOST EFFECTIVE action in response to the situation.

44. Select the LEAST EFFECTIVE action in response to the situation.

Situation 23:

Your base uses a computer program to determine the logistics related to supply deliveries. One day, while you are coordinating the arrival and unloading of several concurrent deliveries, the computer system crashes. The computer technician tells you that it could be an hour before the system is up and running again. You can see that there is a long line of trucks waiting to deliver their goods and that the drivers are becoming impatient.

Possible actions:

a. Ask one of your assistants to inform the drivers of the situation and the likely wait time. Offer whatever accommodations you can in the interim.
b. Receive the deliveries despite the computer problems, and keep paper records so you can update the system later.
c. Call your senior officer and ask for advice.
d. Use this opportunity to take your lunch break, somewhere you are unlikely to meet any of the drivers.
e. Encourage the drivers to make any other deliveries they have and then come back later.

45. Select the MOST EFFECTIVE action in response to the situation.

46. Select the LEAST EFFECTIVE action in response to the situation.

Situation 24:

You have developed an idea that you believe will improve the performance of your unit. However, some of the airmen in your unit disagree with this idea, and one has gone so far as to write a letter of complaint to your senior officer without notifying you. You have not yet implemented your idea.

Possible actions:

a. Meet with the letter-writer and other critics, emphasizing that going above your head will not be tolerated in the future.
b. Abandon your idea and ask for suggestions from the airmen who were critical of it.
c. Ignore the critics in you unit, and implement your idea anyway.
d. Harshly punish the letter writer, as a warning to the other airmen.
e. Implement your idea without acknowledging the letter or the criticism of other airmen in the unit.

47. Select the MOST EFFECTIVE action in response to the situation.

48. Select the LEAST EFFECTIVE action in response to the situation.

SITUATION 25:

You received a promotion six months ago and have been excelling in your new job. However, due to forces beyond your control, the quality of your work has decreased over the past few weeks. In part, you have been undermined by recent budget cuts. Unfortunately, your commanding officer does not fully understand the consequences of the budget cuts and has expressed her displeasure with your recent work. She has even suggested that problems in your unit may be a result of poor management on your part.

Possible actions:

a. Ask the commanding officer if you can take a brief leave to refocus.
b. Do not make any excuses, but ask the advice of other officers who are dealing with the same budget constraints.
c. Ask your commanding officer for a list of her specific complaints.
d. Shift the blame for your unit's performance to your subordinates.
e. Remind the commanding officer of the budget constraints, and defend your management style to her.

49. Select the MOST EFFECTIVE action in response to the situation.

50. Select the LEAST EFFECTIVE action in response to the situation.

Physical Science

1. A long nail is heated at one end. After a few seconds, the other end of the nail becomes equally hot. What type of heat transfer does this represent?

a. Advection
b. Conduction
c. Convection
d. Entropy
e. Radiation

2. The measure of energy within a system is called

a. Temperature
b. Convection
c. Entropy
d. Thermodynamics
e. Heat

3. How do two isotopes of the same element differ?

a. They have different numbers of protons.
b. They have different numbers of neutrons.
c. They have different numbers of electrons.
d. They have different charges.
e. They have different atomic numbers.

4. Which type of nuclear process features atomic nuclei splitting apart to form smaller nuclei?

a. Fission
b. Fusion
c. Decay
d. Ionization
e. Chain reaction

5. The process whereby a radioactive element releases energy slowly over a long period of time to lower its energy and become more stable is best described as

a. Combustion
b. Fission
c. Fusion
d. Decay
e. Radioactivity

6. What property of light explains why a pencil in a glass of water appears to be bent?

a. Reflection
b. Refraction
c. The angle of incidence equals the angle of reflection
d. Constructive interference
e. Destructive interference

7. What unit describes the frequency of a wave?

a. Hertz (Hz)
b. Decibels (dB)
c. Meters (m)
d. Meters per second (m/s)
e. Meters per second squared (m/s^2)

8. Which of the following is an example of kinetic energy being converted to potential energy?

a. A child sliding down a slide
b. A cyclist coasting on his way up a hill
c. A pilot deploying airbrakes on approach to land
d. A motorist swerving to avoid a deer
e. A pair of billiard balls colliding and rebounding off each other

9. The boiling of water is an example of

a. Sublimation
b. Condensation
c. Neutralization
d. Chemical change
e. Physical change

10. The center of an atom is called the

a. Nucleus
b. Nuclide
c. Neutrino
d. Electron cloud
e. Electrolyte

11. When a solid is heated and transforms directly to the gaseous phases, this process is called

a. Sublimation
b. Fusion
c. Diffusion
d. Condensation
e. Fission

12. Which scientist was responsible for developing the format of the modern periodic table?

a. Faraday
b. Einstein
c. Hess
d. Mendeleev
e. Oppenheimer

13. The density of a material refers to its:

a. Mass per unit volume
b. Mass per unit length
c. Mass per unit surface area
d. Volume per unit surface area
e. Volume per unit length

14. The precision of a set of experimentally obtained data points refers to

a. How accurate the data points are
b. How many errors the data points contain
c. How close the data points are to each other
d. How close the data points are to the predicted result
e. How close the set of data is to a normal distribution

15. Current, or the amount of electricity that is flowing, is measured in

a. Volts
b. Watts
c. Ohms
d. Farads
e. Amperes

16. A solar eclipse can only occur if

a. The earth and the sun are on the same side of the moon.
b. The earth is between the sun and the moon.
c. The moon is between the earth and the sun.
d. The sun is between the earth and the moon.
e. The moon is full.

17. What property of motion explains why passengers in a turning car feel pulled toward the outside of the turn?

a. Centripetal force
b. Inertia
c. Normal force
d. Impulse
e. Torque

18. According to the ideal gas law, if a certain amount of gas is being held at a constant volume, and the temperature is increased, what will happen?

a. The mass of the gas will increase
b. The pressure of the gas will increase
c. The density of the gas will decrease
d. The mass of the gas will decrease
e. The pressure of the gas will decrease

19. What wave characteristic is related to the loudness of a sound?

a. Frequency
b. Amplitude
c. Wavelength
d. Velocity
e. Period

20. Which of the following scenarios is NOT an example of a person applying work to a book?

a. A book is picked up from the floor and put on a shelf.
b. A book is pushed across a table top.
c. A backpack holding a book is carried across the room.
d. A book is held and then released so that it falls to the ground.
e. A book is thrown vertically into the air.

Table Reading

For each question, select the number that appears in the table at the given coordinates. Recall that the first number in the ordered pair gives the column number, and the second gives the row number. For instance, the ordered pair $(2, -1)$ refers to the number in column 2, row -1, which is 732 in the table.

Use the table below to answer questions 1-40.

	-12	-11	-10	-9	-8	-7	-6	-5	-4	-3	-2	-1	0	1	2	3	4	5	6	7	8	9	10	11	12
-12	987	972	433	251	462	338	836	424	131	773	809	602	261	569	550	952	216	808	891	232	316	623	986	141	488
-11	337	740	563	587	510	138	491	654	775	261	528	986	212	387	837	100	241	114	536	568	673	833	610	398	578
-10	639	122	374	648	229	692	250	767	803	337	725	838	725	144	863	542	928	232	908	809	296	852	284	963	991
-9	280	271	269	575	696	649	637	750	161	366	151	226	577	995	494	106	819	390	618	557	191	993	438	850	751
-8	586	970	977	677	988	166	748	340	833	710	631	207	464	524	279	596	990	621	752	365	355	920	544	122	185
-7	728	206	273	437	636	394	813	161	731	219	494	278	349	423	325	409	631	538	918	134	151	867	624	920	733
-6	714	817	929	377	264	974	300	999	982	348	166	859	667	762	441	226	734	692	302	688	550	589	143	169	860
-5	780	511	934	814	538	712	832	165	315	637	252	800	205	290	557	713	629	764	228	585	594	912	473	651	957
-4	278	232	882	615	475	795	492	763	943	798	519	682	314	471	338	666	996	118	712	879	663	111	593	380	907
-3	576	534	470	835	886	318	738	322	739	284	890	397	683	356	177	839	679	496	344	613	268	179	951	292	204
-2	597	806	779	782	137	601	669	599	486	562	119	331	497	848	701	602	476	253	787	785	212	734	357	810	356
-1	266	142	405	779	792	514	369	731	663	422	328	529	754	122	732	319	332	927	665	438	342	698	714	637	262
0	836	881	121	327	431	710	702	742	966	902	562	733	522	486	608	810	432	843	413	179	219	556	235	330	776
1	928	271	938	525	554	176	714	402	992	199	870	962	595	959	800	851	823	561	568	647	245	652	669	953	121
2	201	464	830	565	678	748	176	382	161	598	909	610	483	902	512	435	607	119	111	710	331	105	430	958	838
3	955	181	865	766	989	835	207	894	836	533	907	137	339	693	166	619	247	882	948	913	701	130	259	361	754
4	258	997	209	333	331	773	987	354	436	837	269	650	263	813	345	137	861	442	394	456	616	521	870	139	974
5	818	390	866	177	144	937	368	823	703	862	512	545	414	571	713	766	818	268	116	494	936	678	237	401	604
6	165	464	708	301	825	992	526	975	649	450	527	507	455	581	287	528	414	338	779	729	284	247	341	972	443
7	206	217	571	346	566	921	741	462	106	647	464	743	480	700	222	139	947	963	392	826	106	661	917	228	502
8	516	409	120	796	838	721	852	106	226	704	231	187	115	827	434	548	683	138	848	824	957	304	998	617	121
9	779	812	809	702	596	844	261	136	301	227	582	378	683	735	910	620	367	483	826	518	905	563	596	521	751
10	477	320	645	916	438	150	787	578	236	734	393	396	156	507	176	236	886	161	676	226	179	812	999	853	167
11	273	514	137	670	965	886	919	657	775	420	354	146	610	639	181	293	476	150	192	558	729	160	955	780	293
12	675	164	725	723	196	262	436	496	880	663	650	765	851	848	620	743	615	248	536	881	122	642	440	307	846

1. $(\mathbf{0}, -\mathbf{1})$

a. 529
b. 754
c. 733
d. 536
e. 486

2. $(\mathbf{7}, -\mathbf{11})$

a. 568
b. 138
c. 348
d. 809
e. 232

3. $(\mathbf{1}, -\mathbf{2})$

a. 122
b. 356
c. 848
d. 331
e. 497

4. $(-\mathbf{9}, -\mathbf{11})$

a. 648
b. 510
c. 587
d. 216
e. 563

5. $(\mathbf{11}, \mathbf{5})$

a. 139
b. 972
c. 237
d. 511
e. 401

6. $(-\mathbf{9}, -\mathbf{1})$

a. 792
b. 782
c. 405
d. 779
e. 327

7. $(\mathbf{6}, \mathbf{9})$

a. 848
b. 138
c. 826
d. 261
e. 618

8. $(-\mathbf{4}, -\mathbf{3})$

a. 739
b. 322
c. 284
d. 943
e. 679

9. $(\mathbf{2}, -\mathbf{5})$

a. 557
b. 441
c. 290
d. 762
e. 382

10. $(-\mathbf{7}, -\mathbf{10})$

a. 649
b. 692
c. 250
d. 510
e. 273

11. $(\mathbf{11}, -\mathbf{12})$

a. 398
b. 578
c. 488
d. 972
e. 141

12. $(\mathbf{4}, -\mathbf{10})$

a. 241
b. 100
c. 803
d. 882
e. 928

13. $(-\mathbf{8}, \mathbf{9})$

a. 596
b. 844
c. 702
d. 566
e. 438

14. $(\mathbf{10}, \mathbf{7})$

a. 661
b. 917
c. 341
d. 998
e. 571

15. $(-\mathbf{5}, -\mathbf{11})$

a. 424
b. 654
c. 803
d. 114
e. 511

16. $(-\mathbf{6}, -\mathbf{11})$

a. 836
b. 536
c. 169
d. 491
e. 817

17. $(\mathbf{3}, -\mathbf{5})$

a. 713
b. 226
c. 637
d. 511
e. 496

18. $(-\mathbf{7}, \mathbf{7})$

a. 741
b. 462
c. 721
d. 992
e. 921

19. $(-\mathbf{4}, -\mathbf{5})$

a. 999
b. 982
c. 315
d. 763
e. 629

20. $(-\mathbf{4}, -\mathbf{1})$

a. 663
b. 422
c. 486
d. 731
e. 471

21. $(-\mathbf{5}, \mathbf{8})$

a. 852
b. 462
c. 138
d. 166
e. 106

22. $(\mathbf{8}, -\mathbf{1})$

a. 212
b. 219
c. 792
d. 207
e. 342

23. $(-\mathbf{11}, \mathbf{9})$

a. 409
b. 809
c. 812
d. 320
e. 141

24. $(\mathbf{8}, -\mathbf{2})$

a. 268
b. 212
c. 342
d. 137
e. 678

25. $(\mathbf{5}, -\mathbf{2})$

a. 253
b. 787
c. 927
d. 599
e. 557

26. $(\mathbf{12}, -\mathbf{11})$

a. 568
b. 578
c. 991
d. 398
e. 337

27. $(\mathbf{0}, -\mathbf{10})$

a. 725
b. 151
c. 337
d. 838
e. 121

28. $(\mathbf{8}, \mathbf{7})$

a. 661
b. 957
c. 826
d. 824
e. 106

29. $(-\mathbf{11}, \mathbf{10})$

a. 812
b. 514
c. 320
d. 645
e. 137

30. $(-\mathbf{3}, \mathbf{5})$

a. 862
b. 512
c. 450
d. 837
e. 322

31. $(-\mathbf{2}, -\mathbf{6})$

a. 859
b. 252
c. 601
d. 166
e. 787

32. $(-\mathbf{11}, -\mathbf{5})$

a. 817
b. 934
c. 511
d. 780
e. 114

33. $(-\mathbf{7}, \mathbf{11})$

a. 150
b. 262
c. 886
d. 217
e. 558

34. $(\mathbf{10}, \mathbf{5})$

a. 866
b. 161
c. 678
d. 237
e. 401

35. $(\mathbf{3}, \mathbf{7})$

a. 139
b. 222
c. 548
d. 683
e. 913

36. $(\mathbf{7}, \mathbf{3})$

a. 710
b. 913
c. 701
d. 111
e. 613

37. $(\mathbf{0}, \mathbf{2})$

a. 595
b. 339
c. 438
d. 843
e. 483

38. $(\mathbf{2}, \mathbf{5})$

a. 441
b. 762
c. 253
d. 599
e. 713

39. $(\mathbf{6}, -\mathbf{3})$

a. 344
b. 712
c. 738
d. 343
e. 434

40. $(\mathbf{10}, -\mathbf{12})$

a. 610
b. 968
c. 986
d. 433
e. 440

Instrument Comprehension

1. Which of the answer choices represents the orientation of the plane?

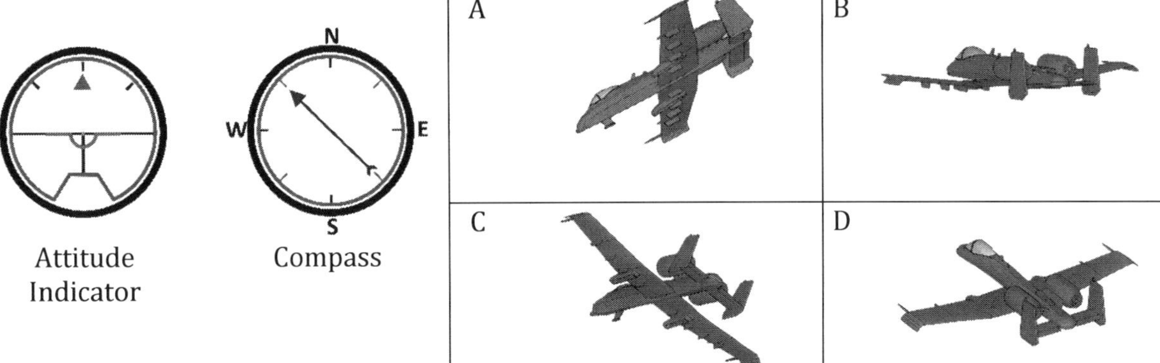

2. Which of the answer choices represents the orientation of the plane?

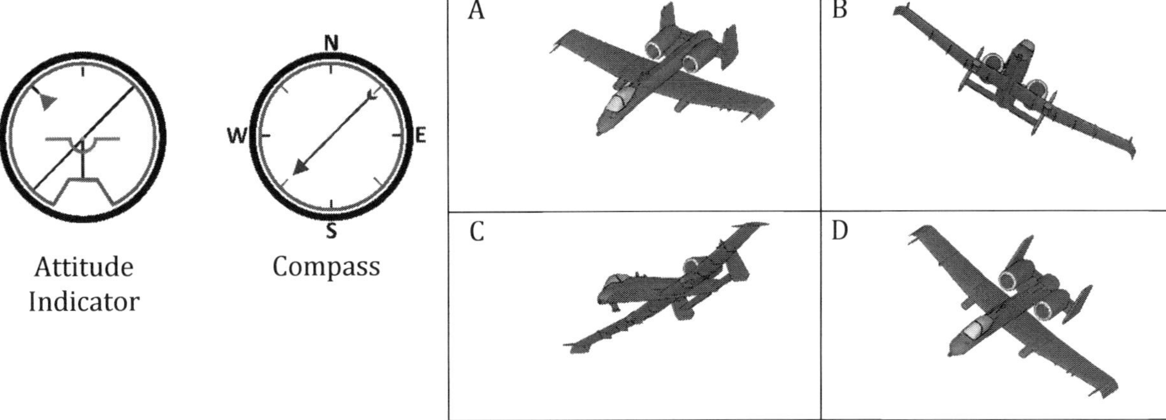

3. Which of the answer choices represents the orientation of the plane?

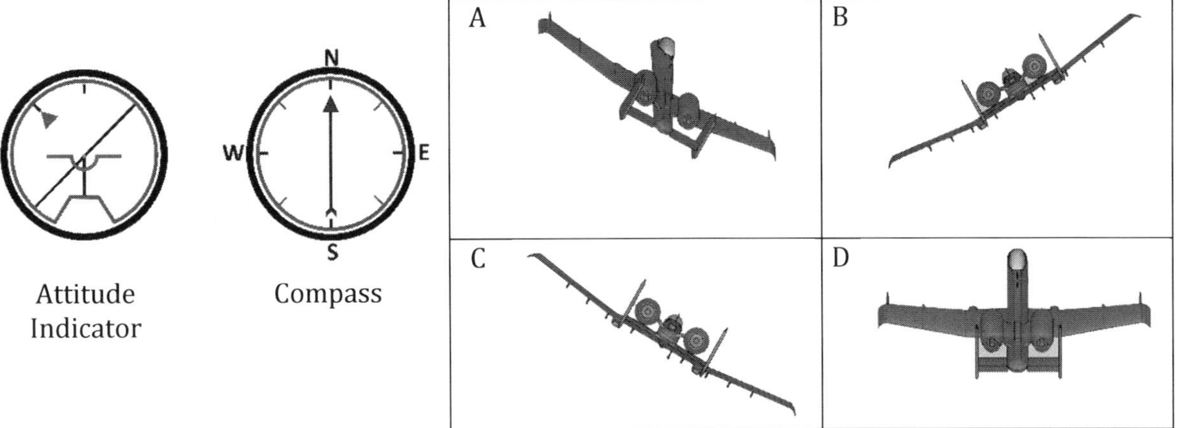

4. **Which of the answer choices represents the orientation of the plane?**

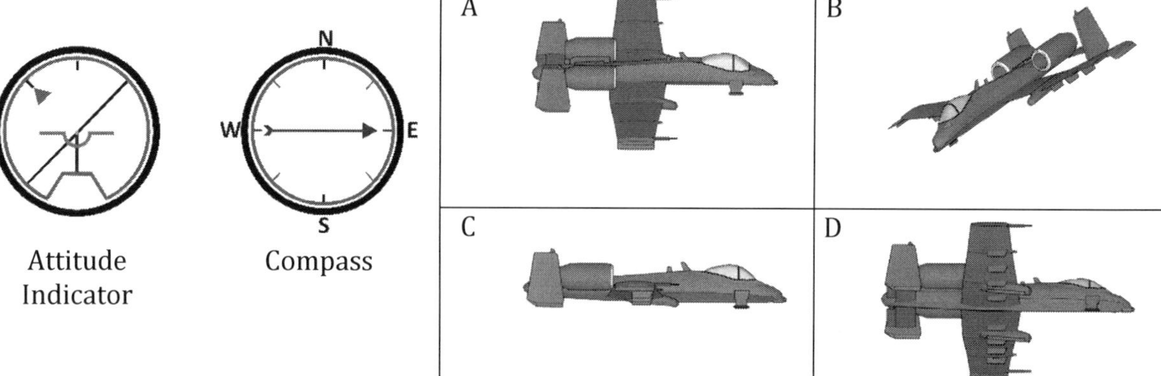

5. **Which of the answer choices represents the orientation of the plane?**

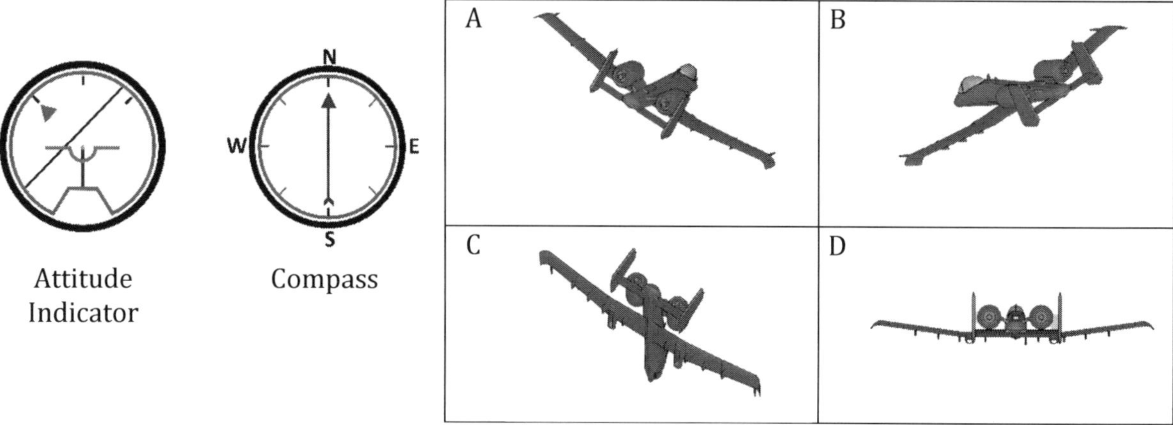

6. **Which of the answer choices represents the orientation of the plane?**

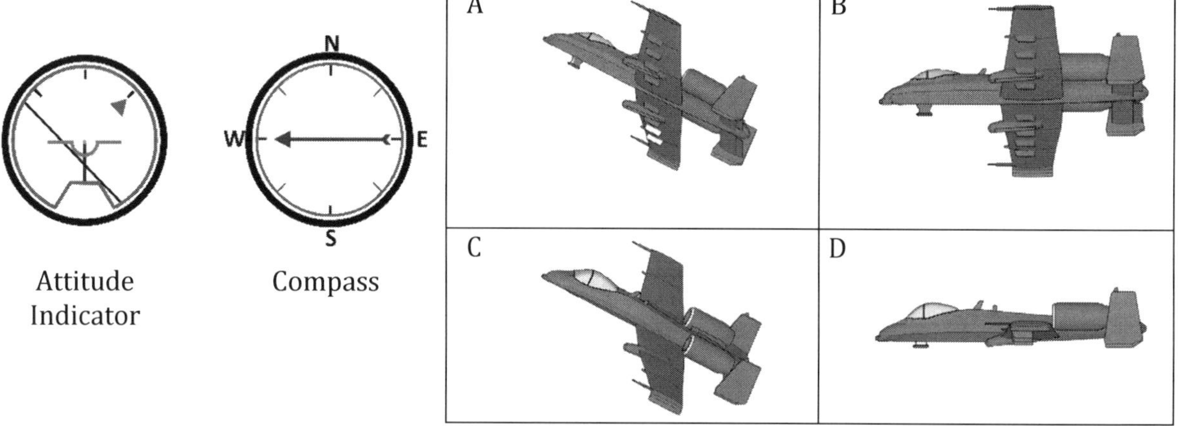

7. Which of the answer choices represents the orientation of the plane?

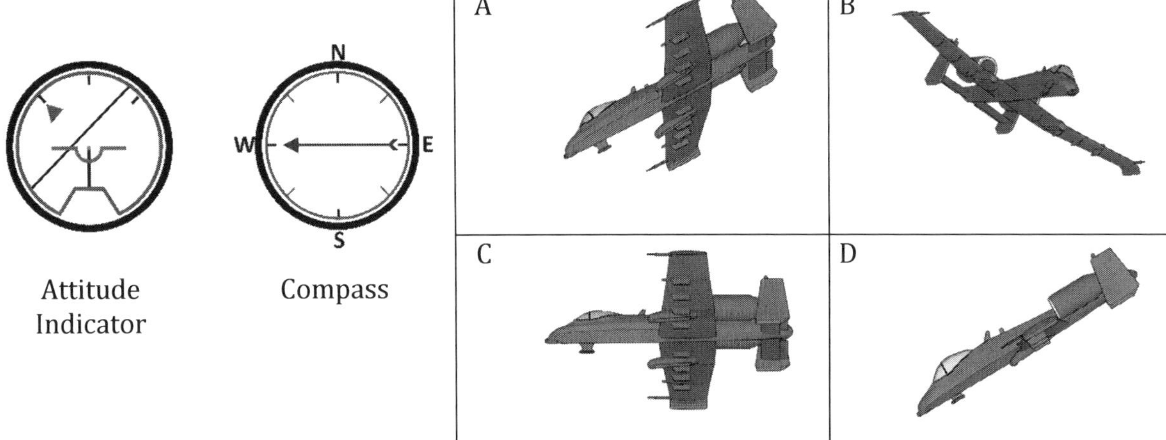

8. Which of the answer choices represents the orientation of the plane?

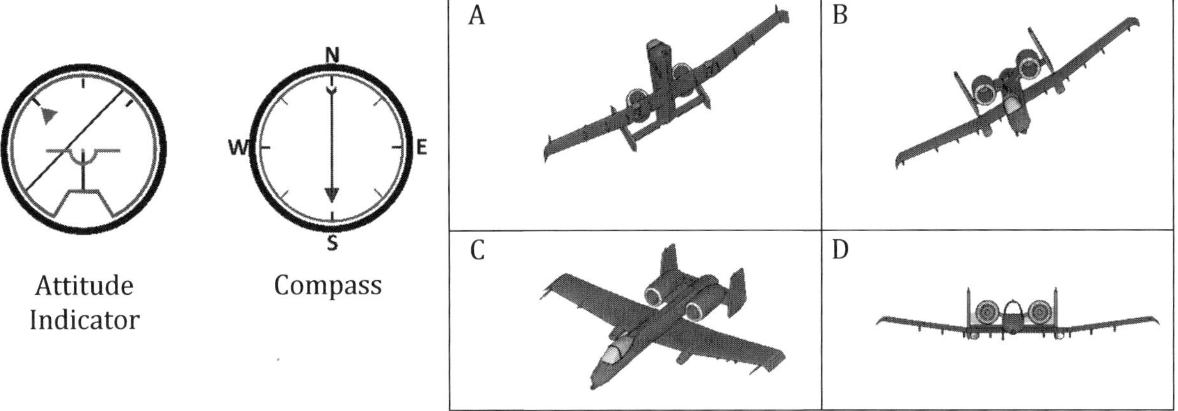

9. Which of the answer choices represents the orientation of the plane?

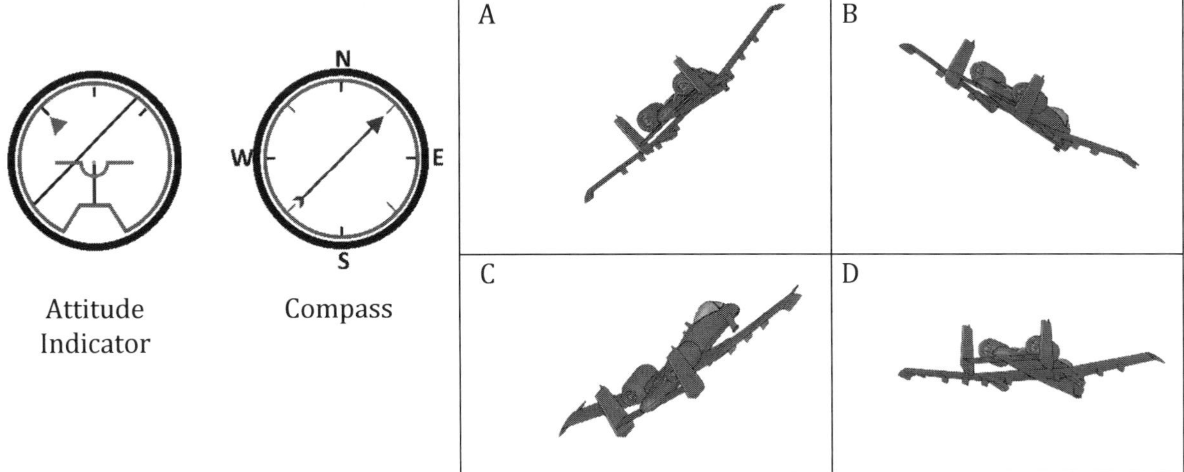

10. Which of the answer choices represents the orientation of the plane?

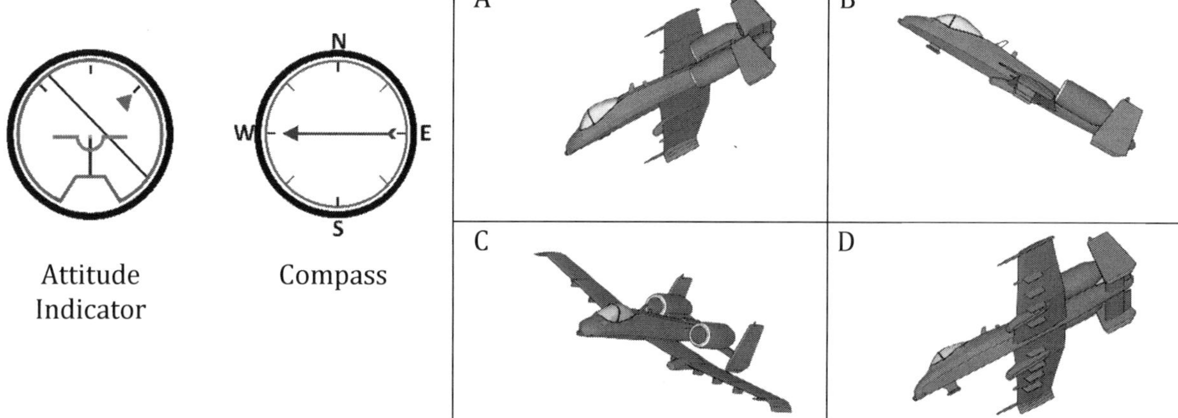

11. Which of the answer choices represents the orientation of the plane?

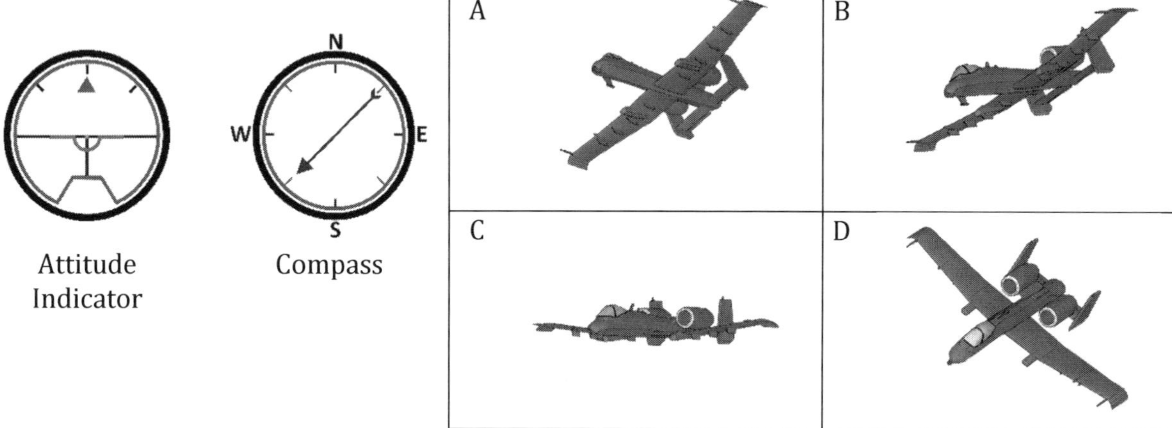

12. Which of the answer choices represents the orientation of the plane?

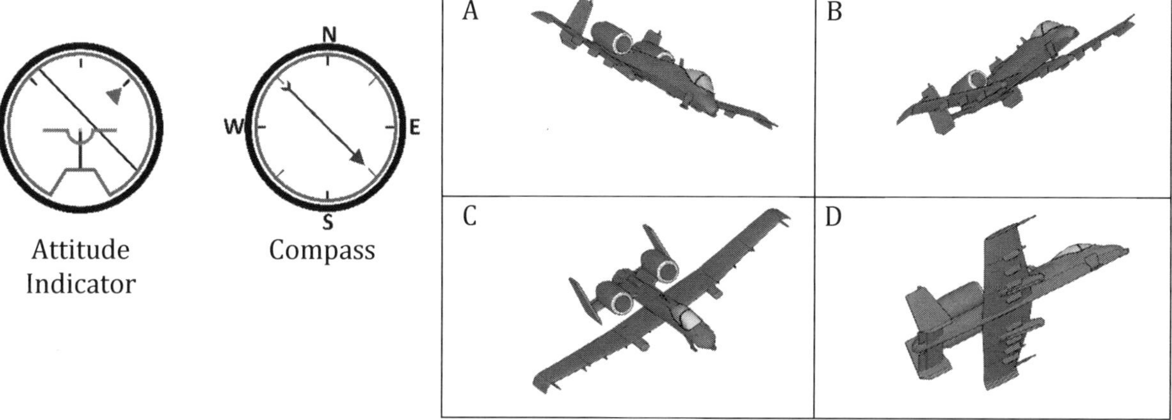

13. Which of the answer choices represents the orientation of the plane?

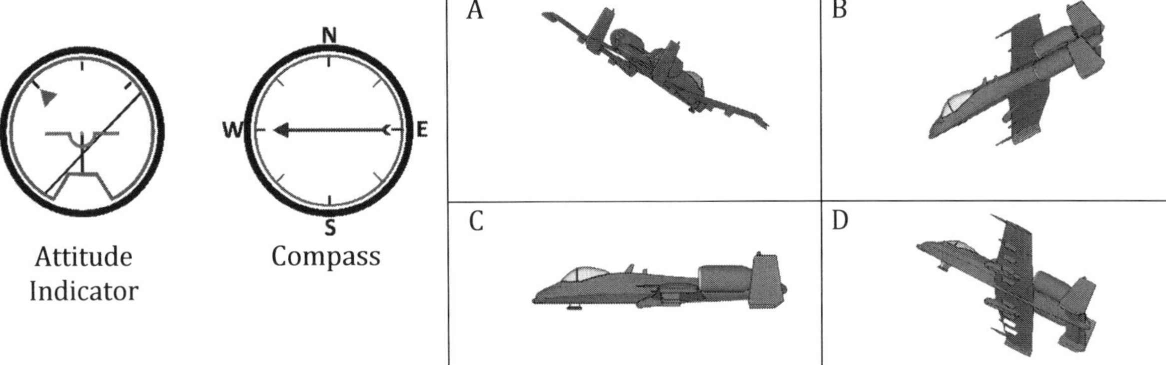

Attitude Indicator

Compass

14. Which of the answer choices represents the orientation of the plane?

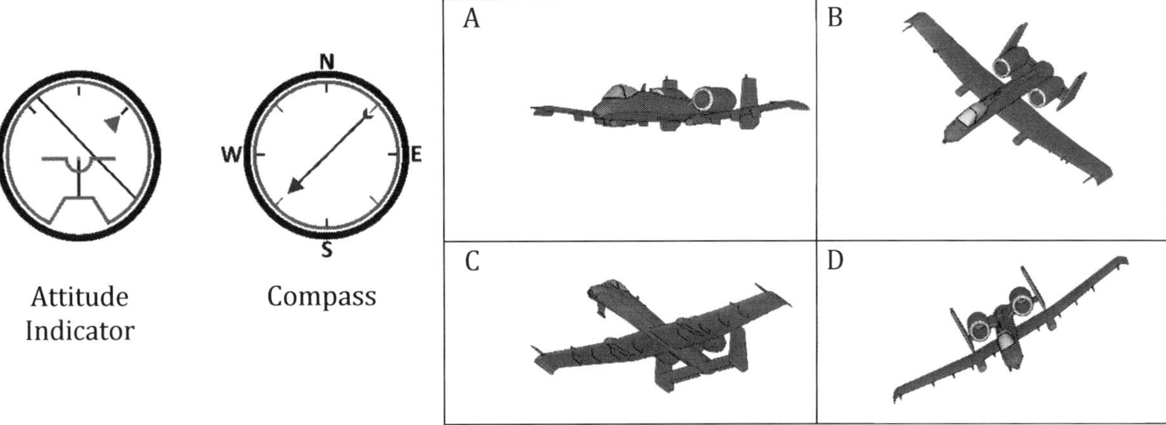

Attitude Indicator

Compass

15. Which of the answer choices represents the orientation of the plane?

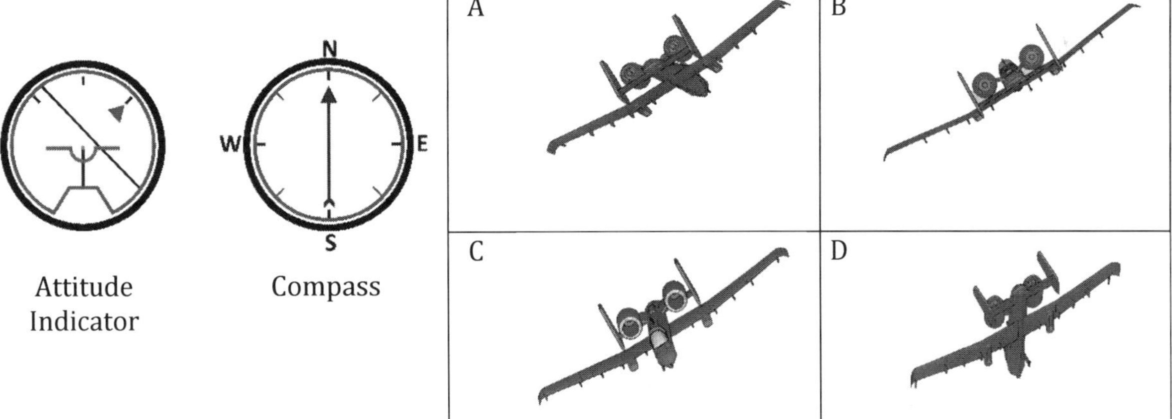

Attitude Indicator

Compass

16. Which of the answer choices represents the orientation of the plane?

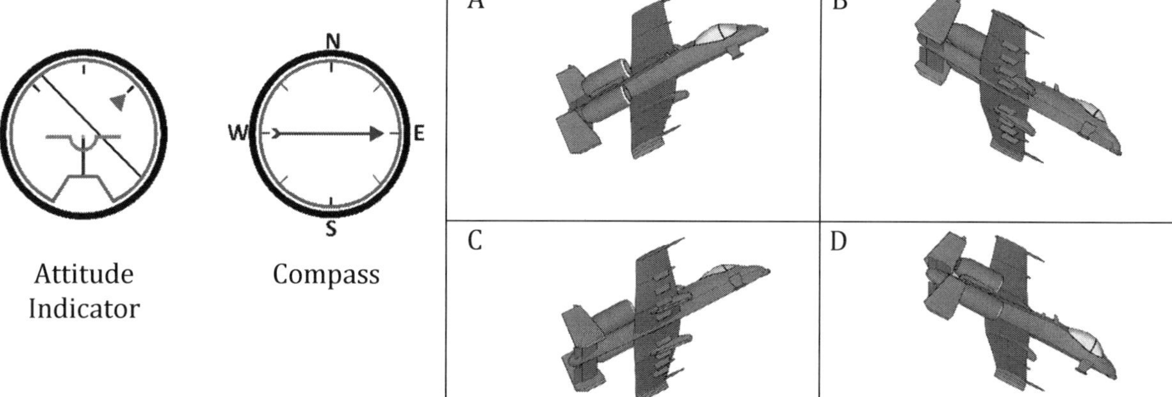

17. Which of the answer choices represents the orientation of the plane?

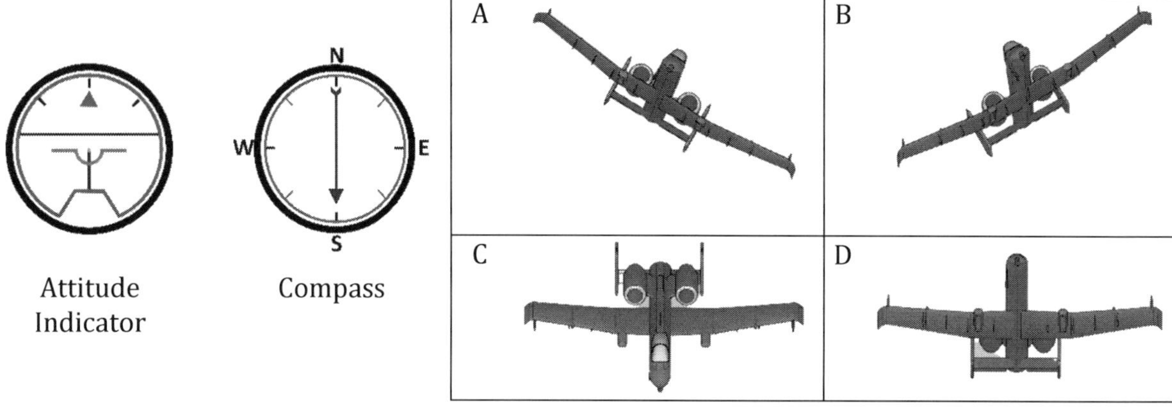

18. Which of the answer choices represents the orientation of the plane?

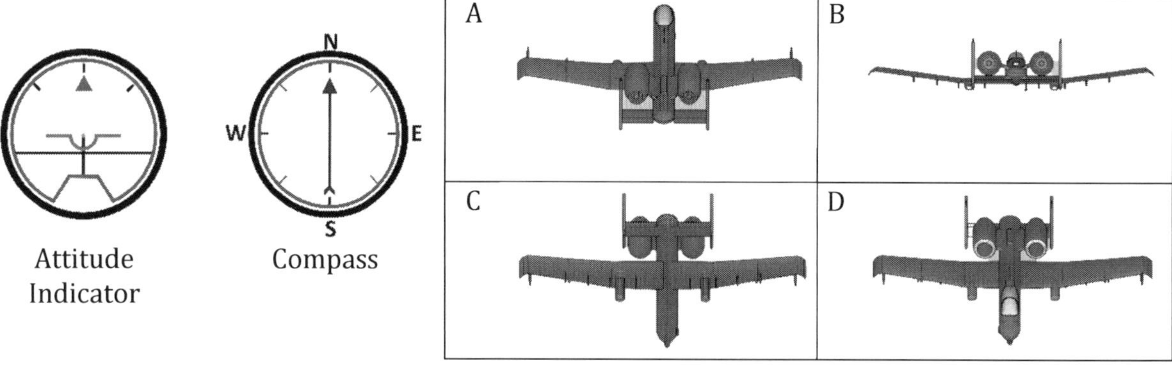

19. Which of the answer choices represents the orientation of the plane?

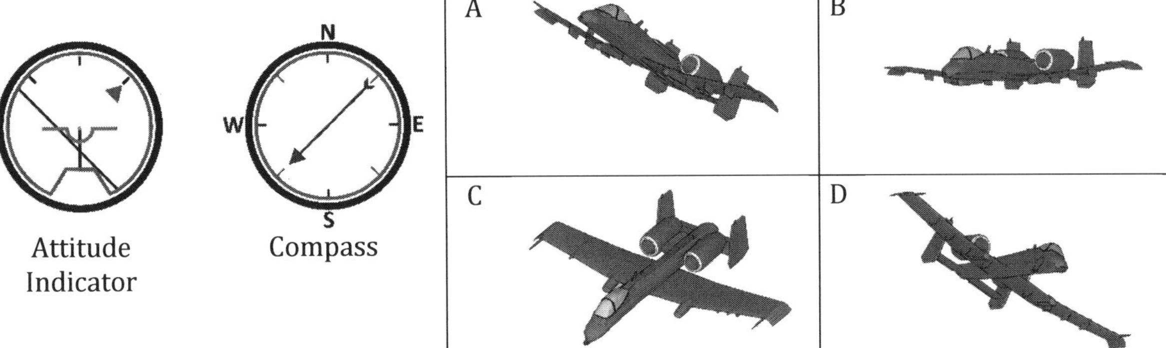

20. Which of the answer choices represents the orientation of the plane?

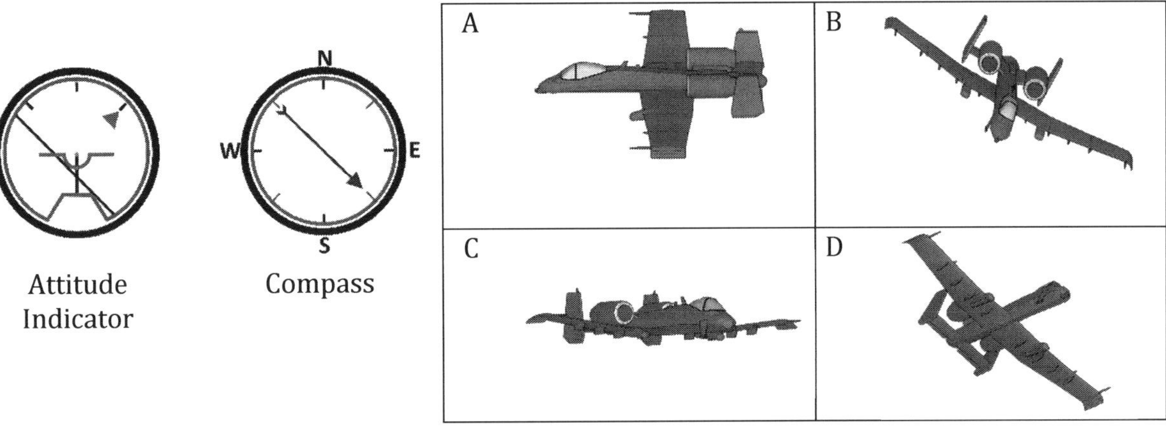

21. Which of the answer choices represents the orientation of the plane?

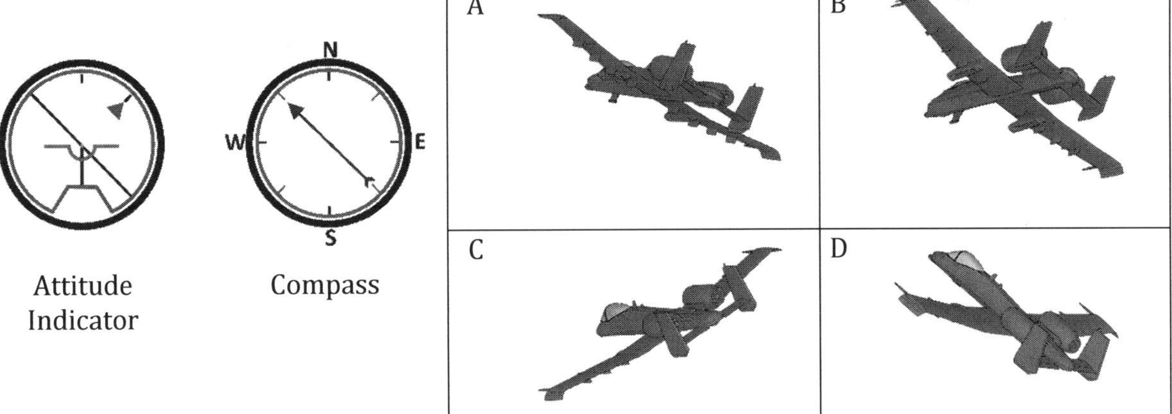

22. Which of the answer choices represents the orientation of the plane?

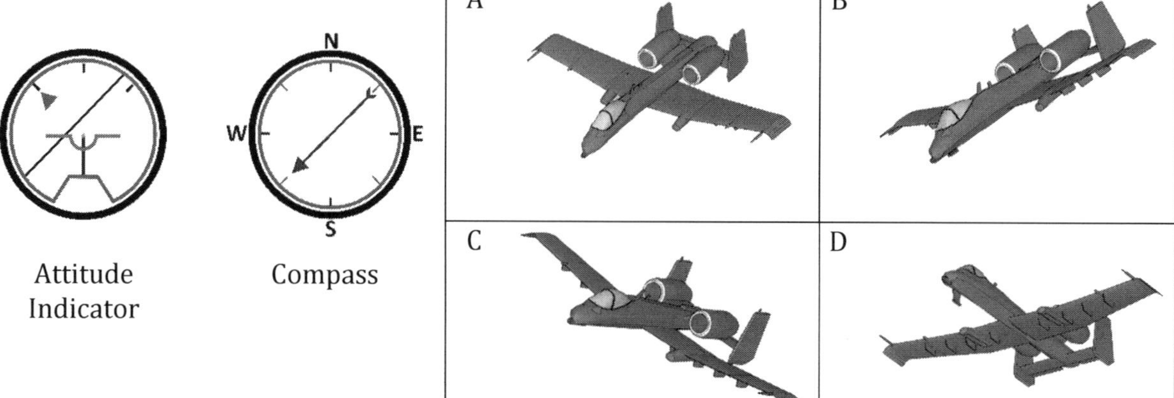

23. Which of the answer choices represents the orientation of the plane?

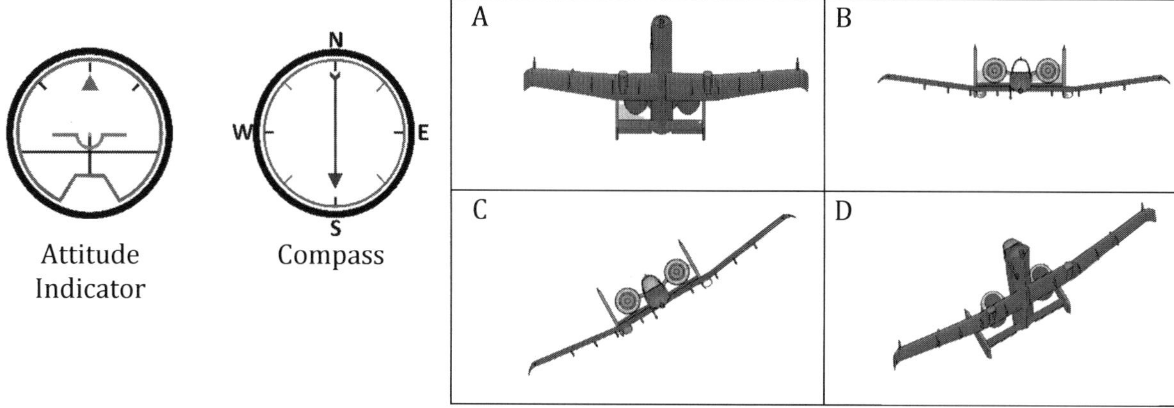

24. Which of the answer choices represents the orientation of the plane?

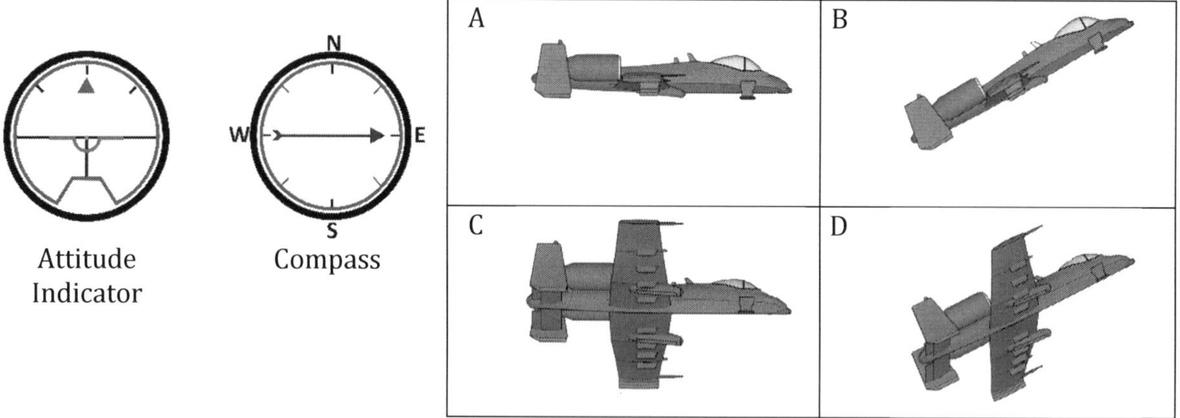

25. Which of the answer choices represents the orientation of the plane?

Attitude Indicator

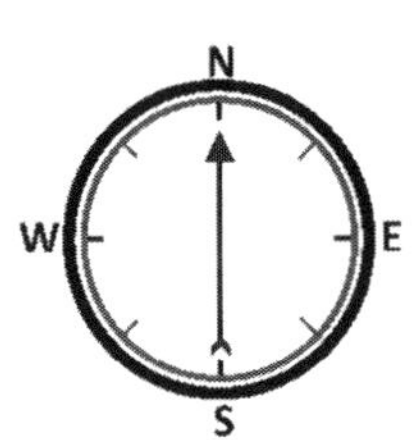

Compass

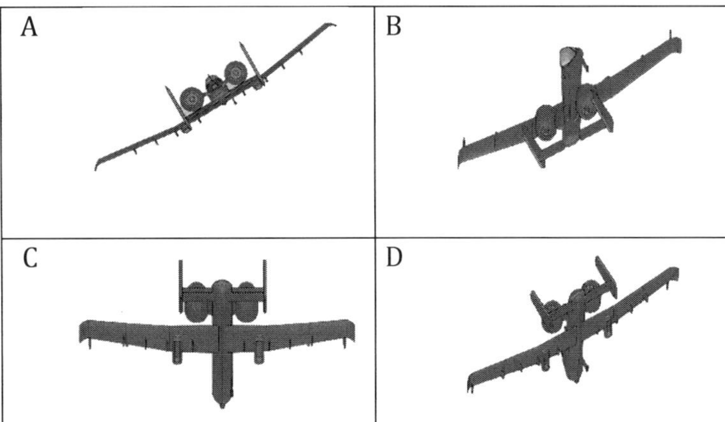

Block Counting

The explanations to these problems use terms like "top," "left," and "front" to refer to the faces of the blocks. This terminology can be confusing due to the angled view of the block arrangements, so the illustration below is provided to help you keep these terms straight.

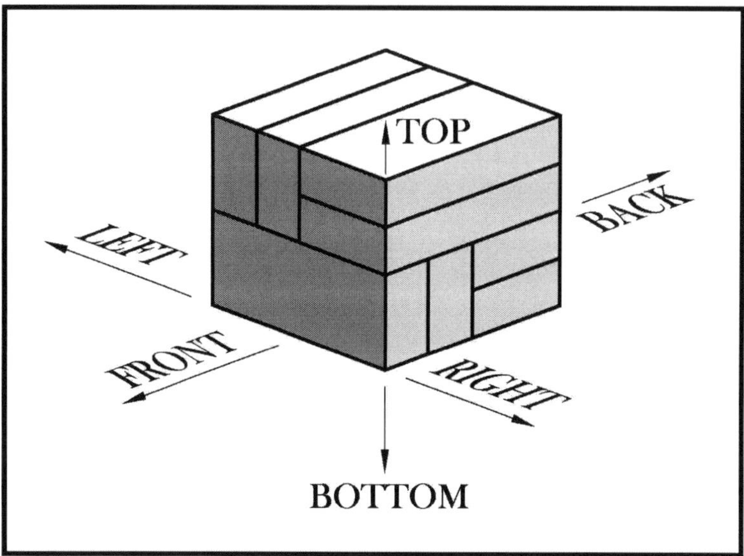

Once you understand these terms, proceed to the practice problems below. As a reminder, all the blocks in the images are intended to be the same size and shape, regardless of how much of each block is shown.

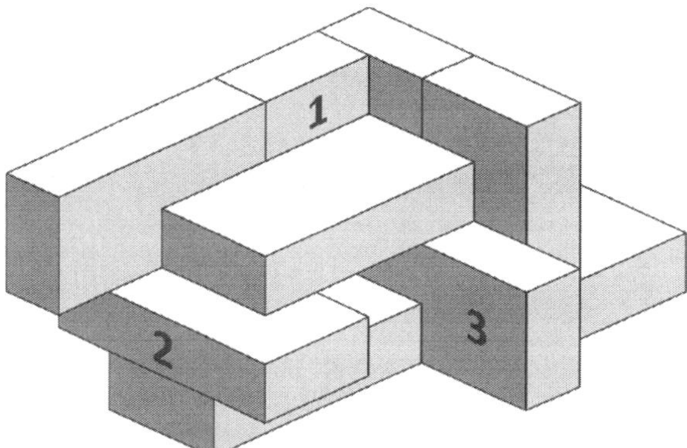

1. How many blocks are touching block 1 in the figure above?

2. How many blocks are touching block 2 in the figure above?

3. How many blocks are touching block 3 in the figure above?

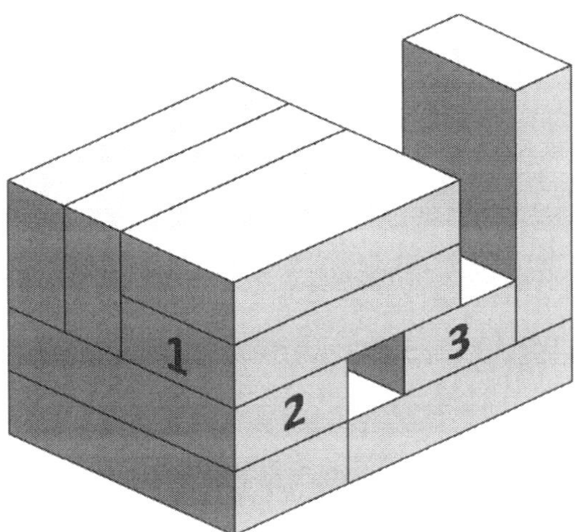

4. How many blocks are touching block 1 in the figure above?

5. How many blocks are touching block 2 in the figure above?

6. How many blocks are touching block 3 in the figure above?

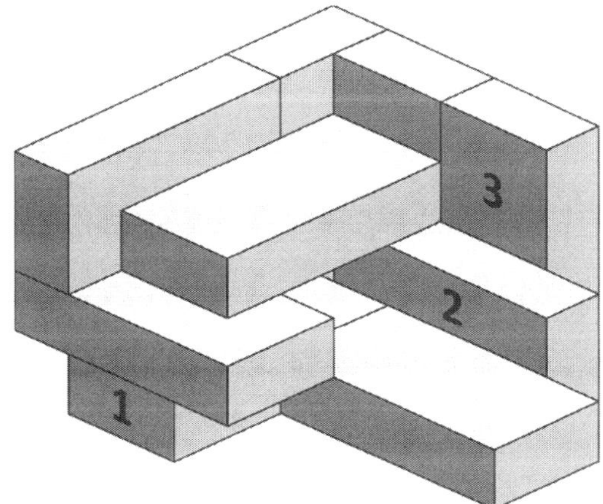

7. How many blocks are touching block 1 in the figure above?

8. How many blocks are touching block 2 in the figure above?

9. How many blocks are touching block 3 in the figure above?

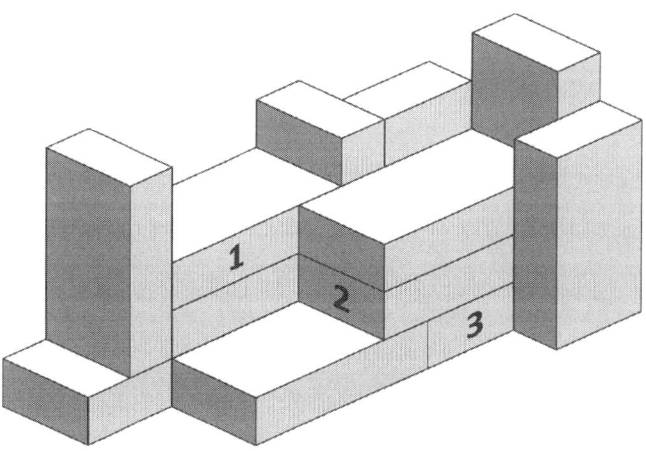

10. How many blocks are touching block 1 in the figure above?

11. How many blocks are touching block 2 in the figure above?

12. How many blocks are touching block 3 in the figure above?

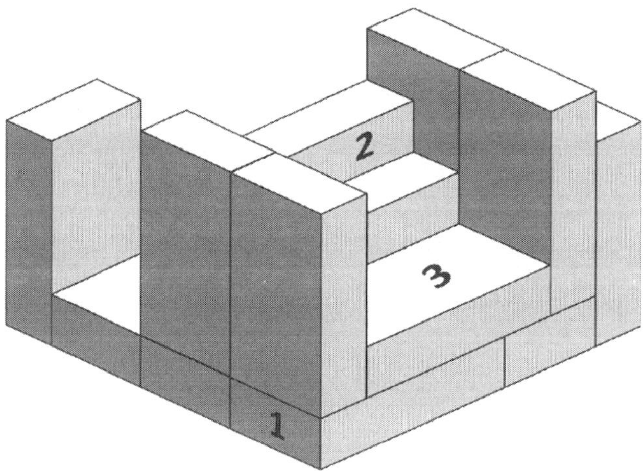

13. How many blocks are touching block 1 in the figure above?

14. How many blocks are touching block 2 in the figure above?

15. How many blocks are touching block 3 in the figure above?

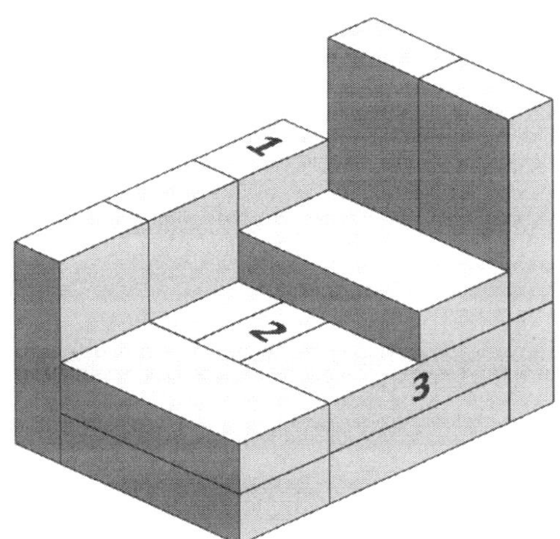

16. How many blocks are touching block 1 in the figure above?

17. How many blocks are touching block 2 in the figure above?

18. How many blocks are touching block 3 in the figure above?

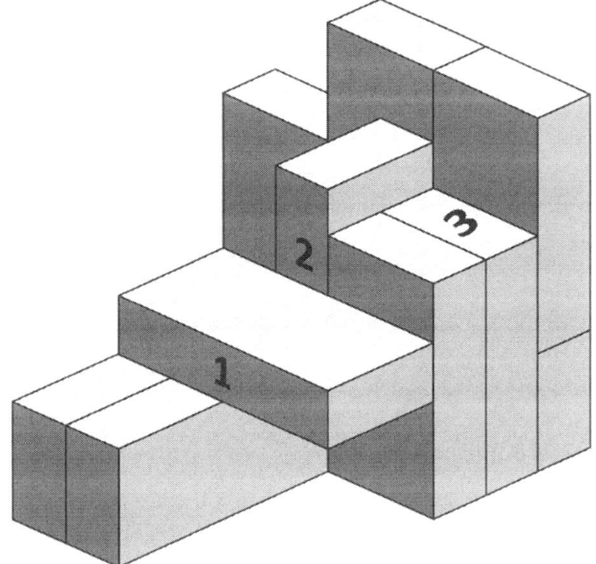

19. How many blocks are touching block 1 in the figure above?

20. How many blocks are touching block 2 in the figure above?

21. How many blocks are touching block 3 in the figure above?

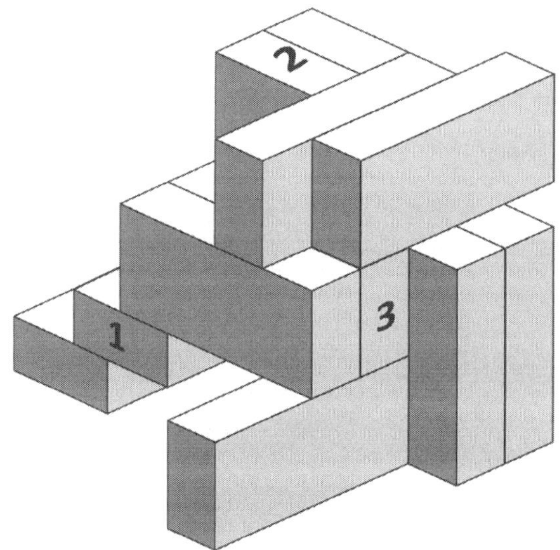

22. How many blocks are touching block 1 in the figure above?

23. How many blocks are touching block 2 in the figure above?

24. How many blocks are touching block 3 in the figure above?

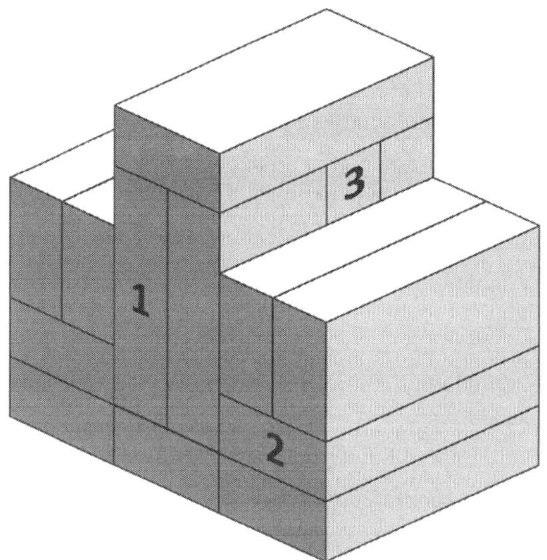

25. How many blocks are touching block 1 in the figure above?

26. How many blocks are touching block 2 in the figure above?

27. How many blocks are touching block 3 in the figure above?

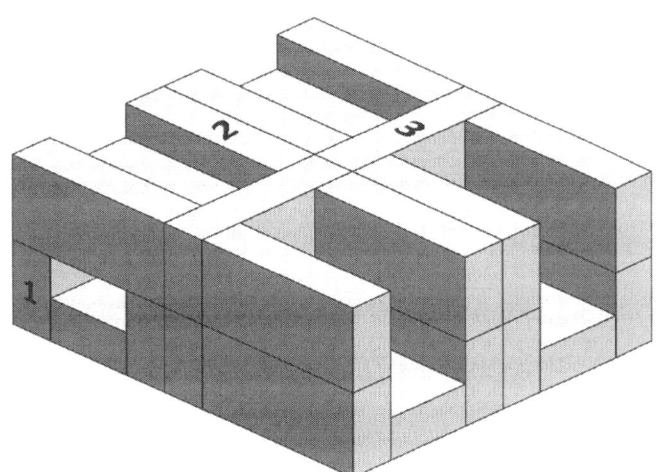

28. How many blocks are touching block 1 in the figure above?

29. How many blocks are touching block 2 in the figure above?

30. How many blocks are touching block 3 in the figure above?

Aviation Information

1. From approximately how far away should a Visual Approach Slope Indicator be visible at night?

a. Five miles
b. Ten miles
c. Twenty miles
d. Thirty miles
e. Fifty miles

2. Which of the following is NOT one of the forces a pilot must manage during flight?

a. Thrust
b. Gravity
c. Drag
d. Lift
e. Torque

3. Which control affects the angle of the main rotor blades of a helicopter?

a. Collective
b. Throttle
c. Cyclic
d. Directional control system
e. None of the above

4. What is the flight attitude?

a. The environment immediately around the plane
b. The morale of the flight crew
c. The position of the plane in motion
d. The inclination of the elevators
e. The positions of the ailerons

5. The curvature of an airfoil is known as the

a. Bank
b. Position
c. Camber
d. Angle
e. Attitude

6. Which of the following is considered one of the primary flight controls?

a. Elevators
b. Leading edge devices
c. Flaps
d. Spoilers
e. Trim tabs

7. What is the term in aviation for movement around the plane's longitudinal axis?

a. Stalling
b. Rolling
c. Pitching
d. Leaning
e. Yawing

8. What is the primary determinant of air pressure in the flight envelope?

a. The altitude at which the plane is flying
b. The camber of the wings
c. The amount of lift that the airfoils can create
d. The pitch of the elevators
e. The humidity of the air

9. A plane is said to have conventional landing gear when the third wheel is

a. Aligned with the second wheel
b. Under the tail
c. Directly behind the first wheel
d. Under the nose
e. Underneath the cockpit

10. Which of the following is NOT part of the empennage?

a. Rudder
b. Trim tab
c. Elevator
d. Aileron
e. Horizontal stabilizer

11. A glider would be most likely to have a

a. Delta wing
b. Triangular wing
c. Forward swept wing
d. Backward swept wing
e. Straight wing

12. Which of the following is NOT considered part of a plane's basic weight?

a. Crew
b. Fuel
c. External equipment
d. Internal equipment
e. Fuselage

13. The support structure that runs the length of the fuselage in a monocoque plane is called a

a. Counter
b. Former
c. Truss
d. Stringer
e. Bulkhead

14. Which control is used to manipulate the elevators on an airplane?

a. Throttle
b. Rudder
c. Joystick
d. Pedals
e. Collective

15. Which maneuver is appropriate when a pilot needs to descend quickly onto a shorter-than-normal runway?

a. Descent at minimum safe airspeed
b. Idle
c. Partial power descent
d. Glide
e. Stall

16. In aviation, which of the following is NOT one of the possible functions of a spoiler?

a. Diminishing lift
b. Raising the nose
c. Increasing drag
d. Reducing adverse yaw
e. Enabling descent without speed reduction

17. The vertical axis of a plane extends upward through the plane's

a. Cockpit
b. Tail
c. Landing gear
d. Center of mass
e. Geometric center

18. When is trimming necessary?

a. When the plane is ascending or descending
b. After the elevators have been deflected upwards
c. After the ailerons have been adjusted
d. After the elevators have been deflected downwards
e. After any change in the flight condition

19. How far away is an approaching plane when the Runway Centerline Lighting System lights become solid red?

a. Five hundred feet
b. One thousand feet
c. Three thousand feet
d. Five thousand feet
e. One mile

20. What is the Coriolis force?

a. The extra lift generated by a helicopter once it has exited its own downwash
b. The force that spins the rotors of a helicopter even when there is no power from the engine
c. The greater downwash at the rear half of the rotor disc, as compared with the front
d. The phenomenon in which the effects of a force applied to a spinning disc occur ninety degrees later
e. The change in rotational speed caused by the shift of the weight towards or away from the center of the spinning object

Answer Key and Explanations for Test #1

Verbal Analogies

1. B: Rash. Chastise and reprimand are synonyms. The answer choice synonym for impetuous is rash.

2. C: Femur. The humerus is a bone in the arm; the femur is a bone in the leg.

3. A: Quotient. A quotient is the result of division as a product is the result of multiplication.

4. C: Asparagus. As a sweater is something one wears, asparagus is something one eats.

5. A: Famished. As a person who is impecunious needs money, so a person who is famished needs food.

6. A: Protest. Denigrate and malign are synonyms. The answer choice synonym for demur is protest.

7. D: Generous. Obeisance and deference are synonyms. The answer choice synonym for munificent is generous.

8. D: Sow. A female goat is a nanny and a female pig is a sow.

9. B: Paucity. Cache and reserve are synonyms. The answer choice synonym for dearth is paucity.

10. E: Refuge. Arable and farmable are synonyms. The answer choice synonym for asylum is refuge.

11. A: Peripatetic. Myriad and few are antonyms. The answer choice antonym for stationary is peripatetic.

12. A: Flagon. As a mansion is a large house, so a flagon is a large bottle.

13. B: Synonyms. As a dictionary is a collection of definitions, so a thesaurus is a collection of synonyms.

14. B: Stubborn. Abstruse and esoteric are synonyms. The answer choice synonym for adamant is stubborn.

15. C: Herd. A group of bees is called a hive, and a group of cattle is called a herd.

16. E: Meridian. A parallel is a line of latitude, while a meridian is a line of longitude.

17. B: Provocation. Prevention and deterrence are synonyms. The answer choice synonym for incitement is provocation.

18. A: Gauge. Value and worth are synonyms. The answer choice synonym for measure is gauge.

19. A: Oppose. Enervate and energize are antonyms. The answer choice antonym for espouse is oppose.

20. D: The analogy is tool to worker. A carpenter uses a hammer, just as a doctor uses a stethoscope.

21. B: The analogy describes characteristic location. An armoire is usually kept in a bedroom, just as a desk is usually kept in an office.

22. C: This analogy describes a food source to animal relationship. Just as plankton is a food source for whales, so is bamboo a food source for pandas.

23. C: The analogy is geographic location. Just as the tundra is located in the Arctic regions, so are savannas located in tropic regions.

24. A: This is an analogy of relative degree. *Parched* is a more intense degree of *thirsty,* just as *famished* is a more intense degree of *hungry.*

25. E: This is an analogy based on antonyms. *Felicity,* or happiness, is the opposite of *sadness,* just as *ignominy,* or disgrace, is the opposite of *honor.*

Arithmetic Reasoning

1. C: To calculate his new hourly rate, add his raise to his original hourly rate.

$$\$15.23 + \$2.34 = \$17.57$$

Therefore, the man's new hourly rate is $17.57.

2. A: To answer this question, calculate half of 140 acres.

$$140 \div 2 = 70$$

The size of the remaining forest is 70 acres.

3. C: First, calculate how many cows he has after selling 45.

$$360 - 45 = 315$$

Then, calculate how many cows he has after buying 85 more.

$$315 + 85 = 400$$

The farmer now has 400 cows.

4. C: First, find the total cost of the items.

$$\$6.65 + \$159.23 = \$165.88$$

Then, calculate how much each friend will have to pay by dividing the total cost by the number of friends.

$$\$165.88 \div 4 = \$41.47$$

Each friend will have to pay $41.47.

5. A: Each earns $135, so to find the total earned, that amount must be multiplied by the number of workers.

$$135 \times 5 = 675$$

Therefore, the total amount earned by the five workers for one day of work is $675.

6. B: Currently, there are two men for every woman. If the number of women is doubled, then the new ratio is $2 : 2$. This is equivalent to $1 : 1$.

7. D: One gallon of paint can paint three rooms, so to find out how many rooms 28 gallons can paint, multiply that number by 3.

$$28 \times 3 = 84$$

Therefore, 28 gallons of paint can paint 84 rooms.

8. C: First, calculate the length of the second office.

$$20 + 6 = 26$$

The second office is 26 feet long. Then, add both values together to get the combined length.

$$26 + 20 = 46$$

The combined length of the two offices is 46 feet.

9. C: First, calculate her score on the second test.

$$99 - 15 = 84$$

Then, calculate her score on the third test.

$$84 + 5 = 89$$

Therefore, she made an 89 on the third test.

10. E: Each notebook costs $1.50. To find the cost of each notebook, we must divide the total amount of money earned, $45.00, by the number of notebooks sold, 30. When we divide 45 by 30, we know that 30 can "fit" into 45 one time, with a remainder of 15. We can turn our remainder into a fraction by making our remainder the numerator and our divisor the denominator, creating the fraction $\frac{15}{30}$, or $\frac{1}{2}$. When working with money, 1 whole and $\frac{1}{2}$ represents one and a half dollars, or $1.50. Giselle charged $1.50 for each notebook.

11. B: The perimeter of a rectangle can be found using the formula $P = 2l + 2w$, where l is the length and w is the width.

$$P = 2(35\text{ ft}) + 2(88\text{ ft}) = 70\text{ ft} + 176\text{ ft} = 246\text{ ft}$$

Therefore, the perimeter of the room is 246 feet.

12. B: First, find the total before taxes.

$$\$7.50 + \$3.00 = \$10.50$$

Then, calculate 6% of the total.

$$\$10.50 \times 0.06 = \$0.63$$

Finally, add the tax to find how much he pays in all.

$$\$10.50 + \$0.63 = \$11.13$$

Therefore, he pays $11.13.

13. A: If there are x squares in the drawing, then there are $x + 16$ circles. Since we know there are 36 total circles and squares, we can set up the following equation and solve it for x.

$$\begin{aligned} x + (x + 16) &= 36 \\ 2x + 16 &= 36 \\ 2x &= 20 \\ x &= 10 \end{aligned}$$

Therefore, there are 10 squares in the drawing.

14. B: Calculate 0.5% of \$450.

$$0.5\% \times \$450$$

To multiply a percentage by a number, convert the percentage to a decimal and then multiply as usual.

$$0.005 \times \$450 = \$2.25$$

She will earn \$2.25 in interest for the month.

15. B: The volume of a rectangular prism can be found by multiplying the length by the width by the height.

$$V = 9 \text{ in} \times 4 \text{ in} \times 5 \text{ in} = 180 \text{ in}^3$$

Therefore, the volume of the tissue box is 180 cubic inches.

16. B: First, calculate 3% of 250 pounds.

$$250 \times 0.03 = 7.5$$

Calculate how much she weighs at the end of the first week.

$$250 - 7.5 = 242.5$$

Calculate 2% of 242.5.

$$242.5 \times 0.02 = 4.85$$

Add the two values together to get the total number of pounds she lost.

$$7.5 + 4.85 = 12.35$$

Therefore, she lost 12.35 pounds after two weeks.

17. C: To start, we can write our ratio in fractional form as $\frac{2 \text{ cups of water}}{6 \text{ cups of flour}}$. We know Josie wants to lessen the flour to only 2 cups, making our proportion $\frac{2 \text{ cups of water}}{6 \text{ cups of flour}} = \frac{x \text{ cups of water}}{2 \text{ cups of flour}}$. To find the value of x, we can cross multiply the two diagonal values we know, 2 and 2, and divide their product by the remaining value, 6. $2 \times 2 = 4$, and $4 \div 6 = \frac{4}{6}$, which simplifies to $\frac{2}{3}$. This means Josie should use $\frac{2}{3}$ of a cup of water for every 2 cups of flour.

18. B: The woman has four days to earn \$250. To find the amount she must earn each day, divide the amount she must earn by 4.

$$\$250 \div 4 = \$62.50$$

Therefore, she must earn \$62.50 each day.

19. D: Find the volume of a cube by taking the cube of any side length.

$$5^3 = 5 \times 5 \times 5 = 125$$

Therefore, the volume of the cube is 125 cm^3.

20. C: To calculate this value, divide the number of dogs (48) by the number of workers that are available to care for them (4).

$$48 \div 4 = 12$$

Each worker must look after 12 dogs.

21. D: Start by setting up a proportion to solve by cross multiplication: $\frac{1\text{ inch}}{60\text{ feet}} = \frac{10\text{ inches}}{x\text{ feet}}$. When the numbers are cross multiplied, you get $x = 600$ feet. Now we need to convert 600 feet to yards. There are 3 feet in 1 yard, so divide 600 by 3 to find the number of yards between the two points: $600 \div 3 = 200$. Therefore, the two points are 200 yards apart.

22. A: To find out how much he has remaining, subtract both the amounts that he spent from the original amount ($50.00).

$$\$50.00 - \$15.64 - \$7.12 = \$27.24$$

The man has $27.24 left after going to the mall.

23. C: First, figure out how many points the first woman will earn.

$$3 \times 5 = 15$$

Then, figure out how many points the second woman will earn.

$$6 \times 5 = 30$$

Finally, add these two values together.

$$30 + 15 = 45$$

Therefore, the two women will have a combined total of 45 points.

24. C: Since we are told that 30% of the equipment are cardio machines and that 40% of the cardio machines are treadmills, we need to multiply 30% and 40% to find the percentage of gym equipment that are treadmills. To multiply percentages, first convert them to decimals and then multiply as usual.

$$30\% \times 40\% = 0.3 \times 0.4 = 0.12$$

Finally, convert this decimal to a percentage.

$$0.12 = 12\%$$

Therefore, 12% of the gym equipment is treadmills.

25. B: We start by adding together the fraction of boxes that contain pretzels and the fraction of boxes that contain chips.

$$\frac{1}{3} + \frac{1}{4} = \frac{4}{12} + \frac{3}{12} = \frac{7}{12}$$

Therefore, $\frac{7}{12}$ of the boxes contain pretzels and chips. Subtract this from the total fraction of snack boxes.

$$1 - \frac{7}{12} = \frac{12}{12} - \frac{7}{12} = \frac{5}{12}$$

Therefore, $\frac{5}{12}$ of the snack boxes contain granola bars.

Word Knowledge

1. A: Spoiled has a number of meanings, and one of them is ruined. If you said somebody spoiled your fun, it would convey the same meaning as saying somebody ruined your fun.

2. B: An oath is a promise. For example, if you make an oath to keep a secret, you are promising to keep that secret.

3. B: When you inquire about something, you are asking about it or requesting more information. For example, if you told somebody you inquired about a job, it would mean you asked about it.

4. C: If you say that you comprehend something, it is the same as saying you understand it. For example, saying you comprehend what another person is saying is the same as saying you understand them.

5. A: To say that something is apparent implies that it is clear or obvious. For example, saying that it is apparent that somebody wants a job is the same as saying it is clear they want the job.

6. C: "Silent" or "silence" indicates quiet and calm. To enjoy the silence of the night is to enjoy the complete quiet of the night.

7. E: "Absolutely," when used to describe a feeling or state of mind, means completely or totally. For example, saying you are absolutely certain that you made the right decision means you are completely certain.

8. D: Something that has been modified has been changed. Saying you modified your plans means that you changed them.

9. A: Something that is delicate can also be described as fragile. Saying that a crystal figurine is delicate means it is fragile.

10. B: Festivities are commonly known as celebrations. Attending festivities implies that you are attending a celebration or party.

11. B: To say that someone is *exhausted* means he or she is tired. Usually, "exhausted" is a word used to describe extreme tiredness.

12. B: To cleanse something is to clean or wash it. Saying you cleansed your face or clothes is the same as saying you washed them.

13. A: To battle something is to fight it. To say that two armies battled each other means they fought each other.

14. C: To wander is to roam. To say someone wandered around a mall is to say they roamed or walked around aimlessly, without a specific goal or destination in mind.

15. E: Something that is done abruptly is done suddenly and without warning. For example, saying the car stopped abruptly means it stopped suddenly.

16. A: Somebody who has been tricked has been conned. To trick somebody is to con them, which implies that dishonest methods are being used to convince them to do something they wouldn't normally do.

17. C: When used as an adjective, *extremely* has the same meaning as very. Saying somebody is extremely happy and saying they are very happy conveys the same meaning.

18. A: To have doubts is to have uncertainties or hesitations. To say that someone is doubtful about something means that they are uncertain.

19. D: To describe something as peculiar is to say it is strange or out of the ordinary. For example, saying you are in a strange situation or saying you are in a peculiar situation conveys the same meaning.

20. B: Describing somebody as courteous implies that they are polite and well-mannered. Polite and courteous both convey the same meaning.

21. C: When somebody says they are troubled by something, they mean that they are bothered by it.

22. A: Perspiration is another word for sweat. Saying somebody is perspiring is the same as saying they are sweating.

23. B: Tremble is another word for shake. To say somebody or something trembled means that it shook or shuddered.

24. A: Adhered is often used as another word for stuck. For example, to say a piece of tape adhered to the wall conveys the same meaning as saying the piece of tape stuck to the wall.

25. D: When something is described as tidy, it usually means that it is neat and that things are in their proper place. Saying a house is tidy and saying it is neat conveys the same meaning.

Mathematics Knowledge

1. C: We can write the problem as a system of two linear equations. Let x be the number of gold coins and y be the number of silver coins. Since there are fifty coins total, we have $x + y = 50$ as one of the equations. If each gold coin weighs 12 ounces, then the total weight in ounces of the gold coins is $12x$. Similarly, the total weight in ounces of the silver coins is $8y$. Since all the coins together weigh 30 pounds, which is equal to $30 \times 16 = 480$ ounces, we have $12x + 8y = 480$. Because each term in this equation is divisible by 4, we can divide the whole equation by 4 to get $3x + 2y = 120$. This is not a required step, but does make the numbers a little smaller and more manageable.

We now have two equations: $x + y = 50$ and $3x + 2y = 120$. There are a number of ways to solve a system of equations like this. One is to the substitution method. We can solve the first equation for y to get $y = 50 - x$, and then substitute this into the second equation to get $3x + 2(50 - x) = 120$. After distributing the 2, we get $3x + 100 - 2x = 120$. Combining like terms gives $x + 100 = 120$. Finally, subtracting 100 from both sides yields $x = 20$. Thus, the number of gold coins is 20.

2. C: First, move all the variable terms to one side and the constants to the other side, and combine like terms.

$$3x - 30 = 45 - 2x$$

$$3x + 2x = 45 + 30$$

$$5x = 75$$

Then, divide both sides by 5 to solve for x.

$$\frac{5x}{5} = \frac{75}{5}$$

$$x = 15$$

3. A: To calculate the value of this expression, substitute –3 for x each time it appears in the expression.

$$3(-3)^3 + (3(-3) + 4) - 2(-3)^2$$

According to the order of operations, any operations inside of parentheses must be done first.

$$3(-3)^3 + (-9 + 4) - 2(-3)^2$$

$$3(-3)^3 + (-5) - 2(-3)^2$$

Then, simplify any exponents.

$$3(-27) + (-5) - 2(9)$$

Next, perform any multiplication.

$$-81 - 5 - 18$$

Finally, subtract from left to right.

$$-81 - 5 - 18 = -104$$

4. B: First, we must calculate the length of one side of the square. Since we know the perimeter is 8 cm, and that a square has 4 equal sides, the length of each side can be calculated by dividing the perimeter (8 cm) by 4.

$$8 \div 4 = 2$$

The length of one side of the square is 2 cm. The formula for the area of a square is length squared.

$$A = 2^2 = 4$$

Therefore, the area of the square is 4 cm^2.

5. D: To simplify the expression, use the exponent rule $(x^m)^n = x^{m\times n}$.

$$(3x^{-2})^3 = (3)^3 (x^{-2})^3 = 27x^{-6}$$

6. C: $16x^2 - 64$ is a difference of squares, which means it can be factored using the formula $a^2 - b^2 = (a + b)(a - b)$.

$$16x^2 - 64x = (4x)^2 - (8)^2 = (4x + 8)(4x - 8)$$

Therefore, $16x^2 - 64$ written in factored form is $(4x + 8)(4x - 8)$.

7. D: One way to find the solution is by using the substitution method. Solve the first equation for x.

$$x = 9 - y$$

Substitute this expression into the second equation for x and solve for y.

$$(9 - y) + 2y = 13$$
$$9 + y = 13$$
$$y = 4$$

Now, plug this value into the first equation and solve for x.

$$x + 4 = 9$$
$$x = 5$$

Therefore, the simultaneous solution is $x = 5, y = 4$.

8. D: To simplify this expression, recall the law of exponents for multiplication.

$$x^n x^m = x^{n+m}$$

Apply this property to each variable in the expression.

$$x^2x^7 = x^{2+7} = x^9$$

$$y^{12}y^3 = y^{12+3} = y^{15}$$

Multiply the coefficients and substitute the variable multiplication into the expression.

$$(3x^27x^7) + (2y^39y^{12}) = 21x^9 + 18y^{15}$$

9. C: The area of a triangle can be calculated by using the following formula.

$$A = \frac{1}{2}bh$$

Substitute the values given in the question into the equation.

$$A = \frac{1}{2}(12)(12) = 72$$

Therefore, the area of the triangle is 72 cm^2.

10. C: First, subtract 27 from both sides of the equation to isolate x.

$$\frac{x}{3} + 27 = 30$$

$$\frac{x}{3} + 27 - 27 = 30 - 27$$

$$\frac{x}{3} = 3$$

Next, multiply both sides by 3.

$$\frac{x}{3} \times 3 = 3 \times 3$$

$$x = 9$$

11. C: First, subtract 7 from both sides to isolate x.

$$\frac{x}{3} + 7 = 35$$

$$\frac{x}{3} + 7 - 7 = 35 - 7$$

$$\frac{x}{3} = 28$$

Then, multiply both sides by 3 to solve for x.

$$\frac{x}{3} \times 3 = 28 \times 3$$

$$x = 84$$

12. A: To simplify the expression, start by distributing the 3s.

$$3\left(\frac{6x-3}{3}\right)-3(9x+9)$$

$$6x-3-27x-27$$

Then, combine like terms.

$$(6x-27x)+(-3-27)$$

$$-21x-30$$

Since this isn't one of the answer choices, manipulate it to match one of the choices given. Factor out a –3 from each term.

$$-3(7x+10)$$

13. B: To simplify this expression, recall the law of exponents for division.

$$\frac{x^n}{x^m}=x^{n-m}$$

Apply this property to each variable in the expression.

$$\frac{x^{18}}{x^5}=x^{18-5}=x^{13}$$

$$\frac{t^6}{t^2}=t^{6-2}=t^4$$

$$\frac{w^3}{w^2}=w^{3-2}=w$$

$$\frac{z^{20}}{z^{19}}=z^{20-19}=z$$

Then, divide the coefficients.

$$50\div 5=10$$

Now, multiply each part together.

$$10x^{13}t^4wz$$

14. B: A triangle has three angles that add up to 180 degrees. An acute angle is less than 90 degrees, so the sum of three acute angles could equal 180 degrees. For instance, they could all be 60 degrees. An obtuse angle is more than 90 degrees, so the sum of three obtuse angles would be more than 180 degrees. Therefore, choice A is incorrect. Right angles are 90 degrees, so the sum of three right angles would be 270 degrees. Therefore, choice C is incorrect. A triangle cannot have four angles. Therefore, choice D is incorrect. Finally, a triangle cannot have a 200-degree angle, since 200 degrees is more than 180 degrees. Therefore, choice E is incorrect.

15. D: To find the value of this expression, substitute the given values for x and y into the expression and simplify.

$$3(4)(2) - 12(2) + 5(4)$$

$$24 - 24 + 20$$

$$20$$

16. A: Setting the cost of shipping equal to the amount received gives us the equation $3{,}000 + 100x = 400x$. Subtract $100x$ from both sides to get $3{,}000 = 300x$, then divide both sides by 300 to see that $x = 10$. Therefore, the least number of computers that must be shipped and sold is 10.

17. A: First, factor this equation.

$$x^2 - 13x + 42 = 0$$

$$(x - 6)(x - 7) = 0$$

The expression on the left side of the equation is equal to zero when either $(x - 6)$ or $(x - 7)$ equals zero, so solve the two equations $x - 6 = 0$ and $x - 7 = 0$.

$$x - 6 = 0 \qquad\qquad x - 7 = 0$$

$$x = 6 \qquad\qquad x = 7$$

Therefore, the solution is $x = 6, 7$.

18. A: First, add 5 to both sides of the equation to isolate x.

$$x^2 - 5 = 20$$

$$x^2 - 5 + 5 = 20 + 5$$

$$x^2 = 25$$

Then, take the square root of both sides to solve for x.

$$\sqrt{x^2} = \sqrt{25}$$

$$x = \pm 5$$

Only 5 is listed as an answer choice, so the correct answer is $x = 5$.

19. A: First, add 25 to both sides to isolate x.

$$\frac{1}{4}x - 25 \geq 75$$

$$\frac{1}{4}x - 25 + 25 \geq 75 + 25$$

$$\frac{1}{4}x \geq 100$$

Then, multiply both sides by 4 to solve for x.

$$4 \times \frac{1}{4}x \geq 4 \times 100$$

$$x \geq 400$$

20. D: First, gather the like terms on opposite sides of the equation.

$$-3q + 12 \geq 4q - 30$$

$$12 \geq 7q - 30$$

$$42 \geq 7q$$

Then, divide both sides by 7 to solve for q.

$$\frac{42}{7} \geq \frac{7q}{7}$$

$$6 \geq q$$

The inequality can be flipped to match the formatting of the answer choices, giving the inequality $q \leq 6$.

21. B: Use the FOIL method (first, outside, inside, and last) to expand the polynomial multiplication.

$$12x^2 - 18x + 20x - 30$$

Then, combine like terms to simplify the expression.

$$12x^2 + 2x - 30$$

22. E: To solve the equation, start by simplifying the division on the left side.

$$72 \div 8 = x - 17$$
$$9 = x - 17$$

Then, add 17 to both sides.

$$26 = x$$

Therefore, the value of x is 26.

23. B: The perimeter of a figure is the sum of all its sides. Since a rectangle's width and length will be the same on opposite sides, the perimeter of a rectangle can be calculated by using the following formula.

$$P = 2w + 2l$$

Substitute the numbers given in the question.

$$P = 2(7) + 2(9)$$

$$P = 14 + 18$$

$$P = 32$$

Therefore, the perimeter of the rectangle is 32 cm.

24. D: First, subtract 10 from both sides to isolate x.

$$\frac{2}{3}x + 10 = 16$$

$$\frac{2}{3}x + 10 - 10 = 16 - 10$$

$$\frac{2}{3}x = 6$$

Then, multiply both sides by the reciprocal of $\frac{2}{3}$ to solve for x.

$$\frac{3}{2} \times \frac{2}{3}x = 6 \times \frac{3}{2}$$

$$x = 9$$

25. A: This expression can be simplified by grouping and combining like terms. First, group like terms together.

$$6x + 2y - 3 + 4x + 5y + 6$$

$$(6x + 4x) + (2y + 5y) + (-3 + 6)$$

Then, simplify the expression.

$$10x + 7y + 3$$

Reading Comprehension

1. A: Explaining the qualities of air that may affect flight is the primary purpose of the passage.

2. C: The best definition for *inversely* as it is used in the second paragraph is *in the opposite direction*. The author is indicating that the density of air decreases as the temperature rises, and increases as the temperature falls.

3. D: A pilot can expect the air density to decrease as the plane gains altitude. At the end of the second paragraph, the author states that a gain in altitude will usually lead to a decrease in air density, no matter what changes there may be in the temperature.

4. B: The author would most likely agree that air density is more important than relative humidity. Though the passage states that humidity can have an effect on aircraft performance, the author admits that it is not considered an essential factor. Indeed, humidity is just one of three factors (along with pressure and temperature) that affect air density.

5. C: The most likely reason why there is no chart for assessing the effects of humidity on density altitude is that humidity does not affect flight performance very much. The author mentions several times that flight performance is not significantly affected by humidity, and so it is seems that a special chart for this purpose would be unnecessary.

6. D: *Influences on Climb Performance* would be the best title for this passage. The passage surveys the various factors that affect climb performance and the choices made by pilots as they gain altitude, both during take-off and while the aircraft is already in flight.

7. E: The best definition for *pronounced* as it is used in the second paragraph is *noticeable*. The author is stating that the weight of an aircraft has a significant impact on aircraft performance. In this sentence *pronounced* is being used as an adjective, but it can also be used as a verb, meaning *spoke* or *said*.

8. C: An increase in weight means that the angle of attack must be higher in order to maintain altitude. Greater weight diminishes reserve power, lowers the climb rate, diminishes the maximum rate of climb, and increases drag.

9. B: The author would most likely agree that at the end of a long journey a plane will have a higher maximum rate of climb. The maximum rate of climb of a plane increases as the weight decreases, and the weight of a plane will decrease as it burns off fuel over the course of a long journey.

10. A: A helicopter that weighs two tons and has rotor blades that cover five hundred square feet would have a disc loading measure of eight pounds per square foot. Pounds per square foot is the standard measure for disc loading. There are two thousand pounds in a ton. Disc loading is calculated by dividing the weight of the helicopter by the area covered by the rotor blades.

11. B: Discussing the interrelationships of airspeed, power, and pitch attitude is the primary purpose of the passage. Answer choices *C* and *D* are partially correct, but they leave out large sections of the passage and therefore do not comprehensively describe the purpose or the content of the passage.

12. A: *Inadvertently*, as it is used in the fifth paragraph, most nearly means *unintentionally*. The author is indicating that a pilot can enter the region of reversed command without meaning to, if he or she attempts to climb out of ground effect without first attaining normal climb pitch attitude and airspeed.

13. B: Most flight occurs in the region of normal command. In the region of normal command, increasing power increases the airspeed, and decreasing power decreases the airspeed. This information is given in the last sentence of the second paragraph.

14. E: The author would most likely agree that as the speed of flight decreases, the power required to maintain altitude increases. This inverse relationship between required power and airspeed is expressed in the last sentence of the first paragraph.

15. D: The best title for this passage would be *Power Requirements During Flight*. The passage discusses how the need for and effects of changes in power are influenced by factors such as airspeed, pitch attitude, and altitude.

16. E: The primary purpose of the passage is to describe the factors that influence landing distance. The passage begins by discussing the minimum and normal landing distances and goes on to cover influences on landing distance, as for instance gross weight, wind, and density altitude.

17. B: When making a normal landing, a pilot will rely on aerodynamic drag in order to avoid wearing down the brakes and tires. This point is made several times in the third paragraph of the passage.

18. A: The best definition for *principal* as it is used in the fifth paragraph is *most important*. The author is trying to make the point that gross weight has an enormous effect on landing distance.

19. C: A heavier plane must be landed at a higher airspeed to avoid hitting the runway with too much force. This idea is explored in the fourth paragraph. In order to generate an amount of lift sufficient for a smooth landing, a higher airspeed must be maintained.

20. C: The author would most likely agree that gross weight and minimum landing distance are positively correlated. The information in the passage makes it clear that as gross weight rises, minimum landing distance increases.

21. D: The primary purpose of the article is to discuss aeronautical decision making, or ADM. The article does give some examples of decision-making strategies, but these are given in the context of a description of ADM, not as the main body of the article.

22. D: The passage explains that aviation safety is distinct from other areas of safety because there is a much smaller margin for error. In other words, even small accidents in aviation can be catastrophic, because of the risks inherent in flight.

23. A: The closest definition for *conjunction* as it is used in the second paragraph is *combination*. The author is stating that the FAA manuals worked well when combined with the usual flight training.

24. A: The author would most likely agree that the body of knowledge about ADM is increasing, and this will have a positive effect on flight safety. The article details the efforts to improve ADM and suggests that these have already improved flight safety a great deal.

25. E: For a pilot, reading the account of a recent aviation accident is an opportunity for an indirect learning experience. The passage distinguishes between direct learning experiences, which are events in one's own life, and indirect learning experiences, which are things that happen to others.

Situational Judgment

1. C (Most effective)

2. A (Least effective)

3. A (Most effective)

4. C (Least effective)

5. E (Most effective)

6. B (Least effective)

7. D (Most effective)

8. A (Least effective)

9. E (Most effective)

10. C (Least effective)

11. B (Most effective)

12. C (Least effective)

13. A (Most effective)

14. B (Least effective)

15. E (Most effective)

16. B (Least effective)

17. C (Most effective)

18. A (Least effective)

19. A (Most effective)

20. B (Least effective)

21. B (Most effective)

22. D (Least effective)

23. A (Most effective)

24. C (Least effective)

25. B (Most effective)

26. E (Least effective)

27. D (Most effective)

28. A (Least effective)

29. B (Most effective)

30. C (Least effective)

31. E (Most effective)

32. B (Least effective)

33. A (Most effective)

34. D (Least effective)

35. D (Most effective)

36. C (Least effective)

37. A (Most effective)

38. D (Least effective)

39. E (Most effective)

40. A (Least effective)

41. B (Most effective)

42. C (Least effective)

43. E (Most effective)

44. A or C (Least effective)

45. A (Most effective)

46. D (Least effective)

47. A (Most effective)

48. B (Least effective)

49. B (Most effective)

50. D (Least effective)

Physical Science

1. B: A long nail or other type of metal, substance, or matter that is heated at one end and then the other end becomes equally hot is an example of conduction. Conduction is energy transfer by neighboring molecules from an area of hotter temperature to cooler temperature.

2. E: The measure of energy within a system is called heat.

3. B: They have a different number of neutrons. The distinguishing feature of an isotope is its number of neutrons. Two different isotopes of the same element will have the same number of protons but different numbers of neutrons.

4. A: Fission is a nuclear process where atomic nuclei split apart to form smaller nuclei. Nuclear fission can release large amounts of energy, emit gamma rays and form daughter products. It is used in nuclear power plants and bombs.

5. D: The process whereby a radioactive element releases energy slowly over a long period of time to lower its energy and become more stable is best described as decay. The nucleus undergoing decay spontaneously releases energy, most commonly through the emission of an alpha particle, a beta particle, or a gamma ray.

6. B: Light within a single medium travels in a straight line. When it changes to a different medium, however, the light rays bend according to the refractive index of each substance. Light coming from the submerged portion of the pencil is refracted as it passes through the air-water barrier, giving the perception of a bent pencil.

7. A: Hertz (Hz) is a unit of measure used for frequency, often described as 1 cycle/second. In the context of wave motion, it is the number of complete waves that pass a given point in one second.

8. B: A cyclist coasting up a hill is trading his speed for increased altitude. This is an example of kinetic energy being converted to potential energy. The other options are examples of potential energy being converted to kinetic, kinetic energy being dissipated, and conservation of kinetic energy.

9. E: Phase changes such as boiling, melting, and freezing are physical changes. No chemical reaction takes place when water is boiled.

10. A: The center of an atom is known as the nucleus. It is composed of protons and neutrons.

11. A: Sublimation is the process of a solid changing directly into a gas without entering the liquid phase.

12. D: Mendeleev was able to connect the trends of the different elements' behaviors and develop a table that showed the periodicity of the elements and their relationship to each other.

13. A: Density is mass per unit volume, typically expressed in units such as g/cm^3, or kg/m^3.

14. C: The closer the data points are to each other, the more precise the data. This does not mean the data is accurate, but rather that the results are reproducible.

15. E: Current is measured in units of amperes or amps.

16. C: In order for a solar eclipse to occur, the moon must come directly between the earth and the sun, blocking the sun's light from the earth.

17. B: Inertia is the tendency of objects that are in motion to continue moving in the same direction. The turning car initiates a change in direction, but the passengers' mass wants to continue going straight, causing them to feel a pull in that direction. This phenomenon is sometimes referred to as centrifugal force.

18. B: According to the ideal gas law, when volume is held constant, the temperature of a gas is directly proportional to the pressure of the gas. Thus, when the temperature is increased, the pressure will also increase.

19. B: The amplitude of a sound wave is what determines how loud the sound is perceived by the ear.

20. D: In all of the other examples, there is a person applying work to the book, either directly, by being picked up, pushed, or thrown, or indirectly, by being carried in a backpack. In the example of a book being released so that it falls, the only work being applied to the book is being done by gravity.

Table Reading

1. B
2. A
3. C
4. C
5. E
6. D
7. C
8. A
9. A
10. B
11. E
12. E
13. A
14. B
15. B
16. D
17. A
18. E
19. C
20. A
21. E
22. E
23. C
24. B
25. A
26. B
27. A
28. E
29. C
30. A
31. D
32. C
33. C
34. D
35. A
36. B
37. E
38. E
39. A
40. C

Instrument Comprehension

1. B: The instruments show that the aircraft is flying level with its wings level and is on a NW heading. This is represented by choice B.

2. C: The instruments show that the aircraft is flying level with its wings banked right and is on a SW heading. This is represented by choice C.

3. C: The instruments show that the aircraft is flying level with its wings banked right and is on a N heading. This is represented by choice C.

4. A: The instruments show that the aircraft is flying level with its wings banked right and is on a E heading. This is represented by choice A.

5. C: The instruments show that the aircraft is descending with its wings banked right and is on a N heading. This is represented by choice C.

6. C: The instruments show that the aircraft is ascending with its wings banked left and is on a W heading. This is represented by choice C.

7. A: The instruments show that the aircraft is descending with its wings banked right and is on a W heading. This is represented by choice A.

8. B: The instruments show that the aircraft is descending with its wings banked right and is on a S heading. This is represented by choice B.

9. B: The instruments show that the aircraft is descending with its wings banked right and is on a NE heading. This is represented by choice B.

10. A: The instruments show that the aircraft is descending with its wings banked left and is on a W heading. This is represented by choice A.

11. C: The instruments show that the aircraft is flying level with its wings level and is on a SW heading. This is represented by choice C.

12. A: The instruments show that the aircraft is descending with its wings banked left and is on a SE heading. This is represented by choice A.

13. D: The instruments show that the aircraft is ascending with its wings banked right and is on a W heading. This is represented by choice D.

14. B: The instruments show that the aircraft is descending with its wings banked left and is on a SW heading. This is represented by choice B.

15. D: The instruments show that the aircraft is descending with its wings banked left and is on a N heading. This is represented by choice D.

16. B: The instruments show that the aircraft is descending with its wings banked left and is on a E heading. This is represented by choice B.

17. C: The instruments show that the aircraft is descending with its wings level and is on a S heading. This is represented by choice C.

18. A: The instruments show that the aircraft is ascending with its wings level and is on a N heading. This is represented by choice A.

19. A: The instruments show that the aircraft is ascending with its wings banked left and is on a SW heading. This is represented by choice A.

20. D: The instruments show that the aircraft is ascending with its wings banked left and is on a SE heading. This is represented by choice D.

21. C: The instruments show that the aircraft is flying level with its wings banked left and is on a NW heading. This is represented by choice C.

22. B: The instruments show that the aircraft is descending with its wings banked right and is on a SW heading. This is represented by choice B.

23. A: The instruments show that the aircraft is ascending with its wings level and is on a S heading. This is represented by choice A.

24. A: The instruments show that the aircraft is flying level with its wings level and is on a E heading. This is represented by choice A.

25. C: The instruments show that the aircraft is descending with its wings level and is on a N heading. This is represented by choice C.

Block Counting

1. 5: 1 on the front, 1 on the back, 3 on the right.

2. 3: 2 on the top, 1 on the bottom.

3. 5: 1 on the front, 2 on the back, 1 on the left, 1 on the top.

4. 4: 1 on the left, 1 on the top, 2 on the bottom.

5. 4: 3 on the top, 1 on the bottom.

6. 5: 1 on the back, 3 on the top, 1 on the bottom.

7. 3: 1 on the back, 1 on the right, 1 on the top.

8. 5: 2 on the front, 2 on the back, 1 on top.

9. 2: 1 on the front, 1 on the left.

10. 4: 1 on the front, 1 on the back, 1 on the right, 1 on the bottom.

11. 8: 1 on the back, 3 on the left, 1 on the right, 1 on the top, 2 on the bottom,

12. 6: 1 on the front, 1 on the back, 2 on the left, 1 on the right, 1 on the top.

13. 4: 1 on the back, 1 on the left, 2 on the top.

14. 4: 1 on the front, 1 on the back, 1 on the right, 1 on the bottom.

15. 5: 1 on the front, 1 on the back, 1 on the left, 2 on the bottom.

16. 3: 1 on the front, 2 on the right.

17. 7: 2 on the front, 1 on the back, 1 on the left, 2 on the right, 1 on top.

18. 5: 1 on the front, 1 on the back, 1 on the left, 1 on the top, 1 on the bottom.

19. 4: 2 on the back, 2 on the bottom.

20. 6: 2 on the front, 2 on the back, 2 on the right.

21. 4: 1 on the front, 2 on the back, 1 on the left.

22. 5: 4 on the top, 1 on the bottom.

23. 4: 1 on the front, 1 on the back, 1 on the right, 1 on the bottom.

24. 7: 1 on the front, 2 on the back, 2 on the top, 2 on the bottom.

25. 6: 1 on the back, 2 on the left, 1 on the right, 1 on the top, 1 on the bottom.

26. 6: 3 on the left, 2 on the top, 1 on the bottom.

27. 9: 2 on the front, 1 on the back, 2 on the left, 2 on the right, 1 on the top, 1 on the bottom.

28. 5: 1 on the back, 1 on the right, 3 on top.

29. 5: 1 on the front, 1 on the back, 1 on the right, 2 on the bottom.

30. 7: 1 on the front, 3 on the left, 2 on the right, 1 on the bottom.

Aviation Information

1. C: A Visual Approach Slope Indicator should be visible from approximately twenty miles away at night. A Visual Approach Slope Indicator (VASI) is a common feature at large airports. This system helps guide the approaching pilot to the runway. The pilot will see white lights at the lower border of the glide path, and red lights at the upper border. In normal conditions, the lights of the VASI system should be visible for three to five miles during the day and for twenty miles at night. If the VASI system is working properly, the plane will be safe so long as it stays within ten degrees of the extended runway centerline and four nautical miles of the runway threshold.

2. E: Torque is not one of the forces a pilot must manage during flight. The four forces a pilot must manage are lift, gravity, thrust, and drag. Lift pushes the plane up, gravity pulls the plane down, thrust propels the plane forward, and drag holds the plane back. The overall admixture of these forces as they operate on the plane is called the flight envelope.

3. A: The collective affects the angle of the main rotor blades of a helicopter. It is a long tube that extends from the floor of the cockpit. In most helicopters, it is situated on the pilot's left. The collective has two parts: a handle that can be raised or lowered, to control the pitch of the blades; and a throttle, to control the torque of the engine. The handle is the part that affects the angle of the main rotor blades. When it is raised, the leading edge of the blade is raised higher than the trailing edge.

4. C: The flight attitude is the position of a plane in motion. The flight attitude is described in terms of its position with respect to three axes: vertical, lateral, and longitudinal. The vertical axis runs up through the plane's center of gravity. A plane's position with respect to this axis is known as its yaw. The lateral axis of a plane runs from wingtip to wingtip, and the motion of the plane around this axis is known as pitch. The longitudinal axis, finally, is an imaginary line extending from the nose of the plane to its tail. The position of the plane in relation to the longitudinal axis is called roll. The attitude of the plane is controlled with the joystick, rudder pedals, and throttle.

5. C: The curvature of an airfoil is known as the camber. An airfoil (wing) is considered to have a high camber if it is very curved. A related piece of wing terminology is the mean camber line, which runs along the inside of the wing, such that the upper and lower wings are equal in thickness.

6. A: The elevators are considered one of the primary flight controls. The elevators are responsible for the plane's pitch, or movement around the lateral axis. The other primary flight controls are the ailerons and the rudder. The ailerons control the roll, or movement around the longitudinal axis, while the rudder controls the yaw, or movement around the vertical axis. The secondary flight controls are the flaps, spoilers, leading edge devices, and trim systems.

7. B: In aviation, the term for movement around the plane's longitudinal axis is rolling. The longitudinal axis runs from the nose of the plane to its tail. For the most part, the plane's roll is controlled by the joystick. By moving the stick to the right or left, the pilot dips the wings.

8. A: The altitude at which the plane is flying is the primary determinant of air pressure in the flight envelope. The most important elements of the flight envelope are the temperature, air pressure, and humidity. The conditions in the atmosphere have a great deal of influence over the amount of lift created by the airfoils. Greater air pressure is the same as greater air density. A plane will generate greater lift when it is in cool air, because cool air is more dense than warm air.

9. B: A plane is said to have conventional landing gear when the third wheel is under the tail. Typically, a plane's landing gear will consist of three wheels or sets of wheels. Two of these are under either wing or on opposing sides of the fuselage. In the conventional arrangement, the third wheel, or wheel set, is under the tail, while in the tricycle arrangement it is under the nose. This third wheel can rotate, which will make it possible for the plane to turn while moving on the ground.

10. D: An aileron is not part of the empennage. The empennage, otherwise known as the tail assembly, includes the elevators, vertical and horizontal stabilizers, rudders, and trim tabs. A fixed wing aircraft will typically have both vertical and horizontal stabilizers, which are immobile surfaces that extend from the back of the fuselage. The horizontal stabilizers have mobile surfaces along their trailing edges; these surfaces are called the elevators. The elevators deflect up and down to raise or lower the nose of the plane. The rudder is a single, large flap connected by a hinge to the vertical stabilizer. The rudder's back-and-forth motion controls the motion of the plane with respect to its vertical axis. The trim tabs, finally, are connected to the trailing edges of one or more of the primary flight controls (i.e., ailerons, elevators, rudder).

11. E: A glider would be most likely to have a straight wing. A straight wing may be tapered, elliptical, or rectangular. This planform (wing shape) is common in aircraft that move at extremely low speeds. A straight wing is often found on sailplanes and gliders. The swept wing, on the other hand, is appropriate for high-speed aircraft. The wing may be swept forward or back. This will make the plane unstable at low speeds, but will produce much less drag. A swept wing requires high-speed takeoff and landing. The delta wing, which is also known as the triangular wing, has a straight trailing edge and a high angle of sweep. This allows the plane to take off and land at high speeds.

12. A: The crew is not considered part of a plane's basic weight. The basic weight is the aircraft plus whatever internal or external equipment will remain on the plane during its journey. The crew is not included in the basic weight, though it is a part of the operating weight (basic weight plus crew), gross weight (total weight of the aircraft at any particular time), landing gross weight (weight of the plane and its contents upon touchdown), and zero fuel weight (weight of the airplane when it has no usable fuel).

13. D: The support structure that runs the length of the fuselage in a monocoque plane is called a stringer. In a monocoque plane, the fuselage is supported by stringers, formers, and bulkheads. Stringers and formers are generally made out of the same material, though they run perpendicular to one another (that is, formers run in circles around the width of the fuselage). Bulkheads are the walls that divide the sections of the fuselage. The other style of fuselage, known as a truss, is composed of triangular groupings of aluminum or steel tubing.

14. C: The joystick is used to manipulate the elevators. When the stick is pulled back, the elevators deflect upwards. This decreases the camber of the horizontal tail surface, which moves the nose up and pushes the tail down. Pushing the joystick forward, on the other hand, pushes the elevators down, which creates an upward force on the tail by increasing the camber of the horizontal tail surface.

15. A: When a pilot needs to descend quickly onto a shorter-than-normal runway, he or she will descend at the minimum safe airspeed. A descent at the minimum safe airspeed is achieved by slightly lifting the nose and moving the plane into the landing configuration. During such a descent, the plane should not exceed 1.3 times the stall speed. This technique is appropriate for landing quickly on a short runway because the rate of descent is much faster. However, if the rate of descent should become too great, the pilot should be ready to increase power.

16. B: Raising the nose is not one of the possible functions of a spoiler. Spoilers can diminish lift and reduce drag, which enables the plane to descend without reducing its speed. However, spoilers also control the plane's roll, partly by reducing any adverse yaw. A pilot uses the spoiler in this way by raising the spoiler on the side of the turn. That side will thereby have less lift and more drag, making it drop. The plane will then bank and yaw in the intended direction. When the pilot raises both of the spoilers at the same time, the plane will descend without losing any speed. Another incidental benefit of spoilers is improved brake performance, which occurs because the plane has lift and is pushed down towards the ground.

17. D: The vertical axis of a plane extends up through the plane's center of gravity. Movement around this axis is called yawing. The position of a plane is also described with respect to the lateral and longitudinal axes. The lateral axis extends from wingtip to wingtip. The longitudinal axis runs from the nose of the plane to its tail.

18. E: Trimming is necessary after any change in the flight condition. Trimming is the adjustment of the trim tabs, which are small flaps that extend from the trailing edges of the elevators, rudder, and ailerons. Trimming generally occurs after the pilot has achieved the desired pitch, power, attitude, and configuration. The trim tabs are then used to resolve the remaining control pressures. A small plane may only have a single tab, which is controlled with a small wheel or crank.

19. B: When the Runway Centerline Lighting System lights become solid red, an approaching plane is one thousand feet away. A Runway Centerline Lighting System is a line of white lights every fifty feet or so along the centerline. The lights change their color and pattern as the plane nears the runway. When the plane gets within 3,000 feet of the runway, the lights blink red and white. Within a thousand feet, the lights will turn solid red.

20. E: The Coriolis force is the change in rotational speed caused by the shift of the weight towards or away from the center of the spinning object. This phenomenon has an important application for helicopters, in which the rotor will move faster or will require less power to maintain its speed when the weight is closer to the base of the blade. The other answer choices are similarly related to helicopters. The extra lift generated by a helicopter once it has exited its own downwash is known as translational lift. The force that spins the rotors of a helicopter even when there is no power from the engine is autorotation. Greater downwash at the rear half of the rotor disc, as compared to the front half, is the result of applying the lateral cyclic. The phenomenon in which the effects of a force applied to a spinning disc occur ninety degrees later is called gyroscopic precession.

AFOQT Practice Test #2

To take this additional AFOQT practice test, visit our online resources page:
mometrix.com/resources719/afoqt-27353

How to Overcome Test Anxiety

Just the thought of taking a test is enough to make most people a little nervous. A test is an important event that can have a long-term impact on your future, so it's important to take it seriously and it's natural to feel anxious about performing well. But just because anxiety is normal, that doesn't mean that it's helpful in test taking, or that you should simply accept it as part of your life. Anxiety can have a variety of effects. These effects can be mild, like making you feel slightly nervous, or severe, like blocking your ability to focus or remember even a simple detail.

If you experience test anxiety—whether severe or mild—it's important to know how to beat it. To discover this, first you need to understand what causes test anxiety.

Causes of Test Anxiety

While we often think of anxiety as an uncontrollable emotional state, it can actually be caused by simple, practical things. One of the most common causes of test anxiety is that a person does not feel adequately prepared for their test. This feeling can be the result of many different issues such as poor study habits or lack of organization, but the most common culprit is time management. Starting to study too late, failing to organize your study time to cover all of the material, or being distracted while you study will mean that you're not well prepared for the test. This may lead to cramming the night before, which will cause you to be physically and mentally exhausted for the test. Poor time management also contributes to feelings of stress, fear, and hopelessness as you realize you are not well prepared but don't know what to do about it.

Other times, test anxiety is not related to your preparation for the test but comes from unresolved fear. This may be a past failure on a test, or poor performance on tests in general. It may come from comparing yourself to others who seem to be performing better or from the stress of living up to expectations. Anxiety may be driven by fears of the future—how failure on this test would affect your educational and career goals. These fears are often completely irrational, but they can still negatively impact your test performance.

Elements of Test Anxiety

As mentioned earlier, test anxiety is considered to be an emotional state, but it has physical and mental components as well. Sometimes you may not even realize that you are suffering from test anxiety until you notice the physical symptoms. These can include trembling hands, rapid heartbeat, sweating, nausea, and tense muscles. Extreme anxiety may lead to fainting or vomiting. Obviously, any of these symptoms can have a negative impact on testing. It is important to recognize them as soon as they begin to occur so that you can address the problem before it damages your performance.

The mental components of test anxiety include trouble focusing and inability to remember learned information. During a test, your mind is on high alert, which can help you recall information and stay focused for an extended period of time. However, anxiety interferes with your mind's natural processes, causing you to blank out, even on the questions you know well. The strain of testing during anxiety makes it difficult to stay focused, especially on a test that may take several hours. Extreme anxiety can take a huge mental toll, making it difficult not only to recall test information but even to understand the test questions or pull your thoughts together.

Effects of Test Anxiety

Test anxiety is like a disease—if left untreated, it will get progressively worse. Anxiety leads to poor performance, and this reinforces the feelings of fear and failure, which in turn lead to poor performances on subsequent tests. It can grow from a mild nervousness to a crippling condition. If allowed to progress, test anxiety can have a big impact on your schooling, and consequently on your future.

Test anxiety can spread to other parts of your life. Anxiety on tests can become anxiety in any stressful situation, and blanking on a test can turn into panicking in a job situation. But fortunately, you don't have to let anxiety rule your testing and determine your grades. There are a number of relatively simple steps you can take to move past anxiety and function normally on a test and in the rest of life.

Physical Steps for Beating Test Anxiety

While test anxiety is a serious problem, the good news is that it can be overcome. It doesn't have to control your ability to think and remember information. While it may take time, you can begin taking steps today to beat anxiety.

Just as your first hint that you may be struggling with anxiety comes from the physical symptoms, the first step to treating it is also physical. Rest is crucial for having a clear, strong mind. If you are tired, it is much easier to give in to anxiety. But if you establish good sleep habits, your body and mind will be ready to perform optimally, without the strain of exhaustion. Additionally, sleeping well helps you to retain information better, so you're more likely to recall the answers when you see the test questions.

Getting good sleep means more than going to bed on time. It's important to allow your brain time to relax. Take study breaks from time to time so it doesn't get overworked, and don't study right before bed. Take time to rest your mind before trying to rest your body, or you may find it difficult to fall asleep.

Along with sleep, other aspects of physical health are important in preparing for a test. Good nutrition is vital for good brain function. Sugary foods and drinks may give a burst of energy but this burst is followed by a crash, both physically and emotionally. Instead, fuel your body with protein and vitamin-rich foods.

Also, drink plenty of water. Dehydration can lead to headaches and exhaustion, especially if your brain is already under stress from the rigors of the test. Particularly if your test is a long one, drink water during the breaks. And if possible, take an energy-boosting snack to eat between sections.

Along with sleep and diet, a third important part of physical health is exercise. Maintaining a steady workout schedule is helpful, but even taking 5-minute study breaks to walk can help get your blood pumping faster and clear your head. Exercise also releases endorphins, which contribute to a positive feeling and can help combat test anxiety.

When you nurture your physical health, you are also contributing to your mental health. If your body is healthy, your mind is much more likely to be healthy as well. So take time to rest, nourish your body with healthy food and water, and get moving as much as possible. Taking these physical steps will make you stronger and more able to take the mental steps necessary to overcome test anxiety.

Mental Steps for Beating Test Anxiety

Working on the mental side of test anxiety can be more challenging, but as with the physical side, there are clear steps you can take to overcome it. As mentioned earlier, test anxiety often stems from lack of preparation, so the obvious solution is to prepare for the test. Effective studying may be the most important weapon you have for beating test anxiety, but you can and should employ several other mental tools to combat fear.

First, boost your confidence by reminding yourself of past success—tests or projects that you aced. If you're putting as much effort into preparing for this test as you did for those, there's no reason you should expect to fail here. Work hard to prepare; then trust your preparation.

Second, surround yourself with encouraging people. It can be helpful to find a study group, but be sure that the people you're around will encourage a positive attitude. If you spend time with others who are anxious or cynical, this will only contribute to your own anxiety. Look for others who are motivated to study hard from a desire to succeed, not from a fear of failure.

Third, reward yourself. A test is physically and mentally tiring, even without anxiety, and it can be helpful to have something to look forward to. Plan an activity following the test, regardless of the outcome, such as going to a movie or getting ice cream.

When you are taking the test, if you find yourself beginning to feel anxious, remind yourself that you know the material. Visualize successfully completing the test. Then take a few deep, relaxing breaths and return to it. Work through the questions carefully but with confidence, knowing that you are capable of succeeding.

Developing a healthy mental approach to test taking will also aid in other areas of life. Test anxiety affects more than just the actual test—it can be damaging to your mental health and even contribute to depression. It's important to beat test anxiety before it becomes a problem for more than testing.

Study Strategy

Being prepared for the test is necessary to combat anxiety, but what does being prepared look like? You may study for hours on end and still not feel prepared. What you need is a strategy for test prep. The next few pages outline our recommended steps to help you plan out and conquer the challenge of preparation.

Step 1: Scope Out the Test

Learn everything you can about the format (multiple choice, essay, etc.) and what will be on the test. Gather any study materials, course outlines, or sample exams that may be available. Not only will this help you to prepare, but knowing what to expect can help to alleviate test anxiety.

Step 2: Map Out the Material

Look through the textbook or study guide and make note of how many chapters or sections it has. Then divide these over the time you have. For example, if a book has 15 chapters and you have five days to study, you need to cover three chapters each day. Even better, if you have the time, leave an extra day at the end for overall review after you have gone through the material in depth.

If time is limited, you may need to prioritize the material. Look through it and make note of which sections you think you already have a good grasp on, and which need review. While you are studying, skim quickly through the familiar sections and take more time on the challenging parts.

Write out your plan so you don't get lost as you go. Having a written plan also helps you feel more in control of the study, so anxiety is less likely to arise from feeling overwhelmed at the amount to cover.

STEP 3: GATHER YOUR TOOLS

Decide what study method works best for you. Do you prefer to highlight in the book as you study and then go back over the highlighted portions? Or do you type out notes of the important information? Or is it helpful to make flashcards that you can carry with you? Assemble the pens, index cards, highlighters, post-it notes, and any other materials you may need so you won't be distracted by getting up to find things while you study.

If you're having a hard time retaining the information or organizing your notes, experiment with different methods. For example, try color-coding by subject with colored pens, highlighters, or post-it notes. If you learn better by hearing, try recording yourself reading your notes so you can listen while in the car, working out, or simply sitting at your desk. Ask a friend to quiz you from your flashcards, or try teaching someone the material to solidify it in your mind.

STEP 4: CREATE YOUR ENVIRONMENT

It's important to avoid distractions while you study. This includes both the obvious distractions like visitors and the subtle distractions like an uncomfortable chair (or a too-comfortable couch that makes you want to fall asleep). Set up the best study environment possible: good lighting and a comfortable work area. If background music helps you focus, you may want to turn it on, but otherwise keep the room quiet. If you are using a computer to take notes, be sure you don't have any other windows open, especially applications like social media, games, or anything else that could distract you. Silence your phone and turn off notifications. Be sure to keep water close by so you stay hydrated while you study (but avoid unhealthy drinks and snacks).

Also, take into account the best time of day to study. Are you freshest first thing in the morning? Try to set aside some time then to work through the material. Is your mind clearer in the afternoon or evening? Schedule your study session then. Another method is to study at the same time of day that you will take the test, so that your brain gets used to working on the material at that time and will be ready to focus at test time.

STEP 5: STUDY!

Once you have done all the study preparation, it's time to settle into the actual studying. Sit down, take a few moments to settle your mind so you can focus, and begin to follow your study plan. Don't give in to distractions or let yourself procrastinate. This is your time to prepare so you'll be ready to fearlessly approach the test. Make the most of the time and stay focused.

Of course, you don't want to burn out. If you study too long you may find that you're not retaining the information very well. Take regular study breaks. For example, taking five minutes out of every hour to walk briskly, breathing deeply and swinging your arms, can help your mind stay fresh.

As you get to the end of each chapter or section, it's a good idea to do a quick review. Remind yourself of what you learned and work on any difficult parts. When you feel that you've mastered the material, move on to the next part. At the end of your study session, briefly skim through your notes again.

But while review is helpful, cramming last minute is NOT. If at all possible, work ahead so that you won't need to fit all your study into the last day. Cramming overloads your brain with more information than it can process and retain, and your tired mind may struggle to recall even previously learned information when it is overwhelmed with last-minute study. Also, the urgent nature of cramming and the stress placed on your brain contribute to anxiety. You'll be more likely to go to the test feeling unprepared and having trouble thinking clearly.

So don't cram, and don't stay up late before the test, even just to review your notes at a leisurely pace. Your brain needs rest more than it needs to go over the information again. In fact, plan to finish your studies by noon or early afternoon the day before the test. Give your brain the rest of the day to relax or focus on other things, and get a good night's sleep. Then you will be fresh for the test and better able to recall what you've studied.

Step 6: Take a Practice Test

Many courses offer sample tests, either online or in the study materials. This is an excellent resource to check whether you have mastered the material, as well as to prepare for the test format and environment.

Check the test format ahead of time: the number of questions, the type (multiple choice, free response, etc.), and the time limit. Then create a plan for working through them. For example, if you have 30 minutes to take a 60-question test, your limit is 30 seconds per question. Spend less time on the questions you know well so that you can take more time on the difficult ones.

If you have time to take several practice tests, take the first one open book, with no time limit. Work through the questions at your own pace and make sure you fully understand them. Gradually work up to taking a test under test conditions: sit at a desk with all study materials put away and set a timer. Pace yourself to make sure you finish the test with time to spare and go back to check your answers if you have time.

After each test, check your answers. On the questions you missed, be sure you understand why you missed them. Did you misread the question (tests can use tricky wording)? Did you forget the information? Or was it something you hadn't learned? Go back and study any shaky areas that the practice tests reveal.

Taking these tests not only helps with your grade, but also aids in combating test anxiety. If you're already used to the test conditions, you're less likely to worry about it, and working through tests until you're scoring well gives you a confidence boost. Go through the practice tests until you feel comfortable, and then you can go into the test knowing that you're ready for it.

Test Tips

On test day, you should be confident, knowing that you've prepared well and are ready to answer the questions. But aside from preparation, there are several test day strategies you can employ to maximize your performance.

First, as stated before, get a good night's sleep the night before the test (and for several nights before that, if possible). Go into the test with a fresh, alert mind rather than staying up late to study.

Try not to change too much about your normal routine on the day of the test. It's important to eat a nutritious breakfast, but if you normally don't eat breakfast at all, consider eating just a protein bar. If you're a coffee drinker, go ahead and have your normal coffee. Just make sure you time it so that the caffeine doesn't wear off right in the middle of your test. Avoid sugary beverages, and drink enough water to stay hydrated but not so much that you need a restroom break 10 minutes into the test. If your test isn't first thing in the morning, consider going for a walk or doing a light workout before the test to get your blood flowing.

Allow yourself enough time to get ready, and leave for the test with plenty of time to spare so you won't have the anxiety of scrambling to arrive in time. Another reason to be early is to select a good seat. It's helpful to sit away from doors and windows, which can be distracting. Find a good seat, get out your supplies, and settle your mind before the test begins.

When the test begins, start by going over the instructions carefully, even if you already know what to expect. Make sure you avoid any careless mistakes by following the directions.

Then begin working through the questions, pacing yourself as you've practiced. If you're not sure on an answer, don't spend too much time on it, and don't let it shake your confidence. Either skip it and come back later, or eliminate as many wrong answers as possible and guess among the remaining ones. Don't dwell on these questions as you continue—put them out of your mind and focus on what lies ahead.

Be sure to read all of the answer choices, even if you're sure the first one is the right answer. Sometimes you'll find a better one if you keep reading. But don't second-guess yourself if you do immediately know the answer. Your gut instinct is usually right. Don't let test anxiety rob you of the information you know.

If you have time at the end of the test (and if the test format allows), go back and review your answers. Be cautious about changing any, since your first instinct tends to be correct, but make sure you didn't misread any of the questions or accidentally mark the wrong answer choice. Look over any you skipped and make an educated guess.

At the end, leave the test feeling confident. You've done your best, so don't waste time worrying about your performance or wishing you could change anything. Instead, celebrate the successful completion of this test. And finally, use this test to learn how to deal with anxiety even better next time.

Review Video: Test Anxiety
Visit mometrix.com/academy and enter code: 100340

Important Qualification

Not all anxiety is created equal. If your test anxiety is causing major issues in your life beyond the classroom or testing center, or if you are experiencing troubling physical symptoms related to your anxiety, it may be a sign of a serious physiological or psychological condition. If this sounds like your situation, we strongly encourage you to seek professional help.

Online Resources

Due to our efforts to try to keep this book to a manageable length, we've created a link that will give you access to all of your online resources:

mometrix.com/resources719/afoqt-27353

It's Your Moment, Let's Celebrate It!

Share your story @mometrixtestpreparation